Great Cases
in
Psychoanalysis

Great Cases
in
Psychoanalysis

EDITED

with Introduction and Notes

BY

HAROLD GREENWALD, PH.D.

Jason Aronson, Inc. New York

ACKNOWLEDGMENTS

THE GIRL WHO COULDN'T BREATHE, THE WOMAN WHO FELT PERSECUTED, reprinted from *Studies in Hysteria* by Sigmund Freud, translated by A. A. Brill, Beacon Press, by permission of the Trustees U/W of A. A. Brill Deceased. THE MAN WHO LOVED CORSETS, reprinted by kind permission of The Hogarth Press and The Institute of Psychoanalysis from *The Selected Papers on Psychoanalysis* by Dr. Karl Abraham. THE UNKNOWN MURDERER, reprinted from *The Compulsion to Confess* by Theodor Reik, copyright 1945, 1959 by Theodor Reik; used by permission of the publishers, Farrar, Straus and Cudahy, Inc. THE GIRL WHO COULDN'T STOP EATING, reprinted from *The Fifty Minute Hour* by Robert Lindner, copyright 1954, Rinehart & Company, Inc. THE ANXIOUS YOUNG WOMAN AND THE RETIRED BUSINESS MAN, reprinted from *Two Essays on Analytical Psychology*, Volume 7 of the *Collected Works of C. G. Jung*, translated by R. F. C. Hull, copyright 1953, by Bollingen Foundation. THE EVER-TIRED EDITOR, reprinted from *Self-Analysis* by Karen Horney, copyright 1942, W. W. Norton & Company, Inc. THE INEFFICIENT WIFE, reprinted from *Clinical Studies in Psychiatry* by Harry Stack Sullivan, copyright 1956 by William Alanson White Psychiatric Foundation (permission of W. W. Norton & Co., Inc.). THE ANGRY ADOLESCENT, reprinted from *Counseling and Psychotherapy*, copyright 1942 by Carl R. Rogers, Houghton Mifflin Company. BRIEF THERAPY OF A PSYCHOSOMATIC CASE, reprinted from *Psychosomatic Case Book* by Grinker & Robbins, copyright 1954, McGraw-Hill Book Company, Inc.

CONTENTS

Introduction

This is a book of case histories gathered from the writings of the leaders of the psychoanalytic movement, and selected with the objective of portraying the history of the development of psychoanalysis. Some of the case histories are written by the founders of schools of psychoanalysis, and some by the most prominent contributors to the development of the particular school or movement they represent.

I feel that these case histories are both a useful and a logical way of presenting such a history, and that here, as in all sincere writing, there is explicit that effort to understand humanity which is the root of all psychoanalysis, for no matter what fine theories psychoanalysists spin, the truth and value of their theories rest on the results obtained in the consultation room.

The schools, and the personalities of the founders and leaders of the schools of psychoanalytic thought, as well as their theories, can best be studied in the context of the treatment situation. These case histories take us into the consultation rooms of the great analysts of the last fifty years and show us what they heard, and what they did with their patients.

For the professional therapist or student, whether he be psychiatrist, psychologist or social worker, these cases will illustrate the therapeutic methods employed by the masters in our field. Many of the analysts represented in this book had to be therapists with excellent insight in order to make an imprint strong enough to gather about them the followers necessary for the establishment of a school. My experiences in teaching a seminar in classical case histories at the National Psychological Association for Psychoanalysis has shown that a careful study of actual cases is one of the richest learning experiences for either student or practitioner.

Perhaps most important of all, these case histories, by helping us to understand others, should serve to help us understand ourselves.

Rarely has a science owed so much to one man as the science of psychoanalysis owes to Sigmund Freud. Dissatisfied with the lack of results obtained in the treatment of neurosis by the physiological methods practiced by physicians of his day, Freud turned to psychology for a possible solution and developed both a theory of the mind and a method of treating its disorders. He saw mental illness as being a result of the struggle between the individual's need to gratify his instinctual wishes and society's prohibition against their direct gratification. Society's condemnation of these instinctual drives was, he believed, so great that frequently the individual did not permit himself even to be conscious of them but consigned them to the vast unconscious part of mental life.

Broadly speaking, Freud labelled this unconscious animal part of our nature the "id." Another unconscious area of the mind became the "super ego," a hidden conscience which attempts to control the id. The rational, self-preservative part of the mind he called the "ego," which attempts to resolve the continuous conflict between the id and the super ego. Mental illness was a result of the ego's failure to resolve the conflict successfully, according to Freud.

His treatment, which actually preceded the development of his theory, consisted of making the patient conscious of the sometimes frightful struggle that raged between the id and the super ego, thus strengthening the ego's ability to resolve the conflict. His method of bringing the unconscious areas of the mind into consciousness consisted of exploring the patient's unconscious through the use of free association, dream interpretation, and interpreting the relationship between the analyst and patient as it developed during the course of the analysis. With some modifications all analysts still use his basic method of interpreting unconscious conflicts, though many disagree with some of his theories about the structure of the mind.

Freud was supported by Karl Abraham, who studied the stages through which the individual developed in his efforts to find instinctual gratification. Sandor Ferenczi, another close associate of Freud's, attempted to find methods of shortening the course of psychotherapy and of applying it to hitherto untreatable cases. Melanie Klein

8

helped develop modifications of psychoanalytic technique to make it possible to treat young children. Theodor Reik applied Freud's methods to the study of special problems like guilt and crime. Robert Lindner followed Reik in applying psychoanalysis to the criminal and delinquent as well as by writing about his cases in a dramatic form which provoked the interest of a wide lay public in psychoanalysis. All of these psychoanalysts stemmed directly from Freud and, as he did, they emphasized the role that sexual or libidinal drives played in the unconscious of the individual.

The first of his early followers to break from Freud was Alfred Adler. Adler felt that the individual's effort to compensate for feelings of inferiority was the key to understanding the human personality. Later Carl Gustave Jung was also to become dissatisfied with the emphasis on sexuality, and stressed instead the importance of inherited racial memories. Karen Horney and Harry Stack Sullivan, like Adler, put greater emphasis on social rather than instinctual factors. Carl Rogers, without developing a special theory of personality, did develop a simplified technique for the treatment of comparatively mild neurotic disturbances.

Two recent developments in technique are included: the application of modified psychoanalytic technique to the treatment of psychosomatic disturbances, and group psychoanalysis which has both brought the advantages of psychoanalysis to many who previously could not afford it and has also displayed a remarkable ability to uncover aspects of the personality that are sometimes hidden from the individual analyst.

In organizing this material a number of difficulties were faced. I do not pretend that I have solved these difficulties in the only or the best possible way. Since Freud is the unquestioned founder of psychoanalysis, he and his followers occupy the major portion of the book. The first section is therefore devoted to Freud and the Freudians. The second section of the book deals with cases taken from the non-Freudians like Jung and Adler, as well as neo-Freudians like Sullivan and Horney. These are the cases of the people who differed openly with some of Freud's major hypotheses, but nevertheless never denied the influence of the great discoveries made by Freud.

9

The last section, a brief one, contains two of the major new applications of psychoanalytic theory; one to psychosomatic medicine and the other to a new and rapidly growing method of therapy—group psychoanalysis.

Finally, there were some unavoidable omissions. Unfortunately I was not able to obtain case histories written by Otto Rank, who believed that the vicissitudes of birth and separation were responsible for the individual's emotional difficulties; nor from Erich Fromm, whose chief contribution has been to investigate social problems with the tools of psychoanalysis, nor Wilhelm Reich and Fritz Perls.

Among the books I found helpful in making my brief comments and which I recommend to anyone who wishes further information about the various schools are:

A SHORT HISTORY OF PSYCHOTHERAPY
Nigel Walker, Ph.D. The Noonday Press, New York: 1959.

SCHOOLS OF PSYCHOANALYTIC THOUGHT
Ruth Monroe, The Dryden Press, New York: 1955

THEORIES OF PERSONALITY
Calvin Hall and Gardner Lindzey, John Wiley & Sons: 1957

SIGMUND FREUD: LIFE AND WORKS (*3 volumes*)
Ernest Jones, Basic Books, New York: 1954

THE DEATH AND REBIRTH OF PSYCHOLOGY
Ira Progoff, The Julian Press, New York: 1956

BASIC TEACHINGS OF THE GREAT PSYCHOLOGISTS
S. Stansfeld Sargent, Ph.D. Barnes & Noble, Inc., New York, 1951

TROUBLED WOMEN
Edited by Lucy Freeman, World Publishing Company, New York: 1959

THE HEALING OF THE MIND
Reuben Fine, David McKay, New York: 1971

I would like to express my appreciation for the assistance given by my colleague, Tom Levin, and my wife, Ruth Greenwald.

HAROLD GREENWALD, PH.D.
United States International University
San Diego, California 92124

PART I

FREUD
AND
HIS FOLLOWERS

The Girl
Who
Couldn't Breathe

Sigmund Freud, M.D.
translated by A. A. Brill

Miss Katharina

from STUDIES IN HYSTERIA
by Joseph Breuer and Sigmund Freud.
Nervous & Mental Disease Publishing Company. New York 1937. (*First published in 1895.*)

SIGMUND FREUD

Sigmund Freud (1856–1939) discovered psychoanalysis despite himself. He became a physician in order to be able to earn a living while pursuing his studies of physiology. His interest in physiology became concentrated on the brain and the nervous system. Only under the pressure of economic need did he turn to the study of the diseases of the human central nervous system.

In his efforts to understand and treat nervous disorders Freud turned from physiology to psychology. He studied hypnotism but found that therapy accomplished by hypnotism was too temporary. With a family physician, Breuer, he observed that a patient was cured of a hysterical paralysis when she spoke of important episodes in her life which she thought she had forgotten.

While Breuer had used hypnotism to aid in the recovery of forgotten memories, Freud soon abandoned this technique in favor of a new and revolutionary method which he named psychoanalysis. He asked his patients to lie on a couch while he sat behind them, out of sight. At first he asked them to concentrate upon remembering the incidents connected with the first appearance of the symptoms of which they complained; later he was to ask them to tell the story of their lives or of anything which occurred to them no matter how embarrassing or trivial. Basically this fundamental rule is still followed in classical psychoanalysis.

The case of "The Girl Who Couldn't Breathe" was hardly a complete analysis. Freud himself stated that he had no objection to offer should anyone consider the history of the solution of this case as more one of guessing than of analysis. However, since in this case Freud gave an almost verbatim account of what he said and what was said to him, it illustrates the first attempts at psychotherapy.

It is the first case Freud published in which he did not employ hypnosis, and while he did not utilize free association either, the case does show Freud's use of a variety of sophisticated interview techniques which have since become the familiar tools of trained psychologists. Many students take years to learn to do the things that Freud appeared to do intuitively in this case.

14

The Girl
Who
Couldn't Breathe

During the vacation of 189– I made an excursion to the High Tauern (Eastern Alps) in order to forget medicine for a while, and especially the neuroses. I almost succeeded when one day I deviated from the main street to climb an out of the way mountain, which was famous for a beautiful view and for its well kept inn. After exhaustive wandering, I reached the top, and after refreshment and rest, I sat there sunk in the reflection of an enchanting view. I was so forgetful of myself that at first I was loath to refer to myself the question: "Is the gentleman a doctor?" The question was, however, directed to me by a girl of about 18 years, who had displayed a sulky expression while serving my meal, and who was addressed by the hostess as "Katharina." Judging by her dress and bearing, she could not be a servant, but most probably was a daughter or a relative of the hostess.

Having regained my senses, I said, "Yes, I am a doctor. How do you know that?"

"You registered in the guestbook, and then I thought if the doctor now had a little time . . . You see I am nervous, and I have already consulted a doctor in L. . . . who also gave me something, but it has not done me any good."

Well, I was back in the midst of neuroses, for it could hardly be anything else in this large and robust girl with the morose features. It interested me that neuroses should flourish so well at a height of over 2,000 meters, and I, therefore, continued questioning her.

The conversation which then developed between us I shall now reproduce as it impressed itself upon my mem-

15

ory. I shall also endeavor to reproduce her peculiar expressions.

"What are you complaining of?"

"I have so much difficulty in breathing. Not always, but sometimes it catches me so that I believe I am choking."

At first that did not sound like nervousness, but it soon became probable that it might well be a substitutive designation for an anxiety attack. Out of the whole complex of sensations she stressed unduly one of the factors, the difficulty of breathing.

"Sit down and describe to me how such a state of 'difficulty in breathing' feels."

"It suddenly comes upon me. There is first a pressure on my eyes. My head becomes so heavy, and it hums so that I can hardly bear it, and then I become so dizzy that I believe I am falling, and then my chest begins to press together so that I cannot get my breath."

"And do you feel nothing in the throat?"

"The throat becomes laced together as if I choked."

"And you feel nothing else in the head?"

"Yes, it hammers as if it would split."

"Yes, and doesn't that frighten you?"

"I always feel, 'Now, I must die,' and I am otherwise courageous; I go everywhere alone, into the cellar and down over the whole mountain, but on the day that I have this attack, I do not trust myself anywhere. I always believe that someone stands behind me and suddenly grabs me."

It was really an anxiety attack, and to be sure, initiated by the signs of an hysterical aura, or better expressed, it was an hysterical attack, the content of which was anxiety. Might it not have an additional content?

"When you have the attack, do you always think of the same thing, or do you see something before you?"

Perhaps we have here found a way by which we can advance quickly to the nucleus of the situation.

"Do you recognize the face? I mean is it a face which you have really once seen?"

"No."

"Do you know how you got these attacks?"

"No."

"When did you first get them?"

"The first time two years ago when I was still with my aunt on the other mountain. She had an inn there before; we have now been here for a year and a half, but they always come again."

Should I attempt an analysis here? To be sure, I did not dare to transplant hypnosis to this height, but perhaps we will succeed with simple conversation. I must have been fortunate in my guessings. I have often seen anxiety in young girls as a result of fear which strikes the virginal mind when the world of sexuality reveals itself to it for the first time.[1]

I, therefore, said: "If you do not know it, I will tell you what I believe is the cause of your attacks. At that time, two years ago, you had seen or heard something which embarrassed you much, something that you would rather not have seen."

Thereupon, she exclaimed: "Heavens, yes, I caught my uncle with my cousin Francisca!"

"What is the story about this girl? Will you tell it to me?"

"One can tell everything to a doctor. You may know, therefore, that my uncle, the husband of my aunt, whom you saw, at that time kept an inn with my aunt on the mountain. Now they are divorced and it is my fault that they are divorced, because through me it became known that he had something to do with Francisca."

"Yes, how did you come to discover this?"

"It was this way. Two years ago, two gentlemen once came up the mountain and wanted to get something to eat. My aunt was not at home and Francisca, who always did the cooking, could not be found anywhere. Nor could we find my uncle. We looked for them every-

---

[1] I shall quote here the case where I first recognized this causal relation. I treated a young woman for a complicated neurosis, who repeatedly refused to admit that she contracted her anxiety in her married life. She argued that already as a girl she had suffered attacks of anxiety which ended with fainting. But I remained firm in my conviction. When we became better acquainted, she one day suddenly said, "Now, I will also tell you whence my anxiety states came as a young girl. At that time I slept in a room next to my parents; the door was open and a night light was burning on the table. There I saw a number of times how my father went into my mother's bed and I heard something which excited me very much. Thereupon, I got my attacks."

17

where until the boy, Alois, my cousin, said, 'In the end, Francisca will be found with father.' Then we both laughed, but we thought nothing bad thereby. We went to the room where my uncle lived and that was locked. That seemed peculiar. Then Alois said: 'On the path there is a window from which you can look into the room.' We got on the path, but Alois would not go to the window. He said he was afraid. Then, I said 'You stupid boy; I will go. I am not afraid of anything.' Nor did I think of anything bad. I looked in, the room was quite dark, but then I saw my uncle and Francisca, and he was lying on her."

"Well?"

"I immediately left the window and leaned against the wall and got the difficulty in breathing which I have had since then. My senses left me. My eyes closed tight and my head hammered and hummed."

"Did you tell it to your aunt immediately on the same day?"

"Oh, no, I said nothing."

"But why were you so frightened when you found them both together? Did you understand anything? Did you know what had happened?"

"Oh, no. At that time I understood nothing. I was only sixteen years old. I do not know what frightened me."

"Fräulien Katharina, if you could now recall what went through your mind at the time that you got the first attack, what you thought at that time, it would help you."

"Yes, if I could, but I was so frightened that I forgot everything."

(Translated in the language of our "preliminary communication," it means: The affect itself created the hypnoid state, the products of which remained in the ego consciousness without any associative relations.)

"Tell me, Katharina, is the head that you always see with the difficulty of breathing the head of Francisca, as you saw it then at that time?"

"Oh, no, hers is not so horrible, and moreover, it is a man's head."

"Or, perhaps, it is your uncle's?"

"But, I did not even see his face distinctly. It was too dark in the room, and why should he at that time have had such a terrifying face?"

18

"You are right." (The leads suddenly seemed closed. Perhaps something will be found on continuing the story.)

"And what happened later?"

"Well, the two of them must have heard some noise. They soon came out. I felt quite bad the whole time. I always had to think about it. Then, two days later it was Sunday when there was a lot to do and I worked the whole day, and Monday morning I again had dizziness and vomiting and remained in bed, and for three days I vomited continually."

We have often compared the hysterical symptomatology to picture writing, the reading of which we understood only after we discovered some bi-lingual cases. According to this alphabet, vomiting signified disgust. I, therefore, said to her: "If you vomited three days later, I believe you felt disgust when you looked into the room."

"Yes, I surely was disgusted," she said reflectingly. "But, at what?"

"Perhaps you saw something naked. How were these two persons in the room?"

"It was too dark to see anything and both of them had their clothes on. Yes, if I only knew at what I was disgusted at that time."

Nor did I know, but I requested her to keep on relating what came to her mind with the assured expectation that something would come to her mind, which I needed for the explanation of the case.

She then related that she finally told the aunt of her discovery because she found that the latter had changed, and she imagined that there was some secret behind it; thereupon, there ensued angry scenes between the uncle and the aunt, and the children heard things that opened their eyes to some things, which they had better not have heard. Finally, the aunt decided to leave the uncle with Francisca, who, meanwhile had become pregnant, and departed with the children and her niece to take over the management of another inn. But then to my astonishment, she dropped this thread and began to relate two series of older stories, which went back to two or three years before the traumatic event. The first series contained occasions during which the same uncle had made sexual advances to her when she was only 14 years old. She told how she once made a tour with him in the

19

winter into the valley, when they stayed overnight at an inn. He remained in the inn drinking and playing cards, while she, becoming sleepy, retired early into the room which they occupied together. She did not sleep soundly when he came up, but then she fell asleep again, only to awake suddenly and "feel his body" in bed. She jumped up, reproached him: "What are you up to uncle? Why don't you remain in your bed?" He attempted to joke about it, and said, "Go, you stupid goose, be quiet. You don't even know how good this is." "I don't want anything good from you. You don't even let me sleep." She remained standing at the door, ready to flee out to the path, until he stopped and fell asleep. Then, she returned to bed and slept until morning. From the mode of her defense it would seem that she did not recognize the attack as sexual. Being asked whether she knew what he was up to, she answered "At that time, no," but it became clear to her much later. She was irritated because she was disturbed in her sleep, and because she had never heard of such things.

I had to report this event in detail because it has great importance for everything that is to follow.—She then related other experiences of later times, how she had to defend herself against him in an inn when he was very drunk, etc. But to my question whether she had experienced on these occasions anything similar to the difficulty in breathing which happened later, she answered with certainty that she had experienced the pressure on the eyes and in the chest on each occasion, but not as strongly as at the scene of the discovery.

Immediately after the conclusion of this series of memories she began to relate a second series, which treated of events wherein her attention was called to something between her uncle and Francisca. She related how she and the whole family once spent a night in their clothing on a haystack. She was awakened, as a result of some noise, and she believed that she observed that the uncle, who was lying between her and Francisca, moved away and Francisca changed her position. She spoke of how at another time she spent the night in the village, N. She and her uncle were in one room and Francisca next door to them. During the night she suddenly awoke and saw a long, white form at the door in the act of turning the door knob:

"Heavens, uncle, is that you? What are you doing at the door?"—"Be quiet, I am only looking for something."—"But, you can only go out by the other door."—"I just made a mistake," etc.

I asked her whether at that time she had any suspicions. "No, I thought nothing about it. It struck me as peculiar, but I made nothing out of it."—Whether she had anxiety on this occasion?—She believed yes, but at the present time she was not so sure of it.

After she finished these two series of stories, she stopped. She looked as if changed. The sulky, suffering features were vivified, her look was cheerful, she felt lighter and elated. Meanwhile, the understanding of her case dawned upon me; what she related last, seemingly without any plan, explains excellently her behavior at the scene of the discovery. At that time she carried with her two series of experiences which she recalled, which she did not understand, and which did not help her in drawing any conclusion. At the sight of the pair in the act of coitus, she immediately connected the new impression with these two series of reminiscences, she began to understand and simultaneously to reject. There then followed a short period of elaboration, "the incubation," and thereupon came the conversion symptoms, the vomiting as a substitute for the moral and physical disgust. With this the riddle was solved. She was not disgusted at the sight of the two, but at a reminiscence which this sight awakened in her and explained everything. This could only be the memory of the nightly attack when she "felt her uncle's body."

After this confession was finished, I said to her: "Now I know what you thought at the time that you looked into the room. You thought 'Now, he does with her what he wished to do with me on that night and the other time.' It disgusted you, because you recalled the feeling how you awakened in the night and felt his body."

She answered: "It is very probable that this disgusted me and that I thought of it at that time."

"Just tell me exactly now that you are a grown-up girl and know everything."

"Yes, now certainly."

21

"Tell me exactly what did you really feel that night of his body?" But she gave me no definite answer. She smiled, perplexed, as if convinced, and like one who must admit that as we have now come to the bottom of the thing, there is nothing more to be said about it. I can imagine the kind of tactile sensation which she later learned to interpret. Her features, too, seemed to express that she agreed with my assumption. But I could not penetrate any deeper into her. At all events, I owe her gratitude for the fact that it was so much easier to talk with her than with the prudish ladies of my city practice, for whom all the *naturalia* are *turpia*.

With this the case would be explained; but wait, whence came the hallucination of the head, which returned in the attack and which inspired her with fear? I asked her about it. As if this conversation had also broadened her understanding, she answered promptly: "Yes, I know that now. The head is the head of my uncle. I recognize it now, but I did not at the time. Later, when all the quarrels were taking place, the uncle expressed a senseless rage against me. He always said that it was all my fault. If I had not blabbered, it would have never come to a divorce. He always threatened that he would do something to me, and when he saw me from a distance, his face became tense with rage and he ran at me with a raised hand. I always ran away from him and always had the greatest anxiety that he might grab me without my seeing him. The face which I then always saw was his face in a rage."

This information reminded me of the fact that the first symptom of the hysteria, the vomiting, had disappeared, but that the anxiety attack remained and was filled with a new content. Accordingly, we dealt with an hysteria, a great part of which was abreacted. For soon thereafter, she actually informed her aunt of her discovery.

"Have you also related the other stories to your aunt, how he appeared to you?"

"Yes, not right away, but later when it was already a question of divorce. My aunt then said: 'We will keep that to ourselves. If he makes any difficulties at the divorce, then we will bring it up.' "

I can understand that from that last period the exciting

22

scenes in the house piled up, when her ailment ceased to awaken her aunt's interest, who was now entirely taken up with her quarrel—that from exactly that time of accumulation and retention, there remained the memory symbol.

I hope that our conversation has done some good to this girl, whose sexual sensibilities were so prematurely traumatized. I did not see her again.

Epicrisis

I have no objection to offer should anyone consider the history of the solution of this case of hysteria as given in this case history more as one of guessing than analysis. To be sure, the patient accepted as probable everything I interpolated into her report, but she was, nevertheless, in no position to recognize it as something that she had experienced. The case of Katharina is typical in this respect, for in every hysteria based on sexual traumas one finds that experiences from a fore-sexual period, which produced no effect on the child, later, as memories, receive traumatic force, when the young girl or the woman gains understanding of her sexual life. The splitting-off of psychic groups is, as it were, a normal process in the development of adolescence, and it is quite comprehensible that their later reception into the ego offers advantageous occasions for psychic disturbances. Moreover, I wish to give expression in this place to a doubt: whether the splitting of consciousness through ignorance is really different from the one through conscious rejection, and whether adolescents do not frequently possess more sexual knowledge than one supposes or than they, themselves, believe.

A further deviation in the psychic mechanism of this case lies in the fact that the scene of the discovery, which we have designated as "auxiliary," deserves also the name, "traumatic." It exerted influences through its own content, and not just through the awakening of the preceding traumatic experience; it unites the characters of an "auxiliary" and a "traumatic" factor. However, I see no reason for giving up in this coincidence an abstract separation, which in other cases corresponds also to a temporal separation. Another peculiarity of Katharina's case, which was, however, known for some time, is shown

23

in the fact that in the conversion the production of the hysterical phenomena did not immediately follow the trauma, but only after an interval of incubation. Charcot had a predilection for calling this interval the "period of psychic elaboration."

The anxiety which Katharina showed in her attacks was hysterical, *i.e.,* it was a reproduction of that anxiety, which appeared at each of the sexual traumas. I am also desisting here from elucidating the process which I have recognized regularly and pertinently in an unusually large number of cases; namely, that the mere presentment of sexual relations in virginal persons, evokes an affect of anxiety.

The Woman Who Felt Persecuted

(1915)

Sigmund Freud, M.D.

translated by Edward Glover

A Case of Paranoia Running Counter to the Psycho-Analytic Theory of the Disease.

Standard Edition of the COMPLETE PSYCHOLOGICAL WORKS OF SIGMUND FREUD, VOL. XIV. The Hogarth Press, London: 1957

SIGMUND FREUD

This case demonstrates Freud's sensitivity to specific detail, his ability to trace such details to their origins and his caution in accepting any item related by a patient at face value. It is a fascinating demonstration of Freud's method of investigation and his tireless search for the psychological mechanisms that determine attitudes and behavior.

While the patient in this case was not actually treated by Freud, it does present Freud's penetrating analysis of one of the most puzzling and destructive of human ailments, paranoia, a mental illness characterized by persistent delusions usually of a suspicious or grandiose nature. This case was of special interest to Freud as a scientist because it seemed to contradict a theory he had developed, namely, that paranoia was a result of the patient's struggle against an intensification of his homosexual trends. Because he does not dare love a person of the same sex, the paranoid transmutes that love to hate and suspicion. In this case a young woman had apparently chanfied her love for a young man into hatred. The task Freud set himself to investigate was whether this apparently heterosexual conflict actually masked a homasexual problem.

Many of the sudden violent outbreaks by hitherto peaceful citizens frequently described in newspapers represent the acting out of paranoid delusions. If paranoia were as visible to the non-psychologically trained person as say, the common cold, many people might be saved much suffering.

One characteristic of the paranoid personality is a tendency to litiginousness, that is, the use of courts to avenge fancied injuries. This case illustrates how one person was so afflicted. It is unfortunate that more attorneys do not have the conscience and perception of the one who consulted Freud in this case.

The Woman
Who
Felt Persecuted
(1915)

Some years ago a well-known lawyer consulted me about a case which had raised some doubts in his mind. A young woman had asked him to protect her from the molestations of a man who had drawn her into a love-affair. She declared that this man had abused her confidence by getting unseen witnesses to photograph them while they were making love, and that by exhibiting these pictures it was now in his power to bring disgrace on her, and force her to resign the post she occupied. Her legal adviser was experienced enough to recognize the pathological stamp of this accusation; he remarked, however, that, as what appears to be incredible often actually happens, he would appreciate the opinion of a psychiatrist in the matter. He promised to call on me again, accompanied by the plaintiff.

(Before I continue the account, I must confess that I have altered the *milieu* of the case in order to preserve the incognito of the people concerned, but that I have altered nothing else. I consider it a wrong practice, however excellent the motive may be, to alter any detail in the presentation of a case. One can never tell what aspect of a case may be picked out by a reader of independent judgment, and one runs the risk of leading him astray.)

Shortly afterwards I met the patient in person. She was thirty years old, a most attractive and handsome girl, who looked much younger than her age and was of a distinctly feminine type. She obviously resented the interference of a doctor and took no trouble to hide her distrust. It was clear that only the influences of her legal

27

adviser, who was present, induced her to tell me the story which follows and which set me a problem that will be mentioned later. Neither in her manner nor by any kind of expression of emotion did she betray the slightest shame or shyness, such as one would have expected her to feel in the presence of a stranger. She was completely under the spell of the apprehension brought on by her experience.

For many years she had been on the staff of a big business concern, in which she held a responsible post. Her work had given her satisfaction and had been appreciated by her superiors. She had never sought any love-affairs with men, but had lived quietly with her old mother, of whom she was the sole support. She had no brothers or sisters; her father had died many years before. Recently an employee in her office, a highly cultivated and attractive man, had paid her attentions and she in turn had been drawn towards him. For external reasons, marriage was out of the question, but the man would not hear of giving up their relationship on that account. He had pleaded that it was senseless to sacrifice to social convention all that they both longed for and had an indisputable right to enjoy, something that could enrich their life as nothing else could. As he had promised not to expose her to any risk, she had at last consented to visit him in his bachelor rooms in the daytime. There they kissed and embraced as they lay side by side, and he began to admire the charms which were now partly revealed. In the midst of this idyllic scene she was suddenly frightened by a noise, a kind of knock or click. It came from the direction of the writing-desk, which was standing across the window; the space between desk and window was partly taken up by a heavy curtain. She had at once asked her friend what this noise meant, and was told, so she said, that it probably came from the small clock on the writing-desk. I shall venture, however, to make a comment presently on this part of her narrative.

As she was leaving the house she had met two men on the staircase, who whispered something to each other when they saw her. One of the strangers was carrying something which was wrapped up and looked like a small box. She was much exercised over this meeting, and on

her way home she had already put together the following notions: the box might easily have been a camera,
and the man a photographer who had been hidden behind
the curtain while she was in the room; the click had been
the noise of the shutter; the photograph had been taken
as soon as he saw her in a particularly compromising
position which he wished to record. From that moment
nothing could abate her suspicion of her lover. She pursued him with reproaches and pestered him for explana-
tions and reassurances, not only when they met but also
by letter. But it was in vain that he tried to convince her
that his feelings were sincere and that her suspicions
were entirely without foundation. At last she called on
the lawyer, told him of her experience and handed over
the letters which the suspect had written to her about
the incident. Later I had an opportunity of seeing some of
these letters. They made a very favorable impression on
me, and consisted mainly in expressions of regret that
such a beautiful and tender relationship should have been
destroyed by this 'unfortunate morbid idea.'

I need hardly justify my agreement with this judgment.
But the case had a special interest for me other than a
merely diagnostic one. The view had already been put forward in psycho-analytic literature that patients suffering
from paranoia are struggling against an intensification of
their homosexual trends—a fact pointing back to a narcissistic object-choice. And a further interpretation had
been made: that the persecutor is at bottom someone
whom the patient loves or has loved in the past. A synthe-
sis of the two propositions would lead us to the necessary conclusion that the persecutor must be of the same
sex as the person persecuted. We did not maintain, it is
true, as universally and without exception valid the thesis
that paranoia is determined by homosexuality; but this
was only because our observations were not sufficiently
numerous; the thesis was one of those which in view of
certain considerations become important only when uni-
versal application can be claimed for them. In psychiatric
literature there is certainly no lack of cases in which the
patient imagines himself persecuted by a person of the
opposite sex. It is one thing, however, to read of such
cases, and quite a different thing to come into personal

29

contact with one of them. My own observations and analyses and those of my friends had so far confirmed the relation between paranoia and homosexuality without any difficulty. But the present case emphatically contradicted it. The girl seemed to be defending herself against love for a man by directly transforming the lover into a persecutor: there was no sign of the influence of a woman, no trace of a struggle against a homosexual attachment.

In these circumstances the simplest thing would have been to abandon the theory that the delusion of persecution invariably depends on homosexuality, and at the same time to abandon everything that followed from that theory. Either the theory must be given up or else, in view of this departure from our expectations, we must side with the lawyer and assume that this was no paranoic combination but an actual experience which had been correctly interpreted. But I saw another way out, by which a final verdict could for the moment be postponed. I recollected how often wrong views have been taken about people who are ill physically, simply because the physician has not studied them thoroughly enough and had thus not learnt enough about them. I therefore said that I could not form an immediate opinion, and asked the patient to call on me a second time, when she could relate her story again at greater length and add any subsidiary details that might have been omitted. Thanks to the lawyer's influence I secured this promise from the reluctant patient; and he helped me in another way by saying that at our second meeting his presence would be unnecessary.

The story told me by the patient on this second occasion did not conflict with the previous one, but the additional details she supplied resolved all doubts and difficulties. To begin with, she had visited the young man in his rooms not once but twice. It was on the second occasion that she had been disturbed by the suspicious noise: in her original story she had suppressed, or omitted to mention, the first visit because it had no longer seemed of importance to her. Nothing noteworthy had happened during this first visit, but something did happen on the day after it. Her department in the business was under the direction of an elderly lady whom she described as follows: 'She has white hair like my mother.' This elderly superior had a great liking for her and treated her with affection, though sometimes she teased her; the girl regarded herself as her particular favorite. On the day after her first visit to the young man's rooms he appeared in the office to discuss some business matter with this elderly lady. While they were talking in low voices the patient suddenly felt convinced that he was telling her about their adventure of the previous day—indeed, that the two of them had for some time been having a love-affair, which she had hitherto overlooked. The white-haired motherly old lady now knew everything, and her speech and conduct in the course of the day confirmed the patient's suspicion. At the first opportunity she took her lover to task about his betrayal. He naturally protested vigorously against what he called a senseless accusation. For the time being, in fact, he succeeded in freeing her from her delusion, and she regained enough confidence to repeat her visit to his rooms a short time—I believe it was a few weeks—afterwards. The rest we know already from her first narrative.

In the first place, this new information removes any doubts as to the pathological nature of her suspicion. It is easy to see that the white-haired elderly superior was a substitute for her mother, that in spite of his youth her lover had been put in the place of her father, and that it was the strength of her mother-complex which had driven the patient to suspect a love-relationship between these ill-matched partners, however unlikely such a relation might be. Moreover, this disposes of the apparent contradiction to the expectation, based on psycho-analytic theory, that the development of a delusion of persecution will turn out to be determined by an over-powerful homosexual attachment. The *original* persecutor—the agency whose influence the patient wishes to escape—is here again not a man but a woman. The superior knew about the girl's love affairs, disapproved of them, and showed her disapproval by mysterious hints. The patient's attachment to her own sex opposed her attempts to adopt a person of the other sex as a love-object. Her love for her mother had become the spokesman of all those tendencies which, playing the part of a 'conscience', seek to

31

arrest a girl's first step along the new road to normal sexual satisfaction—in many respects a dangerous one; and indeed it succeeded in disturbing her relation with men.

When a mother hinders or arrests a daughter's sexual activity, she is fulfilling a normal function whose lines are laid down by events in childhood, which has powerful, unconscious motives, and has received the sanction of society. It is the daughter's business to emancipate herself from this influence and to decide for herself on broad and rational grounds what her share of enjoyment or denial of sexual pleasure shall be. If in the attempt to emancipate herself she falls a victim to a neurosis it implies the presence of a mother-complex which is as a rule over-powerful, and is certainly unmastered. The conflict between this complex and the new direction taken by the libido is dealt with in the form of one neurosis or another, according to the subject's disposition. The manifestation of the neurotic reaction will always be determined, however, not by her present-day relation to her actual mother but by her infantile relations to her earliest image of her mother.

We know that our patient had been fatherless for many years: we may also assume that she would not have kept away from men up the the age of thirty if she had not been supported by a powerful emotional attachment to her mother. This support became a heavy yoke when her libido began to turn to a man in response to his insistent wooing. She tried to free herself, to throw off her homosexual attachment; and her disposition, which need not be discussed here, enabled this to occur in the form of a paranoic delusion. The mother thus became the hostile and malevolent watcher and persecutor. As such she could have been overcome, had it not been that the mother-complex retained power enough to carry out its purpose of keeping the patient at a distance from men. Thus, at the end of the first phase of the conflict the patient had become estranged from her mother without having definitely gone over to the man. Indeed, both of them were plotting against her. Then the man's vigorous efforts succeeded in drawing her decisively to him. She conquered her mother's opposition in her mind and was willing to grant her lover a second meeting. In the later developments the mother did not reappear, but we may safely insist that in this [first] phase the lover had not become the persecutor directly but *via* the mother and in virtue of his relationship to the mother, who had played the leading part in the first delusion.

One would think that the resistance was now definitely overcome, that the girl who until now had been bound to her mother had succeeded in coming to love a man. But after the second visit a new delusion appeared, which, by making ingenious use of some accidental circumstances, destroyed this love and thus successfully carried through the purpose of the mother-complex. It still seems strange that a woman should protect herself against loving a man by means of a paranoic delusion; but before examining this state of things more closely, let us glance at the accidental circumstances that formed the basis of this second delusion, the one aimed exclusively against the man.

Lying partly undressed on the sofa beside her lover, she heard a noise like a click or beat. She did not know its cause, but she arrived at an interpretation of it after meeting two men on the staircase, one of whom was carrying something that looked like a covered box. She became convinced that someone acting on instructions from her lover had watched and photographed her during their intimate *tête-à-tête*. I do not for a moment imagine, of course, that if the unlucky noise had not occurred the delusion would not have been formed; on the contrary, something inevitable is to be seen behind this accidental circumstance, something which was bound to assert itself compulsively in the patient, just as when she supposed that there was a *liaison* between her lover and the elderly superior, her mother-substitute. Among the store of unconscious phantasies of all neurotics, and probably of all human beings, there is one which is seldom absent and which can be disclosed by analysis: this is the phantasy of watching sexual intercourse between the parents. I call such phantasies—of the observation of sexual intercourse between the parents, of seduction, of castration, and others—'primal phantasies'; and I shall discuss in detail elsewhere their origin and their relation to individual experience. The accidental noise was thus merely playing the part of a provoking factor which activated

33

the typical phantasy of overhearing which is a component of the parental complex. Indeed, it is doubtful
whether we can rightly call the noise 'accidental'. As
Otto Rank has remarked to me, such noises are on the
contrary an indispensible part of the phantasy of listening, and they reproduce either the sounds which betray
parental intercourse or those by which the listening child
fears to betray itself. But now we know at once where
we stand. The patient's lover was still her father, but she
herself had taken her mother's place. The part of the
listener had then to be allotted to a third person. We can
see by what means the girl had freed herself from her
homosexual dependence on her mother. It was by means
of a small piece of regression: instead of choosing her
mother as a love-object, she identified herself with her—
she herself *became* her mother. The possibility of this
regression points to the narcissistic origin of her homosexual object-choice and thus to the paranoic disposition
in her. One might sketch a train of thought which would
bring about the same result as this identification: 'If my
mother does it, I may do it too; I've just as good a right
as she has.'

One can go a step further in disproving the accidental
nature of the noise. We do not, however, ask our readers
to follow us, since the absence of any deeper analytic investigation makes it impossible in this case to go beyond
a certain degree of probability. The patient mentioned
in her first interview with me that she had immediately
demanded an explanation of the noise, and had been
told that it was probably the ticking of the small clock on
the writing-desk. I venture, however, to explain what she
told me as a mistaken memory. It seems to me much more
likely that at first she did not react to the noise at all,
and that it became significant only after she met the two
men on the staircase. Her lover, who had probably not
even heard the noise, may have tried, perhaps on some
later occasion when she assailed him with her suspicions,
to account for it in this way: 'I don't know what noise
you can have heard. Perhaps it was the small clock; it
sometimes ticks like that.' This deferred use of impressions and this displacement of recollections often occur
precisely in paranoia and are characteristic of it. But as I

34

never met the man and could not continue the analysis of the woman, my hypothesis cannot be proved.

I might go still further in the analysis of this ostensibly real 'accident'. I do not believe that the clock ever ticked or that there was any noise to be heard at all. The woman's situation justified a sensation of a knock or beat in her clitoris. And it was this that she subsequently projected as a perception of an external object. Just the same sort of thing can occur in dreams. A hysterical woman patient of mine once related to me a short arousal dream to which she could bring no spontaneous associations. She dreamt simply that someone knocked and then she awoke. Nobody had knocked at the door, but during the previous nights she had been awakened by distressing sensations of pollutions: she thus had a motive for awakening as soon as she felt the first real sign of genital excitation. There had been a 'knock' in her clitoris. In the case of our paranoic patient, I should substitute for the accidental noise a similar process of projection. I certainly cannot guarantee that in the course of our short acquaintance the patient, who was reluctantly yielding to compulsion, gave me a truthful account of all that had taken place during the two meetings of the lovers. But an isolated contraction of the clitoris would be in keeping with her statement that no contact of the genitals had taken place. In her subsequent rejection of the man, lack of satisfaction undoubtedly played a part as well as 'conscience'.

Let us consider again the outstanding fact that the patient protected herself against her love for a man by means of a paranoic delusion. The key to the understanding of this is to be found in the history of the development of the delusion. As we might have expected, the latter was at first aimed against the woman. But now, *on this paranoic basis, the advance from a female to a male object was accomplished.* Such an advance is unusual in paranoia; as a rule we find that the victim of persecution remains fixated to the same persons, and therefore to the same sex to which his love-objects belonged before the paranoic transformation took place. But neurotic disorder does not preclude an advance of this kind, and our observation may be typical of many others. There are many similar processes occurring outside paranoia which

35

have not yet been looked at from this point of view, amongst them some which are very familiar. For instance, the so-called neurasthenic's unconscious attachment to incestuous love-objects prevents him from choosing a strange woman as his object and restricts his sexual activity to phantasy. But within the limits of phantasy he achieves the progress which is denied him, and he succeeds in replacing mother and sister by extraneous objects. Since the veto of the censorship does not come into action with these objects, he can become conscious in his phantasies of his choice of these substitute-figures.

These then are phenomena of an attempted advance from the new ground which has as a rule been regressively acquired; and we may set alongside them the efforts made in some neuroses to regain a position of the libido which was once held and subsequently lost. Indeed we can hardly draw any conceptual distinction between these two classes of phenomena. We are too apt to think that the conflict underlying a neurosis is brought to an end when the symptom has been formed. In reality the struggle can go on in many ways after this. Fresh instinctual components arise on both sides, and these prolong it. The symptom itself becomes an object of this struggle; certain trends anxious to preserve it conflict with others which strive to remove it and to re-establish the *status quo ante*. Methods are often sought of rendering the symptom nugatory by trying to regain along other lines of approach what has been lost and is now withheld by the symptom. These facts throw much light on a statement made by C. G. Jung to the effect that a peculiar 'psychical inertia', which opposes change and progress, is the fundamental precondition of neurosis. This inertia is indeed most peculiar; it is not a general one, but is highly specialized; it is not even all-powerful within its own field, but fights against tendencies towards progress and recovery which remain active even after the formation of neurotic symptoms. If we search for the starting-point of this special inertia, we discover that it is the manifestation of very early linkages—linkages which it is hard to resolve—between instincts and impressions and the objects involved in those impressions. These linkages have the effect of bringing the development of the instincts concerned to a standstill. Or in other words, this specialized

36

'psychical inertia' is only a different term, though hardly a better one, for what in psycho-analysis we are accustomed to call a 'fixation'.

The Man
Who
Loved Corsets

(1910)

Karl Abraham, M.D.

translated by Douglas Bryan
and Alix Strachey

*Remarks on the Psycho-Analysis of a case of
Foot and Corset Fetishism.*
SELECTED PAPERS OF KARL ABRAHAM M.D.,
Basic Books, Inc., New York: 1953

KARL ABRAHAM

Karl Abraham (1877–1925) was one of Freud's earliest followers. In 1907, Abraham came to Vienna as a guest of the Psychological Wednesday Society, a small group of men who met to discuss psychoanalysis and from which the vast structure of psychoanalytic organizations had developed. Among other members and early guests of the Society were Adler, Jung, Rank and Ferenczi.

While Abraham practiced psychoanalysis in Berlin, where he became the leader of the small group of German psychoanalysts, he was a member of Freud's inner circle. He was among the first to apply psychoanalysis to the study of psychoses, especially the treatment of depressive states.

Abraham's chief contribution to psychoanalytic theory was his interest in the stages of infantile development; the oral in which the child obtains pleasure from the use of the mouth in sucking and biting; the anal in which the child obtains pleasure from excretory activities, and finally the genital or sexual stage.

Abraham demonstrates his interest in the erotic zones in this case dealing with a form of fetishism (sexual attachment to an object). Parenthetically it is interesting to note that since the knowledge of psychoanalysis has spread to the general public, fetishism as a symptom rarely appears. In this case, written in 1910, the important role that fetishism can play in certain types of emotional difficulties is explained. Abraham states also that in perversions there is a marked reduction in sexual activity—contrary to the common belief that the pervert is a dangerous individual because of his overactive sexual life.

This case also serves to clearly explain and illustrate the mechanisms of repression and partial repression. In using the term repression, the psychoanalyst usually means the exclusion from consciousness of feelings and thoughts which the conscious mind finds unacceptable.

The Man
Who
Loved Corsets
(1910)

It is only latterly that special attention has been paid to
the problems of fetishism by psychoanalysis. Observation
has shown that in many cases fetishism and neurosis are
both present in the same individual. Freud has made a
short reference to this fact, and has traced the phenomena of fetishism back to a special variety of repression
which he has called 'partial repression'. In consequence
of this the once emphasized contrast between neurosis
and fetishism has been done away with.

The analysis of a case of shoe and corset fetishism
which I am going to discuss has led me to certain conclusions regarding the psychogenesis of this form of fetishism; and other cases have confirmed that view.

We must assume that as the basis of such an abnormality there is a specific sexual constitution which is characterized by the abnormal strength of certain component-instincts. Given this, the complex of fetishistic phenomena is formed by the cooperation of two factors,
namely, the partial repression mentioned above, and a
process of displacement which we shall discuss in greater
detail.

I will give as brief an account of the case as possible:
At the time of his analysis the patient was twenty-two
years old and a student at a technical college. At the
commencement of the treatment he handed me an autobiography which dwelt in detail on his sexual life. The
first thing to be noticed in it was that at the age of puberty he differed from other persons of his own age in
that he did not share their sexual interest in women. He

41

experienced no feelings of love in the usual sense towards male persons either. His conscious knowledge of the most important facts of sexuality was acquired very late. As soon as he did obtain such knowledge he had the idea that he would be impotent. He had a strong antipathy to manual self-gratification as carried out by young men of his own age.

His sexual interests turned in another direction. At the age of fourteen he began to tie himself up, and he repeated this performance whenever he was undisturbed at home. He derived pleasure from books whose theme was chaining or binding—for instance, in stories about Red Indians in which the prisoners are tied to a stake and tortured. But he never attempted to bind another person, nor did he like to suffer such treatment at the hands of others.

When he was about fifteen, while staying at a health resort, he saw a boy of eight or ten years of age who immediately attracted his attention on account of the elegant shoes he wore. He wrote in his autobiography: 'Each time I looked at his shoes I felt great pleasure and longed for this opportunity to recur'. On his return home he began to take an interest in elegant shoes, especially those worn by his school-fellows. This interest soon became transferred to women's shoes, and grew in to a passion. 'My eyes were attracted to women's shoes as though by magic force. . . . Ugly shoes repelled me and filled me with feelings of disgust.' Henceforth, the sight of dainty shoes on women induced in him an 'inward joy'. This feeling of pleasure used often to change into violent excitement, especially when he saw patent-leather boots with high heels like those worn by *demi-mondaines*. It was not only the appearance of the shoes that excited him, however, but his vivid mental picture of the discomfort it must cause the person to walk in them. In order to have a direct experience of the feeling of having one's feet painfully compressed he would often wear his own shoes on the wrong foot, forcing his right foot into his left boot, and *vice versa*.

His interest in corsets began soon after his interest in footwear. When he was sixteen he got hold of an old pair of his mother's stays, and used to lace himself tightly in them, and sometimes wear them under his ordinary clothes out of doors. The following description in his autobiography is characteristic: 'If I see women and girls tightly laced and picture to myself the pressure of their corsets on their breasts and body I can get an erection. On those occasions I have often wished I was a woman, for then I could tight-lace myself, wear women's boots and high heels, and stand in front of corset-shops without attracting notice. This is impossible, but I often long to wear women's clothes, stays, and shoes.' Looking out for elegant shoes or tightly-laced waists became his most important sexual activity. This interest occupied the chief place in his vivid daydreams. At night he had frequent erotic dreams about stays, tight-lacing, etc. And, as we have already said, he had a preference for reading stories of a sadistic nature. He had kept everything that related to these propensities strictly secret until he sought the advice of a specialist, who referred him to me for psychoanalysis. From the beginning I was sceptical of a therapeutic result.

Accidental causes, to which in the older literature on the subject great significance in the etiology of fetishistic tendencies is ascribed, could not be discovered in his case. The fact that the patient had as a boy frequently seen his mother put on her stays cannot have had the effect of a psychic trauma. His interest in his mother's corsets or later in boy's shoes was doubtless the expression of a perversion which was already in existence. An etiological significance cannot be ascribed to these circumstances.

What stands out most distinctly in this case and in every one of its kind is the extraordinary reduction in the person's sexual activity. In fact, we can hardly speak of a sexual activity at all in the case of this patient, apart from his earlier attempts at lacing and tying himself up. He had never put into practice any sadistic or other desires towards other people; he gratified his wishes in this direction entirely in phantasy. In practice he had never moved outside the field of auto-erotism.

If, on the one hand, we have found very little evidence of sexual activity in the patient, we have seen, on the other, that his sexual instinct to look was very pronounced. But even that instinct had been diverted from its real sphere of interest. It was not directed to other

43

people's bodies as a whole, nor to their primary and secondary sexual characteristics, but to certain portions of their clothing. It was directed, therefore, not to the naked body but to its covering. And here again the patient had specialized on the footwear and on the constricting garments of the upper part of a woman's body. His sexual desire did not go beyond the viewing of these objects. It is therefore a question of fixation upon a preliminary sexual aim. Nevertheless the sight of women's shoes only excited pleasure in him when they were elegant in form and design; clumsy, ugly footwear made him feel disgusted. We find, therefore, side by side with a sexual overestimation of the fetish, a pronounced tendency towards an emotional rejection of it, just as is the case with neurotics. The high esthetic standard that the shoe-fetishist demands of his sexual object indicates a strong need to idealize it.

Although the patient's sexual activity had been so much reduced, and although his instincts found gratification in the attainment of preliminary sexual aims, it by no means follows that there was a fundamental, primary weakness of the libido in him. Analysis of the neuroses has shown quite clearly that instincts which have originally been excessively strong can be paralyzed through repression. And the analysis of the present case disclosed a similar state of affairs. Numerous facts, only a few of which can be brought forward in this place, showed that the patient's active sadistic component-instincts and his sexual pleasure in looking had originally been abnormally strong. Both instincts, which were in the closest 'confluence' (Adler), had been overtaken by repression.

It appeared, however, that other component instincts had been included in this process of repression. The particular need felt by the fetishist for esthetic value in his sexual object indicates that his libido originally sought certain aims which seem particularly unesthetic to the generality of normal adults and give rise to feelings of disgust in them. Before taking up this analysis I had my attention drawn to a definite sphere of instinctual life. Professor Freud had told me in a private communication that according to his experience repression of the coprophilic (interest in feces [Ed.]) pleasure in smell played a peculiar part in the psychogenesis of foot-fetishism. My own investigations have fully confirmed this view. In the present case of fetishism I found that the patient's pleasure in 'disgusting' bodily odors had been unusually strong originally. Repression of his coprophilic pleasure in smell, his scoptophilia (sexual pleasure in looking. [Ed.]) and his sexual activity had led to the building up of compromise-formations. And it is precisely these compromise-formations that constitute the characteristic peculiarities of foot-fetishism.

There are cases of fetishism in which the sexual anomaly shows itself in an unrepressed, *i.e.* a fully conscious, pleasure in disgusting odors. In this so-called smell-fetishism pleasure is very frequently obtained from the odor of perspiring and unclean feet; and these attract the patient's scoptophilic instincts at the same time. In the present case it turned out that the patient had passed through a stage which corresponded to smell-fetishism, and that after this a peculiar modification had taken place by which his osphresiolagnia (abnormal interest in odors [Ed.]) had been repressed and his pleasure in looking had been sublimated to pleasure in seeing foot-wear which had an æsthetic value.

But how was it that his scoptophilic and osphresiolagnic instincts could turn so markedly to the feet, instead of being directed to the sexual organs and their secretions? Certain observations led me to suspect that both instincts had originally been concerned with the genital zone, but that other erotogenic zones had prematurely entered into competition with it. An ascendancy of this kind of other erotogenic zones (mouth, anus, etc.) is quite familiar to us from the theory of the sexual aberrations as well as from analyses of neuroses and dreams.

And in fact the analysis of the patient showed that the genital zone had quite early been exposed to strong competition from the side of the anal zone. The purely sexual interest of his first period of childhood had given place to an interest in the processes of excretion; and at puberty he had been overtaken by another wave of repression with a similar (feminine) aim. He had retained for an unusually long time those infantile ideas according to which the processes of excretion have the significance of sexual function. The symbolism of his dreams was of a corresponding character. His scoptophilia and his osphre-

45

siolagnia—in so far as they were not displaced on to the feet—were chiefly directed to the function and products of urination and defecation.

The patient's memories of early childhood were chiefly connected with impressions of smell, and only secondarily with impressions of sight. If his attention was directed back to that time certain obsessive ideas would frequently come into his mind. One of these was the smell of iodoform and pyroxylic acid, two substances used by his mother in his younger days. Another was a scene at a seaside resort, in which he saw his mother wading into the water. The real significance of this scene was only explained through his associations, and was this: he had once or twice soiled himself at that time and his mother had taken him into the sea to clean him.

Many memories connected with smell occurred to him out of his later childhood, too. For instance, he remembered finding in his mother's room a packet of hair the odor of which was agreeable to him; and he remembered hugging his mother in order to smell her armpits. He had one more recollection dating from his early childhood in which his younger sister was at his mother's breast and he had touched the other breast with his mouth and had liked the smell of his mother's body.

The patient's fondness for his mother lasted until he was about ten years old, and up to that time he had frequently got into her bed. But at ten his affection gave place to dislike. He became very intolerant of the bodily smell of women. At the same time as his pleasure in smell became repressed his sexual interest turned away from women and attached itself to the nearest male object—his father. In this transference his interest in bodily evacuations came to the fore. His attention was undoubtedly especially directed to these processes through certain peculiarities of his father, who would, for example, often make water before his children. His phantasies were occupied to a great extent with everything that concerned this function in himself and in his father.

Intimately related to his transference on to his father was his wish to be a woman, a wish that persisted, as we know, after puberty. As far as he was conscious, however, this wish was not directed towards fulfilling the sex-

46

ual function of a woman. What he desired was 'to wear laced shoes and corsets like a woman and be able to look at them in shop-windows without attracting notice'. Once or twice at the age of puberty, as has already been said, he had actually worn corsets under his clothes. His wish to be a woman was expressed unconsciously in various ways which have still to be mentioned.

His infantile impulses of rebellion and jealousy were necessarily directed against his father and mother alternately. This attitude was associated in the customary way with death and castration phantasies, the latter being sometimes of an active and sometimes of a passive nature. His active castration phantasies also had as their object his mother, to whom his infantile imagination attributed a male sexual organ. His passive castration phantasies corresponded to his desire to be a woman. They originated in a period in which he held the view that the female sex had originally possessed a penis but had been deprived of it by castration. All these ideas played a large part in his dreams. He used to dream that he had to amputate the finger of a woman, or that he had to carry out an operation on a man (his father), and that afterwards his mother helped him to sew up the wound. In other dreams a child would have to be beheaded. A recurrent dream of his worth mentioning was one in which a man was pursuing him with a knife in his hand. The exceptional development of his castration complex testifies to the original strength of his sado-masochistic impulses.

In the patient's phantasies castration not only had the obvious significance of emasculation, but also had reference to a certain idea that had always interested him particularly, namely, that of being unable to urinate owing to castration. From this point there are connections which lead to another complex of ideas.

All neurotics in whom the anal and urethral zones are especially erotogenic have a tendency to retain their excreta. This tendency was unusually strong in the patient in question. His childhood memories mostly concerned the pleasurable practices he used to indulge in in this direction. A nervous symptom of his—a 'urinary stammer'—was also connected with those practices.

The patient had all his life-long indulged in phantasies

47

in which he was forced to refrain from relieving his needs. For instance, he would like to imagine that he was tied to a stake by Indians and compelled to hold back the contents of his bladder and bowels. A strong masochistic element was present in this phantasy as well. Another of his favorite ideas was that he was an Arctic explorer and was prevented by the terrible cold from opening his clothes even for a short time in order to relieve the calls of Nature. His experiments in tying himself up were also determined, among other things, by the same motives; and it is significant that those practices took place in the w.c. This tying-up, which plays a large part in the phantasies of sadists and masochists, acquired its significance in his case through its association with the functions of evacuation. Tight-lacing caused a pressure on the bowels and bladder which was pleasurable to him; and when he had put on corsets for the first time he had had an erection and had then passed water. One important determinant of this whole lacing-up *motif* was to be found in certain auto-erotic habits of his connected with squeezing-in the genitals.

In this patient the anal zone greatly predominated. In his childhood it had subserved a peculiar auto-erotic practice in which he used to sit down so that the heel of his boot was pressed against the anal region. And in his memories we find a direct connection between foot and anus, in which the heel corresponded more or less to the male organ and the anus to the female organ. This connection was strengthened by his coprophilic pleasure in smell. His auto-erotism found abundant gratification in the odors of his own excretions and secretions. Such odors arising from the skin, the genital region, and the feet were pleasurable to him at an early age. In this way the foot was able to acquire genital significance in his unconscious phantasies. It may be mentioned with regard to his coprophilic pleasure in smell that many of his dreams had their setting in the w.c. or fulfilled anal-erotic desires by means of a transparent symbolism. A characteristic type of dream was one in which he put his nose between two big hemispheres.

It has already been said that the patient's scoptophilic instinct was also chiefly directed on to excrement. He often used to dream of his father and brother in situations of this kind; and water occurred as a symbol in the majority of his dreams, of which the following is an interesting example. He was in a boat with his brother, going through a harbor. In order to get out of the harbor they had to pass through a peculiarly built passage, like a house on the water. Then they got into open water, but suddenly they were on dry land and the boat was passing down a street without touching the ground. Then they were floating along in the air, and a policeman was looking on at them. I will only say a few words about the interpretation of the dream. The word 'harbor' *'Hafen'* contains a double meaning, since in certain dialects *Hafen* means chamber utensil. And the word 'boat' [*'Schiff'*] is very similar to a word vulgarly used for making water [*'Schiffen'*]. The passage out of the harbor reminded the dreamer of the tapering columns of the temple at Philæ. Another association was 'Colossus of Rhodes'. The Colossus represents a man standing with his legs apart over the entrance to the harbor of Rhodes. It reminded the patient of his father, whom he had seen urinating in a similar attitude. His subsequent voyage in the boat in company with his brother, and the part about the boat going through the air, were connected with a childhood memory which concerned a certain not infrequent contest among boys with respect to making water. The exhibitionistic factor in this dream was also of some importance; for the urinating was done in front of a policeman, and we know from experience that in dreams persons in authority signify the father.

The extraordinarily rich dream-material which the patient supplied in the course of his analysis contained a great number of dreams with a similar theme. One can conclude from the amazing variety of these dreams that his phantasies were occupied in quite an unusual degree with a coprophilic pleasure in looking. It may be mentioned that he exhibited the typical character-traits of sublimated anal-erotism; pedantic economy and love of orderliness were especially prominent features.

The degree to which the foot replaced the penis in the patient's mind was clearly seen in certain dreams of his, two of which I will briefly relate. In the one dream he was wearing slippers which were trodden down behind so that his heels were visible. This dream turned out to be

49

an exhibitionistic dream. The heel was exposed to view as the sexual organs are in the ordinary exhibitionistic dream. The affect was the same as in typical exhibition dreams that are accompanied by anxiety. In the other dream he touched a woman with his foot and in this way dirtied her. This dream can be understood without further comment.

It is now clear why the patient took particular interest in the high heels of women's shoes. The heel of the shoe corresponded to the heel of the foot—a part of the body which, in virtue of the displacement referred to, had taken on the significance of a male genital. Thus the patient's predilection for women's feet and their covering, and more especially the heels, prolonged his infantile sexual interest in the supposed penis of the female.

The facts brought forward here only represent a small part of those which his analysis furnished, but they seem to me sufficient to show that the foot can be a substitute for the genitals. The patient's scoptophilic and osphresiophilic instincts, which had been particularly directed to excreta from the first, had undergone far-reaching though certainly very dissimilar alterations. His osphresiophilic instinct had been repressed to a great extent, whereas his scoptophilic instinct had been very much accentuated but at the same time diverted from its original sphere of interest and idealized. To this latter process, which only affected the second of the two instincts in question, we can apply Freud's term of 'partial repression'.

Since having had this case I have more than once had an opportunity of analysing fetishistic traits in neurotics where such traits have formed secondary symptoms; and in every case I have come to the same conclusions concerning the importance of those instincts which formed the basis of the fetishistic symptoms in the present case. On account of this uniformity in my results I do not propose to bring forward new material from these later cases.

A few words must be said about the therapeutic effect of psychoanalysis in the present case and in other cases of fetishism. I did not succeed in removing the fetishistic symptoms in this particular case; but the analytic interpretation succeeded in very greatly diminishing the power which the patient's sexual abnormality had hitherto exercised over him. His power of resistance against the attraction of women's shoes, etc., was considerably increased, and normal sexual instincts often emerged during his analysis. I do not think it impossible that if the treatment had been persevered with, a gradual strengthening of the normal libido would have been achieved.

The therapeutic outlook seems to me more favorable in less pronounced cases, as, for instance, when certain fetishistic symptoms accompany a neurosis. A case of this kind which I analysed recently seemed to show that psychoanalysis can remove both the neurotic and the fetishistic symptoms and can bring about a normal sexual attitude in the patient.

The Brief Analysis

of a

Hypochondriac

(1919)

Sandor Ferenczi, M.D.

translated by Joan Riviere

The Psycho-Analysis of a Case of Hysterical Hypochondria.

From: FURTHER CONTRIBUTIONS TO THE THEORY & TECHNIQUE OF PSYCHO-ANALYSIS. The Hogarth Press, Ltd., London: 1950

53

SANDOR FERENCZI

Sandor Ferenczi (1873–1933) was another one of Freud's earliest students and joined the Psychological Wednesday Society in 1908. He was a Hungarian physician who was one of Freud's closest personal friends from 1908 on.

Ferenczi's chief contributions dealt with his suggestions for psychoanalytic technique. He is especially known for his efforts to develop a more active technique in order to shorten the course of psychoanalysis and to enable the analyst to deal with cases that could not be treated by the more orthodox or passive methods of psychoanalysis.

In this case of hysterical hypochondria written in 1919, Ferenczi demonstrates some of his more active methods. In addition, Ferenczi shows the importance of repressed emotions as a cause of emotional disorder; for example, his patient's repression of the death wishes she felt against her child and her vain attempts to retreat into "insanity". Here, too, there is a demonstration of the wish of many females to possess a penis so that they may be either the equal of men or, as in the case of Ferenczi's patient, to be able to do without men by giving themselves sexual gratification.

In this case also Ferenczi seems to demonstrate that repressed unconscious death wishes may be as pathogenic as repressed sexuality.

The Brief Analysis
of a
Hypochondriac
(1919)

In consequence of the wearisome and slow progress of
its method of cure, psychoanalytic technique entails the
blurring of the general impression of a case, and the individual factors of its complicated connections force themselves on' the attention only intermittently.

In what follows I shall communicate a case whose cure
was very rapid and whose clinical picture (both in form
and content very varied and interesting) unfolded itself
dramatically, almost without interruption, like a series of
cinematograph pictures.

The patient, a pretty young foreigner, was brought to
me for treatment by her relatives, after various other
methods of cure had been tried. She made a very unfavorable impression. Her most prominent symptom was
a very marked *anxiety*. Without being exactly agorapho-
bic (fear of open places [Ed.]), she had for months
been unable to exist without being accompanied at every
moment; if she were left alone, the most intense attacks
of anxiety occurred, even at night she had to waken her
husband or whoever happened to be sleeping with her
and tell them about her ideas and feelings of anxiety for
hours on end. Her complaints were of hypochondriacal
bodily sensations and the fear of death associated with
them. She felt something in her throat, 'points' were
coming out of her scalp (these sensations compelled her
constantly to touch her throat and the skin of her face);
her ears were lengthening, her head was splitting in
front; her heart was palpitating, etc. In each such sensation, for whose occurrence she was constantly looking,

she saw an indication of her approaching death; she had thoughts too of suicide. Her father had died of arteriosclerosis and that now seemed imminent to her; she would also (like her father) become insane, and would have to die in the asylum. She at once constructed a new symptom out of the fact that at the first examination I explored her throat for possible anesthesia (lack of sensation [Ed.]) or hyperesthesia (oversensitivity [Ed.]). She had constantly to stand in front of the mirror and look for changes in her tongue. The first interviews passed in continuous, monotonous complaints about these sensations, and the symptoms seemed to me to be of an unmodifiable, hypochondriacal, insane type, especially as a few such cases were still fresh in my memory.

After some time she seemed to have exhausted herself somewhat, probably because I never tried either to soothe or otherwise influence her, but let her run on with her complaints undisturbed. Slight signs of transference, too, showed themselves; she felt quieter after the interview, awaited the beginning of the next hour with impatience, etc. She grasped very quickly how to 'associate freely,' but the associations changed over at the very first attempt into insanely passionate and theatrical behavior. 'I am N. N.—manufacturer.' (Here she gave her father's name, with visibly heightened self-consciousness.) She then behaved as though she were actually her father giving orders in the yard and shops, swore (pretty roughly and shamelessly too, as is customary in that district); then repeated scenes enacted by her father when he was insane, before he was confined in an asylum. At the end of the hour, however, she was quite well orientated, said good-bye nicely, and let herself be accompanied quietly home.

She began the ensuing hour with the continuation of the above scene; she repeated over and over again: 'I am N. N. I have a penis'. Between whiles she related an infantile scene in which an ugly nurse threatened her with an enema syringe because she would not defecate spontaneously. The hours that now followed were taken up alternately with the hypochondriacal complaints, her father's insane episodes, and soon with passionate transference phantasies. She demanded—in downright peasant speech—to be sexually satisfied, and ranted at her husband who could not do it properly (which, however, did not agree with the truth). Her husband then told me that from this time the patient did actually ask to be sexually satisfied, while she had previously refused it for a considerable period.

After these unburdenings her manic exaltation quieted down and we were able to study the previous history of the case. She related the exciting causes of the illness. The war had broken out, her husband had been called up, she had had to replace him in the business; she could not do this properly, however, as she had constantly to think about her elder daughter (about six years old), and had the idea that something might happen to her at home, so she had constantly to run home to see about it. This elder daughter was born with rickets and a sacro-meningocele which was operated on, so that the little creature lived but her lower extremities and bladder were incurably paralysed. She could only crawl about on all fours, and on account of the incontinence must be changed 'about a hundred times a day'. 'It makes no difference, however, I love her a thousand times more than the second (the healthy!) daughter'. This was confirmed, too, by all those about her; the patient petted this sick child at the expense of the second, healthy one; she would not admit that one should be unhappy about the sick child—'she is so good, so clever, has such a pretty face'.

It was quite soon apparent to me that this was a tremendous effort of repression on the part of the patient; that in reality she yearned unconsciously for the death of her unfortunate child, and was not capable of the increased efforts demanded of her by the war, because of this previous burden. She therefore took refuge in illness.

After careful preparation I explained this conception of her illness to her, whereupon—after vain attempts to precipitate herself once more into insanity or into the transference passion—she gradually managed to let herself become conscious to a certain extent of the great pain and shame which the crippled condition of her child caused her.

I now had recourse to one of the methods of 'active technique'. I sent the patient home for a day, in order that she should have the opportunity of reviving, with the

57

help of her newly won insight, the feelings which her children inspired in her. While at home she devoted herself again passionately to the love and care of the sick child, and then said triumphantly at the next interview: 'You see it is none of it true! I do love only my eldest girl!' and so on. But even in the same interview she had to admit the contrary with bitter tears; corresponding with her impulsively passionate nature there occurred to her sudden compulsive thoughts in which she strangled or hanged this child, or cursed it 'God's lightning strike you'. (This curse was familiar to her from the folklore of her home.)

The remainder of the treatment progressed on the lines of the transference love. The patient showed herself seriously wounded at the purely medical handling of her repeated love declarations, involuntarily indicating her unusually powerful narcissism. We lost a few hours owing to the resistance evoked by this hurt to her conceit and self-love, but this afforded us the opportunity for the reproduction of similar 'insults' of which she had experienced an usual number. I was able to show her that each time one of her numerous sisters had become engaged (she was the youngest), she felt herself injured by the neglect of her person. Her jealousy and revengefulness went so far that out of sheer envy she reported a relative whom she caught with a young man. In spite of her apparent reserve and her introspection she was very self-conscious, and had a high opinion of her own physical and intellectual qualities. To protect herself from the risk of too painful disillusionments she preferred to stand obstinately aside where any competitions with other girls was concerned. Now, too, I understood the extraordinary phantasy to which she gave expression in one of her pseudo-insane attacks; she again represented herself to be her (insane) father, and declared that *she wished to have sexual intercourse with herself.*

Her child's illness influenced her so powerfully only because of her—quite comprehensible—*identification* with her; she herself had formerly at one time had to endure some painful violations of her own bodily integrity. She too came into the world with a physical disability; she squinted, and had in her youth to undergo an operation of which she had stood in the utmost terror,

58

and almost went insane at the thought that she might go blind. Moreover, on account of this squint she had been in her childhood the object of her playfellows' scorn.

We also gradually achieved the interpretation of the individual hypochondriacal sensations. The feeling in her throat was the substitute for the wish that her beautiful alto voice should be heard and admired. The 'points' that 'came out' of her scalp were little vermin, that were once—to her great humiliation—discovered on her head; the 'elongation of the ears' referred to the fact that at school she was once called a 'donkey' by the teacher, and so on.

The most remote covering memory to which we could penetrate was a mutual exhibitionism that had occurred between her and a boy of her own age in the attic of her home, and I do not doubt that behind this scene lies the most powerful impressions affecting the patient. It was probably the *penis jealousy* implanted at that time that rendered her capable of the remarkably successful identification with her father in her attacks of delirium. ('I have a penis', etc.) Finally, the congenital abnormality of her eldest child need not be considered so much the cause of her illness as the fact that she had given birth, not to a boy, but to two girls (creatures without a penis, that could not—like boys—urinate properly). Hence the unconscious horror of her daughter's incontinence. It seems, moreover, that the illness of her first-born began to affect her more powerfully when the second child also proved to be a girl.

The patient returned from a second visit home quite changed. She was reconciled to the idea that she preferred the younger child and that she wished for the death of the sick daughter; she ceased to wail about her hypochondriacal sensations, and occupied herself with planning to return home soon for good. Behind this sudden improvement I discovered the resistance to the cessation of treatment. From the analysis of her dreams I had to conclude that she had a paranoid distrust of her doctor's integrity; she believed that I wanted to prolong the treatment in order to get more money from her. From this point of vantage I tried to find the approach to her anal erotism associated with her narcissism (*cf.* her infantile fear of the enema syringe), but I only partially

59

succeeded. The patient preferred to keep a part of her neurotic peculiarities, and went home practically cured.[1]

Apart from the unusually rapid course of this illness, the epicrisis (summary [Ed.]) of this case presents much of interest. We are dealing here with a mixture of purely hypochondriacal and hysterical symptoms, and at the beginning of the analysis the clinical picture of the illness merged into schizophrenia, while towards the end it showed indications, however slight, of paranoia.

The mechanism of individual hypochondriac paresthesias (disordered sensations, as tingling, itching, etc. [Ed.]) is noteworthy. They were based originally on her narcissistic preference for her own body, but then became—something after the fashion of a 'physical predisposition'—the means of expression of hysterical processes (ideational in origin), for instance, the feeling of the elongation of her ears became the memorial of a psychic trauma.

In this way one observes problems—still unsolved—of the organic basis of conversion hysteria and hypochondria. It seems as though the same stagnation of organ libido—according to the patient's sexual constitution—can have either a purely hypochondriacal or conversion hysteria 'superstructure'. In our case we were dealing apparently with the combination of both possibilities, and the hysterical side of the neurosis rendered possible the

[1] Here are a few more details: the complusive sensation, *my head is splitting open in front,* was the expression of a pregnancy wish displaced 'upwards'. She wished for new children (boys) in place of those she already had (the sick child and the other girl). She was in the habit of repeating constantly, 'There is nothing new again'—pointing to her forehead; this also belonged to the pregnancy complex. The patient had aborted twice—not altogether accidentally—and unconsciously regretted it. The *palpitation* was the memory of libidinal feelings on meeting sympathetic young men who seemed potent to her. (To be potent meant for her, ability to beget *boys* and *healthy* children in general.) The *'points'* that came out were over-determined. They meant not only vermin but (as so often) little children also. Here are two characteristic dreams: 1. *She sees bags hanging up (money bags?).* (Interpretation: If she realizes that she wishes to hang her child she will be able to save further fees.) 2. *One of her sisters is dancing a cake walk; her father is there too.* (Reproduction of her bridal night, when her pleasure was spoiled by the thought that her father was in an institution.)

transference and the psychoanalytic discharge of the hypochondriacal sensations. Where this possibility of discharge does not exist the hypochondriac remains inaccessible and fastens—often insanely—on the sensation and observation of his paresthesia.

Pure hypochondria is incurable; only where—as here —transference neurotic components are present, can one attempt psychotherapeutic influence with any hope of success.

The Child
Who
Couldn't Sleep

(1924)

Melanie Klein

translated by Alix Strachey

An Obsessional Neurosis in a Six-Year-Old Girl.

From: THE PSYCHOANALYSIS OF CHILDREN;
The Hogarth Press, London: 1950.

MELANIE KLEIN

Melanie Klein, a psychologist who trained with both Ferenczi and Abraham, started to practice psychoanalysis in Germany in 1919, went to England in 1926, and there became the leader of one of the two groups into which British Freudian psychoanalyists are divided. The other group is headed by Anna Freud, the daughter of Sigmund Freud.

Melanie Klein and her group believe that even with very young children the analyst should drive straight to the instinctual conflicts which should then be interpreted to the child. Anna Freud, on the other hand, takes the position that the child's defences or expedient ways of dealing with its instinctual drives should be understood, respected, and helpfully modified by the therapist.

When Freud first stated his psychoanalytic theories, one of the causes of resistance to his teachings was disbelief in his theory of infantile sexuality. Freud attempted for the most part to prove the existence of sexual fantasies in children through his analysis of adult neurotics. There was considerable opposition to Freud's theories about the existence of sexual feelings in very young children by those who claimed that the adult neurotic is not an accurate reporter of early feelings and therefore the history of childhood sexual feelings that Freud was getting from his adult neurotic patients could just as easily have been fantasies developed by the patients at a later date. It was not until techniques were developed for the treatment of children that it was possible to explore the existence of sexual feelings and fantasies in such young children by direct observation.

While Freud had attempted to treat a child by talking to one boy's father, and Frau Dr. Hermine von Hug-Hellmuth had treated children over six, it was probably Melanie Klein who first devised a method of treating children as young as three. Since she found such young children unable to cooperate by free-associating in words, she provided them with toys and observed the ways in which they played with them as a means of inferring what unconscious forces were at work. The child, for example, is permitted to play with dolls that represent father, mother, sister or brother, and the way in

64

which the child manipulates these toys is taken as indicative of its unconscious feelings to the members of his family. Following the style of Ferenczi, Mrs. Klein and her followers interpret the meaning of his behavior directly to the child or adult instead of waiting for the patient to arrive at his own insights as do the more "passive" psychoanalysts.

In the following case, Melanie Klein illustrates how the analysis of a child is conducted by utilizing the techniques of play therapy. The child's play seemed to symbolize many of her problems at home.

This case also demonstrates the importance of early analysis to prevent the development of serious mental disorder in the adult.

The Child
Who
Couldn't Sleep
(1924)

Erna, a child of six had a number of severe symptoms. She suffered from sleeplessness, which was caused partly by anxiety (in particular by a fear of robbers and burglars) and partly by a series of obsessional activities. These consisted in lying on her face and banging her head on the pillow, in making a rocking movement, during which she sat or lay on her back, in obsessional thumb-sucking and in excessive masturbation. All these obsessional activities, which prevented her from sleeping at night, were carried on in the day-time as well. This was especially the case with masturbation, which she practised even in the presence of strangers, and, for instance, almost continuously at her kindergarten. She suffered

Note: This chapter is based on a paper read by Melanie Klein at Würzburg in October 1924, at the First Conference of German Psycho-Analysts.

65

from severe depressions, which she would describe by saying: 'There's something I don't like about life.' In her relations to her mother she was over-affectionate, but would at times veer round to a hostile attitude. She completely dominated her mother, left her no freedom of movement and plagued her continually with her love and hatred. As her mother put it: 'She swallows me up.' The child might, too, be fairly described as ineducable. Obsessive brooding and a curiously unchildlike nature were depicted in the suffering look upon the little girl's face. Besides this she made an impression of being unusually precocious sexually. A symptom which first became obvious during the analysis was that she had a very severe inhibition in learning. She was sent to school a few months after her analysis began, and it was soon evident that she was incapable of learning and could adapt herself neither to school nor to her school-fellows. The fact that she herself felt that she was ill—at the very beginning of her treatment she begged me to help her— was of great assistance to me in analysing her.

Erna began her play by taking a small carriage which stood on the little table among the other toys and pushing it towards me. She declared that she had come to fetch me. But she put a toy woman in the carriage instead and added a toy man. The two loved and kissed one another and drove up and down all the time. Next a toy man in another carriage collided with them, ran over them and killed them and then roasted and ate them up. Another time the fight had a different end and the attacking toy man was thrown down; but the woman helped him and comforted him. She got a divorce from her first husband and married the new one. This third person was given the most various parts to play in Erna's games. For instance, the original man and his wife were in a house which they were defending against a burglar; the third person was the burglar, and slipped in. The house burnt down, the man and woman burst and the third person was the only one left. Then again the third person was a brother who came on a visit; but while embracing the woman he bit her nose off. This little man, the third person, was Erna herself. In a series of similar games she represented her wish to oust her father from his position with her mother. On the other hand, in many other

66

games she showed her direct Oedipus wish to get rid of her mother and to win her father. Thus she made a toy teacher give the children violin lessons by knocking his head[1] against the violin, or stand on his head as he was reading out of a book. She then made him throw down book or violin as the case might be and dance with his girl pupil. The two next kissed and embraced each other. At this point Erna asked me all at once if I would allow a marriage between teacher and pupil. Another time a teacher and a mistress—represented by a toy man and woman—were giving the children lessons in manners, teaching them how to bow and curtsy, etc. At first the children were obedient and polite (just as Erna herself always did her best to be good and behave nicely), then suddenly they attacked the teacher and mistress, trampled them underfoot and killed and roasted them. They had now become devils, and gloated over the torments of their victims. But all at once the teacher and mistress were in heaven and the former devils had turned into angels, who, according to Erna's account, knew nothing about ever having been devils—indeed 'they never *were* devils'. God the Father, the former teacher, began kissing and embracing the woman passionately, the angels worshipped them and all was well again—though before long things were sure to go wrong again one way or another.

Erna used very often to play at being mother. I was the child and one of my greatest faults was thumb-sucking. The first thing which I was supposed to put into my mouth was an engine. She had already much admired its gilded lamps, saying, 'They're so lovely, all red and burning', and at the same time putting them into her mouth and sucking them. They stood to her for her mother's breast and her father's penis. These games were invariably followed by outbreaks of rage, envy and aggression against her mother, to be succeeded by remorse and by attempts to make amends and placate her. In playing

[1] Compare her obsessional symptom of banging her head on the pillow. Here is another game which shows clearly that to Erna's unconscious the head had the meaning of a penis: a toy man wanted to get into a car and stuck his head into the window, whereupon the car said to him, 'Better come right inside!' The car stood for her mother inviting her father to have coitus with her.

with bricks, for instance, she would divide them between us so that she had more bricks than I; then she would make up for this by taking fewer herself, but would nevertheless always manage to keep more in the end. If I had to build with my bricks it was only so that she might prove how much more beautiful her building was than mine or so that she might knock mine down, apparently by accident. She would sometimes make a toy man be judge and decide that her house was better than mine. From the details of the game it was apparent that she was giving expression to a long-standing rivalry with her mother in this business about our respective houses. In a later part of her analysis she brought out her rivalry in a direct form.

Besides playing these games she also began cutting out paper and making paper patterns. She told me once that it was 'hash' she was making and that blood was coming out of the paper; upon which she gave a shudder and said she felt bad all at once. On one occasion she talked about 'eye-salad', and on another she said that she was cutting 'fringes' in my nose. She was here repeating the wish to bite off my nose which she had expressed in her very first hour. (And indeed she made a number of attempts to carry out her wish.) By this means she also showed her identity with the 'third person', the toy man who broke in and set fire to the house, etc., and who bit off noses. In her analysis, as in that of other children, cutting out paper proved to be very variously determined. It gave outlet to sadistic and cannibalistic impulses and represented the destruction of her parents' genitals and her mother's whole body. At the same time, however, it expressed her reactive impulses as well, because in the thing cut out—a pretty mat, let us say—what had been destroyed was re-created.

From cutting out paper Erna went on to playing with water. A small piece of paper floating in the basin was a captain whose ship had gone down. He was able to save himself because—so Erna declared—he had something 'long and golden' which held him up in the water. She then tore off his head and announced: 'His head's gone; now he's drowned.' These games with water led deep into the analysis of her oral-sadistic, urethral-sadistic

68

and anal-sadistic phantasies. Thus, for instance, she played at being a washerwoman, and used some pieces of paper to represent a child's dirty linen. I was the child and had to dirty my underclothes over and over again. (Incidentally, Erna brought her coprophilic and cannibalistic impulses clearly to view by chewing up the pieces of paper, which represented excrements and children as well as dirty linen.) As a washerwoman Erna also had many opportunities of punishing and humiliating the child, and played the part of the cruel mother. But since she also identified herself with the child, she was gratifying her masochistic wishes as well. She would often pretend that the mother made the father punish the child and beat it on the bottom. This punishment was recommended by Erna, in her rôle of washerwoman, as a means of curing the child of its love of dirt. Once, instead of the father, a magician came along. He hit the child on the anus and then on the head with a stick, and as he did so a yellowish fluid poured out of the magic wand. On another occasion the child—a quite little one this time—was given a powder to take, which was 'red and white' mixed together. This treatment made it quite clean, and it was suddenly able to talk, and became as clever as its mother.[1] The magician stood for the penis, and hitting with the stick meant coitus. The fluid and the powder represented urine, feces, semen and blood, all of which, according to Erna's phantasies, her mother put inside herself in copulation through her mouth, anus and genitals.

Another time Erna suddenly changed herself from a washerwoman into a fishwife and began to cry her wares. In the course of this game she turned on the water-tap (which she used also to call the 'whipped cream tap') after wrapping some paper round it. When the paper was soaked through and fell into the basin she tore it up and offered it for sale as fish. The compulsive greed with which Erna drank from the water-tap during this game and chewed up the imaginary fish pointed very clearly to the oral envy which she had felt during the primal scene and in her primal phantasies. This envy had affected the development of her character very deeply, and was also a

[1] These phantasies relate to the penis in its 'good' and curative aspect.

central feature of her neurosis.[1] The equation of the fish with her father's penis, as well as with feces and children, was very obvious in her associations. Erna had a variety of fish for sale and amongst them some '*Kokelfish*' or, as she suddenly called them, '*Kakelfish*'.[2] While she was cutting these up she had a sudden wish to defecate, and this showed that the fish were equivalent to feces, while cutting them up was equated with the act of defecation. As the fishwife, Erna cheated me in all sorts of ways. She took large quantities of money from me and gave me no fish in return. I was helpless against her, because she was assisted by a policeman; and together they 'wurled'[3] the money, which also stood for fish, she had got from me. This policeman represented her father with whom she copulated and who was her ally against her mother. I had to look on while she 'wurled' the money, or fish, with the policeman, and then I had to try to get possession of it by stealth. In fact, I had to pretend to do what she herself had wanted to do to her mother when she had witnessed her mother and father having sexual intercourse. These sadistic impulses and phantasies were at the bottom of her severe anxiety in regard to her mother. She repeatedly expressed fear of a 'robber woman' who would 'take out everything inside her.'

The symbolic meaning of the theatre and performances of all kinds, as signifying coitus between the parents, came out very clearly in Erna's analysis. The numerous performances in which she was an actress or a dancer, admired by all the spectators, showed the immense admiration—an admiration mixed with envy—which she had for her mother. Often, too, in identification with her mother, she pretended to be a queen before whom everyone bowed down. In all these representations it was always the child who got the worst of it. Everything which Erna did in the rôle of her mother—the tenderness she showed to her husband, the way in which she dressed herself up and allowed herself to be admired—

[1] We shall discuss later on the connection between Erna's observations of her parents' sexual intercourse and her own neurosis.
[2] '*Kaki*' = 'feces' in nursery German.
[3] An invented word resembling the German word for whipping cream.

70

had one chief purpose, which was to arouse the child's envy and to wound its feelings. Thus, for instance, when she, as queen, had celebrated her marriage with the king, she lay down on the sofa and wanted me, as the king, to lie down beside her. As I refused to do this I had to sit on a little chair by her side instead and hit the sofa with my fist. This she called 'churning', and it meant copulating. Immediately after this she announced that a child was creeping out of her, and she represented the scene in a quite realistic way, writhing about and groaning. Her imaginary child then shared its parents' bedroom and had to be a spectator of sexual intercourse between them. If it interrupted it was beaten, and the mother kept on complaining of it to the father. If she, as the mother, put the child to bed it was only in order to get rid of it and to be able to get back to the father all the sooner. The child was incessantly being maltreated and tormented. It was given gruel to eat that was so nasty as to make it sick, while at the same time its mother and father were enjoying marvelous foods made of whipped cream or a special milk prepared by Dr. Whippo or Whippour—a name compounded from 'whipping' and 'pouring out'. This special food, which was eaten only by the mother and father, was used in endless variations to represent the exchange of substances during coition. Erna's phantasies that in coition her mother, incorporated her father's penis and semen and her father incorporated her, mother's breasts and milk formed the basis of her hatred and envy against her two parents.

In one of Erna's games a 'performance' was given by a priest. He turned on the water-tap, and his partner, a woman dancer, drank from it. The child, called Cinderella, was only allowed to look on and had to remain absolutely motionless. A sudden tremendous outbreak of anger on Erna's part at this point showed with what feelings of hatred her phantasies were accompanied and how badly she had succeeded in dealing with those feelings. Her whole relationship to her mother had been distorted by them. Every educational measure, every act of nursery discipline, every unavoidable frustration, was felt by her as a purely sadistic act on the part of her mother, done with a view to humiliating and ill-treating her.

Nevertheless, in her make-believe of being a mother

71

Erna did show affection to her imaginary child so long as it was still only a baby. Then she would nurse and wash it and be tender to it, and even forgive it when it was dirty. This was because, in her view, she herself had only been treated lovingly as long as she was an infant in arms. To her older 'child' she would be most cruel, and would let it be tortured by devils in a variety of ways and in the end be killed.[1] That the child was also the mother turned into a child, however, was made clear by the following phantasy. Erna played at being a child that had dirtied itself, and I, as the mother, had to scold her, whereupon she became insolent, and out of defiance dirtied herself more and more. In order to annoy the mother still further she vomited up the bad food I had given her. The father was then called in by the mother, but he took the child's side. Next the mother was seized with an illness called 'God has spoken to her'; then the child in turn got an illness called 'mother's agitation' and died of it, and the mother was killed by the father as a punishment. The child then came to life again and was married to the father, who kept on praising it at the expense of the mother. The mother was then brought to life again too, but, as a punishment, was turned into a child by the father with the help of his magic wand; and now she in turn had to suffer all the scorn and ill-treatment to which the child had been subjected before. In her numerous phantasies of this kind about a mother and a child Erna was repeating what she felt her own experiences had been, while on the other hand she was also expressing the sadistic things she would like to do to her mother if the child-mother relationship were reversed.

Erna's mental life was dominated by anal-sadistic phan-

[1] Where, as in this case, the child's fury against its object is really excessive, the fundamental situation is that the super-ego has turned against the id. The ego escapes from this intolerable situation by means of a projection. It presents the object as an enemy in order that the id can destroy it in a sadistic way with the consent of the super-ego. If the ego can effect an alliance between the super-ego and the id by this means, it can for the time being send out the sadism of the super-ego that was directed against the id into the external world. In this way the primary sadistic impulses which are directed against the object are increased by the hatred originally directed against the id.

72

tasies. At a later stage of her analysis, starting, once more, from games connected with water, she produced phantasies in which feces 'baked on' to dirty clothes were cooked and eaten. Again, she played that she was sitting in the lavatory and eating what she produced there, or that we were handing it to one another to eat. Her phantasies about our continually dirtying each other with urine and feces came out more and more clearly in the course of the analysis. In one game she demonstrated that her mother had dirtied herself over and over again and that everything in the room had been turned into feces through her mother's fault. Her mother was accordingly thrown into prison and starved there. She herself then had the job of cleaning up after her mother, and in that connection called herself 'Mrs. Dirt Parade' —that is, a person parading with dirt. Through her love of tidiness she won the admiration and recognition of her father, who set her high above her mother and married her. She did his cooking for him. The drinks and food which they gave one another were once more urine and feces, but this time a good kind instead of a harmful one.—The above will serve as an example of the numerous and extravagant anal-sadistic phantasies which became conscious in the course of her analysis.

Erna, who was an only child, was much occupied in her imagination with the arrival of brothers and sisters. Her phantasies in this context deserve special attention, since, so far as my observations show, they have a general application. Judging from them and from those of other children similarly situated, it would appear that an only child suffers to a far greater extent than other children from the anxiety it feels in regard to the brother or sister whom it is forever expecting, and from the feelings of guilt it has towards them on account of its unconscious impulses of aggression against them in their imaginary existence inside its mother's body, because it has no opportunity of developing a positive relation to them in reality. This fact often makes it more difficult for an only child to adapt itself to society. For a long time Erna used to have attacks of rage and anxiety at the beginning and end of her analytic hour with me, and these were in part occasioned by her meeting the child who came to me for treatment immediately before or after her and who

73

stood to her for the brother or sister whose arrival she was always awaiting.[1] On the other hand, although she got on badly with other children, she felt a great need for their society at times. Her occasional wish for a brother or sister was, I found, determined by a number of motives. (1) The brothers and sisters which she desired meant a child of her own. This wish, however, was soon disturbed by severe feelings of guilt, because it would have meant that she had stolen the child from her mother. (2) Their existence would have reassured her that the attacks she had made in her phantasy on the children which she supposed to be inside her mother had damaged neither them nor her mother, and that consequently the interior of her own body was unharmed. (3) They would afford her the sexual gratification which her father and mother had denied her; and, most important of all, (4) they would be her confederates, not only in sexual doings, but in enterprises against her terrifying parents. They and she together would kill her mother and capture her father's penis.[1]

But these phantasies of Erna's would quickly be followed by feelings of hatred against her imaginary brothers and sisters—for they were, ultimately, only substitutes for her father and mother—and by very severe feelings of guilt on account of the destructive acts she and they had committed against her parents in her phantasies. And she would usually end by having an attack of depression.

These phantasies, too, had their share in making it impossible for Erna to get on to good terms with other children. She shrank from them because she identified them with her imaginary brothers and sisters, so that on the one hand she regarded them as accomplices in her

[1] As Erna had no brothers or sisters in real life, her unconscious fear and jealousy of them which played such an important part in her mental life were only revealed and lived through in the analysis. This is once more an example of the importance of the transference-situation in child analyses.

[1] In my paper, 'Early Stages of the Oedipus Conflict' (1928), I have pointed out that children, in their sexual relations with one another, especially if they are brothers and sisters, have phantasies of being in league together against their parents and often experience a diminution of their anxiety and sense of guilt from this belief.

attacks upon her parents, and on the other she feared them as enemies because of her own aggressive impulses towards those brothers and sisters.

Erna's case throws light on another factor which seems to me to be of general importance. In the first chapter I drew attention to the peculiar relationship that children have to reality. I pointed out that failure in making a correct adaptation to reality could, in analysis, be recognized in the play of quite small children, and that it was necessary in analysis gradually to bring even the youngest child into complete touch with reality. With Erna, even after a good deal of analysis had been done, I had not succeeded in obtaining any detailed information about her real life. I got plenty of material regarding her extravagant sadistic impulses against her mother, but I never heard the least complaint or criticism from her about her *real* mother and what she actually did. Although Erna got to recognize that her phantasies were directed against her own mother—a fact which she had denied at an earlier stage of analysis—and although it became clearer and clearer that she copied her mother in an exaggerated and invidious manner, yet it was difficult to establish the connection between her phantasies and reality. All my efforts to draw her actual life more fully into the analysis remained ineffective, until I had made definite progress in analysing her deepest reasons for wanting to cut herself off from reality. Erna's relationship to reality proved to be largely a façade, and this to a far greater extent than her behavior would have led one to expect. The truth was that she was trying by every means to maintain a dream world in existence and to protect it from reality.[1] For instance, she used to imagine that the toy carriages and coachmen were in her service, that they came at her command and brought her everything she wished, that the toy women were her servants, and so on. Even while these phantasies were in progress she would often be seized with rage and depression. She would then go to the lavatory and there phantasy aloud while she defecated. When she came out of the lavatory she would

[1] Many children make only an *apparent* return to reality when their games are interrupted. Actually they are still occupied with their phantasies.

75

fling herself on to the sofa and begin to suck her thumb passionately, to masturbate and to pick her nose. I succeeded in getting her to tell me the phantasies which accompanied this defecation, thumb-sucking, masturbation and nose-picking. By means of these physical satisfactions and the phantasies bound up with them she was endeavoring forcibly to continue the same day-dreaming situation which she had been keeping up in her game. The depression, anger and anxiety which seized her during her play were due to a disturbance of her phantasies by some incursion of reality. She remembered, too, how greatly she was put out if anyone came near her bed in the morning while she was thumb-sucking or masturbating. The reason for this was not only that she was afraid of being caught, but that she wanted to ward off reality. A *pseudologia,* which appeared during her analysis and grew to fantastic proportions, served the purpose of reshaping to her desires a reality which was intolerable to her. This extraordinary cutting-off of reality—to which end she also employed megalomanic (delusions of grandeur [Ed.]) phantasies—had one cause, I found, in her excessive fear of her parents, especially her mother. It was in order to lessen this fear that Erna was driven to imagine herself as a powerful and harsh mistress over her mother, and this led to a great intensification of her sadism.

Erna's phantasies of being cruelly persecuted by her mother began to show their paranoid character more distinctly. As I have already said, she looked upon every step taken in her education and upbringing, even down to the least details of her clothing, as an act of persecution on the part of her mother. Not only so, but everything else that her mother did—the way she behaved towards her father, the things she did for her own amusement, and soon—were felt by Erna as a persecution of herself. Moreover, she felt herself continually spied upon. One cause of her excessive fixation upon her mother was the compulsion she was under of continually keeping watch over her. Analysis showed that Erna felt responsible for every illness that her mother had, and expected a corresponding punishment because of her own aggressive phantasies. The action of an over-severe and cruel superego in her was apparent in many of the details of her games and phantasies, as they perpetually alternated between the severe, punishing mother and the hating child. It needed a very deep-going analysis to elucidate these phantasies, which were identical with what, in adult paranoiacs, are known as delusions. The experience I have gained since I first wrote down this case-history has led me to the view that the peculiar character of Erna's anxiety, of her phantasies and of her relation to reality, is typical of those cases in which strong paranoic traits are active.

At this point I must draw attention to Erna's homosexual tendencies, which had been excessively strong from early childhood onwards. After a great amount of her hatred of her father, arising out of the Oedipus situation, had been analysed, those tendencies, though undoubtedly diminished, were still very strong and seemed at first incapable of being resolved any further. It was only after obstinate and lengthy resistances had been broken down that the real character and full strength of her persecution phantasies and their relation to her homosexuality came to light. Anal love desires now emerged much clearer in their *positive* form, alternately with her phantasies of persecution. Erna once more played at being a shopwoman (and that what she sold was faeces was obvious from the fact that right at the beginning of the game she had to interrupt it in order to go and defecate). I was a customer and had to prefer her to all other shopkeepers and think her wares particularly good. Then she was the customer and loved me, and in this way she represented an anal love relationship between her mother and herself. These anal phantasies were soon interrupted by fits of depression and hatred which she chiefly directed against me but which were actually aimed at her mother. In this connection Erna produced phantasies of a flea which was 'black and yellow mixed' and which she herself at once recognized as a bit of faeces— dangerous, poisoned faeces, it turned out. This flea, she said, came out of my anus and forced its way into hers and injured her.

In Erna's case I was able to ascertain beyond doubt the presence of phenomena familiar to us as underlying delusions of persecution, *i.e.* a transformation of love for the parent of the same sex into hatred, and an unusual

77

prominence of the mechanism of projection. Further analysis, however, revealed the fact that beneath Erna's homosexual attitude, at an even deeper level, lay an extraordinarily intense feeling of hatred against her mother, derived from her early Oedipus situation and her oral sadism. This hatred had as its result an excessive anxiety which, in its turn, was a determining factor in every detail of her phantasies of persecution. We now came to a fresh lot of sadistic phantasies which in the intensity of their sadism exceeded anything which I had as yet come across in Erna's analysis. This was the most difficult part of the work and taxed Erna's willingness to co-operate in it to the utmost, since it was accompanied by extreme anxiety. Her oral envy of the genital and oral gratifications which she supposed her parents to be enjoying during intercourse proved to be the deepest foundation of her hatred. She gave expression to that hatred over and over again in countless phantasies directed against her parents united in copulation. In these phantasies she attacked them, and especially her mother, by means of her excrements, among other things; and what most deeply underlay her fear of my faeces (the flea), which she thought of as being pushed into her, were phantasies of herself destroying her mother's inside with her own dangerous and poisoned faeces.[1]

After these sadistic phantasies and impulses belonging to a very early stage of development had been further analysed, Erna's homosexual fixation upon her mother was lessened and her heterosexual impulses grew stronger. Up till now the essential determinant of her phantasies had been her attitude of hatred and love towards her mother. Her father had figured chiefly as a mere instrument for coitus; he seemed to derive his whole importance from the mother-daughter relationship.

[1] As I have later found in the course of my analytic work, the child's fears of poisoned and dangerous excrement increase its fixation at the pre-genital levels by being a constant incentive to it to convince itself that those excrements—both its own and those of its objects—are not dangerous but 'good' things. This is why Erna pretended that we were giving one another 'good' anal presents and loved one another. But the states of depression which followed upon these games of supposed love showed that at bottom she was terrified and believed that we—that is, her mother and she—were persecuting and poisoning each other.

In her imagination every sign of affection to him, had served no other purpose than to defraud her, Erna, make her jealous and set her father against her. In the same way, in those phantasies in which she deprived her mother of her father and married him, all the stress had been laid on her hatred of her mother and her wish to mortify her. If in games of this type Erna was affectionate to her husband, it would soon appear that the tenderness was only a pretence, designed to hurt her rival's feelings. At the same time as she made these important steps in her analysis she also moved forward in her relations to him and began to entertain genuine feelings for him of a positive nature. Now that the situation was not governed so completely by hate and fear, the direct Oedipus relationship could establish itself. At the same time Erna's fixation upon her mother was lessened and her relationship to her, which had hitherto been so ambivalent, was improved. This alteration in the girl's attitude to both her parents was based upon great changes in her phantasy-life. Her sadism was diminished, and her phantasies of persecution were far fewer in number and less in intensity. Important changes, too, occurred in her relationship to reality, and these made themselves felt, among other things, in an increased infiltration of reality into her phastasies.

In this period of her analysis, after having represented her ideas of persecution in play, Erna would often say with astonishment: 'But Mother can't *really* have meant to do that? She's very fond of me *really*.' But as her contact with reality became stronger and her unconscious hatred of her mother more conscious, she began to criticize her as a real person with ever greater openness. At the same time her relations with her improved, and hand in hand with this improvement there appeared genuinely motherly and tender feelings in her attitude towards her imaginary child. On one occasion, after having been very cruel to it, she asked in a deeply moved voice: 'Should I *really* have treated my children like that?' Thus the analysis of her ideas of persecution and the diminution of her anxiety had succeeded not only in strengthening her heterosexual position but in improving her relations to her mother and in enabling her to have more maternal feelings herself. I should like to say here that in my

79

opinion the satisfactory regulation of these fundamental attitudes, which determine the child's later choice of a love-object and the whole course of its future life, is one of the criteria of a successful child analysis.

Erna's neurosis had appeared very early in her life. Before she was quite a year old she showed marked signs of illness. (Mentally, she was an unusually precocious child, it may be remarked.) From that time on her difficulties increased continually, so that by the time she was between two and three years old her upbringing had become an insoluble problem, her character was already abnormal, and she was suffering from a definite obsessional neurosis. Yet it was not until she was about four years old that the unusual nature of her masturbatory habits and thumb-sucking was recognized. It will be seen, then, that this six-year-old child's obsessioal neurosis was already a chronic one. Pictures of her at the age of about three show her with the same neurotic, worried look upon her face that she had when she was six.

I should like to impress upon the reader the unusual severity of the case. The obsessional symptoms, which amongst other things deprived the child almost entirely of sleep, the depressions and other signs of illness, and the abnormal development of her character, were only a weak reflection of the entirely abnormal, extravagant and uncurbed instinctual life which lay behind them. The future prospects of an obsessional neurosis which, like this one, had for years been of a progressive character could not be described as other than decidedly gloomy. It may safely be asserted that the only remedy in a case of this kind was a timely treatment by psychoanalysis.

We shall now enter into the structure of the case in greater detail. Erna's training in habits of cleanliness had presented no difficulty and had been completed unusually early, by the time she was a year old. No severity had been necessary: the ambition of a precocious child had been a powerful incentive to the speedy attainment of the required standards of cleanliness.[1] But this outward

[1] What some of the sources of Erna's early ambition in this line were can be inferred from the phantasies in which she outdid her mother in cleanliness and was called 'Mrs. Dirt Parade' by her

success went along with a complete internal failure. Erna's tremendous anal-sadistic phantasies showed to what a degree she remained fixated at that stage and how much hatred and ambivalence flowed from it. One factor in this failure was a constitutionally strong anal-sadistic disposition; but an important part was played by another factor—one which has been pointed out by Freud as having a share in the predisposition to obsessional neurosis, namely, a too rapid development of the ego in comparison with the libido. Besides this, analysis showed that another critical phase in Erna's development had been passed through with only apparent success. She had never got over her weaning. And there was yet a third privation which she underwent subsequently to this. When she was between six and nine months old her mother had noticed with what evident sexual pleasure she responded to the care of her body and especially to the cleansing of her genitals and of her anus. The over-excitability of her genital zone was unmistakable. Her mother therefore exercised greater discretion in washing those parts, and the older and the cleaner the child grew the easier, of course, it was to do so. But the child, who had looked upon the earlier and more elaborate attention as a form of seduction, felt this later reticence as a frustration. This feeling of being seduced, behind which there lay a desire to be seduced, was constantly being repeated all through her life. In every relationship, *e.g.* to her nurse and the other people who brought her up and also in her analysis, she tried to repeat the situation of being seduced or alternately to bring forward the charge that she was being seduced. By analysing this specific transference-situation it was possible to trace her attitude through earlier situations back to the earliest —to the experience of being cared for when she was an infant.

Thus in each of the three events that led to the production of Erna's neurosis we can discern the part played by constitutional factors.[1] It now remains to be seen in what way her experience of the primal scene when she was two and a half combined with those constitutional factors

father and married by him on account of it, while her mother had to starve in prison.

to bring about the full development of her obsessional neurosis. At the age of two and a half, and again at three and a half,[2] she had shared her parents' bedroom during a summer holiday. At these times she had had an opportunity of watching coitus between them. Not only were the effects of this observable in her analysis, but they were definitely established by external evidence. In the summer during which she had made her first observations, a markedly unfavorable change had taken place in her. Analysis showed that the sight of her parents copulating had brought on her neurosis in its full force. It had enormously intensified her sense of frustration and envy in regard to her parents and had raised to an extreme

[1] I have subsequently come to the view that an excessive oral sadism brings on the development of the ego too rapidly and also hastens that of the libido. The constitutional factors in Erna's neurosis which have been referred to above, her over-strong sadism, the too rapid development of her ego and the premature activity of her genital impulses, are thus interconnected.

Since dealing with this case I have been able to discover yet another constitutional factor in the production of a neurosis. This consists in a relative incapacity on the part of the ego to tolerate anxiety. In many instances—and Erna was one of them—the child's sadism very early on arouses a degree of anxiety which the ego cannot adequately master. It must be said in general that the capacity of the ego to master even ordinary amounts of anxiety varies with the individual; and this fact is of aetiological importance in the neuroses.

[2] We have here an interesting analogy to the case described in Freud's 'History of an Infantile Neurosis' (1918). When Erna was five years old, that is, eighteen months after the last occasion on which she had watched her parents copulate, she was with them on a visit to her grandmother, and for a short time during the visit shared their bedroom, but without having an opportunity for observing coitus. Nevertheless, one morning Erna astonished her grandmother by saying: 'Daddy got into bed with Mummy and wiggle-woggled with her'. The child's story remained inexplicable until her analysis showed that she had taken in what she had seen when she was two and a half, and, though she had forgotten it, it had remained stored up in her mind. When she was three and a half these impressions had been revived, but once again forgotten. Finally, eighteen months later, a similar situation (sleeping in her parents' bedroom) had excited in her an unconscious expectation of seeing the same events and had stirred up her earlier experiences. In Erna's case, as in that of the Wolf Man, the primal scene had been completely repressed but had been subsequently reactivated and brought for a moment into consciousness.

82

pitch her sadistic phantasies and impulses against the sexual gratification they were obtaining.[1]

Erna's obsessional symptoms were explained as follows.[2] The obsessive character of her thumb-sucking was caused by phantasies of sucking, biting and devouring her father's penis and her mother's breasts. The penis represented the whole father and the breasts the whole mother.[3] As we have seen, moreover, the head stood for a penis in her unconscious. Her action of banging her head against the pillow was intended to represent her father's movements to coitus. She told me that at night she became afraid of robbers and burglars directly she stopped 'bumping' with her head. She was thus freeing herself from this fear by identifying herself with the object of it.

The structure of her obsessive masturbation was very complicated. She distinguished between various forms of it: a pressing together of her legs which she called 'ranking'; a rocking movement, already mentioned, called 'sculpting', and a pulling at the clitoris, called 'the cupboard game,' in which she 'wanted to pull out something very long'. Further, she used to cause a pressure on her vagina by pulling the corner of a sheet between her legs. Various identifications were operative

---

[1] In his *Hemmung, Symptom und Angst* (1926), Freud has informed us that it is the quantity of anxiety present which determines the outbreak of a neurosis. In my opinion, anxiety is liberated by the destructive tendencies so that the outbreak of a neurosis would, in fact, be a consequence of an excessive increase of those destructive tendencies. In Erna's case it was her heightened hatred, bringing on anxiety, which led to her illness.

[2] Analysis also uncovered the strong melancholic features which her illness presented. In her analysis she used repeatedly to complain of a queer feeling that she often had. She would sometimes wonder, she said, whether she was an animal or not. This feeling proved to be determined by her sense of guilt over her cannibalistic impulses. Her depression, which she used to express in the words, 'There's something I don't like about life', was shown by the analysis to be a genuine *taedium vitae* and to be accompanied by suicidal ideas. It had its roots in the feelings of anxiety and guilt resulting from the oral-sadistic introjection of her love-objects.

[3] Cf. Abraham, 'A Short Study of the Development of the Libido' (1924), Part II.

83

in these different forms of masturbation, according to whether, in the accompanying phantasies, she was playing the active part of her father or the passive one of her mother, or both at once. These masturbation phantasies of Erna's, which were very strongly sado-masochistic, showed a clear connection with the primal scene and with her primal phantasies. Her sadism was directed against her parents in the act of coition, and as a reaction to it she had phantasies of a corresponding masochistic character.

During a whole succession of analytic hours Erna masturbated in these various ways. Owing to the well-established transference, however, it was also possible to induce her to describe her masturbation phantasies in between times. I was able in this way to discover the causes of her obsessive masturbation and thus to free her from it. The rocking movements which began in the second half of her first year sprang from her wish to be masturbated and went back to the manipulations connected with her toilet as an infant. There was a period of the analysis during which she depicted her parents copulating in the most various ways in her games and afterwards gave vent to her full fury over the frustration involved. In the course of these scenes she would never fail to produce a situation in which she rocked herself about in a half-lying or sitting posture, exhibited, and eventually even made open requests to me to touch her genitals or sometimes to smell them. At that time she once astonished her mother by asking her after her bath to lift up one of her legs and pat or touch her underneath, at the same time taking up the position of a child having its genitals powdered—a position which she had not been in for years. The elucidation of her rocking movements led to the complete cessation of the symptom.

Erna's most resistant symptom was her inhibition in learning. It was so extensive that, notwithstanding all the trouble she gave herself, she took two years to master what children ordinarily learn in a few months. This difficulty was more decidedly affected by the later part of her analysis, and when I concluded the treatment it had been reduced, though not entirely done away with.

We have already gone into the favorable change which took place in Erna's relationship to her parents and in her libido position in general as a result of analysis, and have seen how it was only thanks to it that she was able to take the first steps in the direction of social adaptation. Her obsessional symptoms (obsessive masturbation, thumb-sucking, rocking, etc.) were removed, although their severity had been so great that they had been partly responsible for her sleeplessness. With their cure and the material lessening of anxiety, her sleep became normal. Her attacks of depression also passed away.[1]

Notwithstanding these favorable results I did not consider that the analysis was by any means complete when it was broken off for external reasons after 575 hours of treatment, having extended over two and a half years. The extraordinary severity of the case, which was manifested not only in the child's symptoms but in her distorted character and completely abnormal personality, demanded further analysis in order to remove the difficulties from which she still suffered. That she was still in an insufficiently stable condition was shown by the fact that in situations of great strain she had a tendency to relapse into some of her old troubles, though such relapses were always less acute than the original condition. In these circumstances it was always possible that a severe strain, or even the onset of puberty, might bring about a fresh illness or some other trouble.

This opens up a question of first-rate importance, namely, the question of when a child analysis can be said to be completed. In children of the latency age I cannot consider even very good results, such as fully satisfy the people about them, as sufficient evidence that the analysis has been carried through to the end. I have come to the conclusion that the fact that an analysis has brought about a fairly favorable development in the latency period—however important that may be—is not in itself a guarantee that the patient's further development will be completely successful. The transition to puberty, and from it to maturity, seems to me to be the test of whether a child analysis has been carried far enough or not. I will only state here as an empirical fact that analysis ensures the future stability of the child in

[1] When I last had news of her, two and a half years after the end of the analysis, these improvements had been maintained.

85

direct proportion as it is able to resolve anxiety in the deepest mental layers. In this, and in the character of the child's unconscious phantasies, or rather in the changes that have been brought about in them, a criterion is to be found which helps us to judge whether an analysis has been carried sufficiently far.

To return to Erna's case. As has already been said, at the end of the analysis, her phantasies of persecution were greatly reduced both in quantity and intensity. In my opinion, however, her sadism and anxiety could and should have been further diminished in order to prevent the possibility of an illness overtaking her at puberty or when she became grown-up. But since a continuance of the analysis was not at the time possible, its completion was left over for a future period.

I shall now proceed to discuss in connection with Erna's case-history certain questions of general importance, some of which, indeed, first arose out of her analysis. I found that the extensive occupation of her analysis with sexual questions and the freedom which was allowed her in her phantasies and games[1] led to a diminution and not to an increase of sexual excitation and preoccupation with sexual matters. Erna was a child whose unusual sexual precocity had struck everyone around her. Not only the type of phantasies she had but

[1] I have pointed out elsewhere that a child analysis, just as an adult one, must be carried through in abstinence; but as the child is different from the adult, a different criterion must be used. For instance, in taking part in the games and phantasies of the child the analyst gives it a much greater amount of gratification in reality than he does the adult patient; but this amount of gratification is seen to be less than it at first appears to be. For play is a form of expression natural to the child, so that the part the analyst takes in it does not differ in character from the attention with which he follows the verbal expressions of adult patients in describing their phantasies. Furthermore it must be remembered that the gratification which children obtain in their analysis is for the most part one of the imagination. Erna, it is true, did masturbate regularly in her analytic hour over a certain period of time. But she was an exception. We must not forget that in her case obsessional masturbation was present in such measure that she used to masturbate most of the day, sometimes even in the presence of other people. When her compulsion had been considerably lessened, the analytical situation led to a cessation of masturbation during the analytical hours in favor of a mere representation of the masturbation phantasies involved.

86

her behavior and movements were those of a very sensual girl in her puberty. This was shown especially in her provocative behavior towards men and boys. Her behavior in this respect, too, was very much changed for the better during the analysis, and when it was ended she showed a more childlike nature in every way. Further, the result of analysing her masturbation phantasies was to put an end to her obsessive masturbation.[1]

Another analytic principle which I should like to emphasize here is that it is indispensable to make conscious as far as possible the doubts and criticism which the child habors in its unconscious concerning its parents and especially their sexual life. Its attitude to its environment cannot but benefit from this, since, in being brought into consciousness, its unconscious grievances and adverse judgments undergo a test by reality and thus lose their former virulence, and its relations to reality improve. Again, its capacity to criticize its parents consciously is already, as we saw in Erna's case, a result of its improved relations to reality.[2]

Coming now to a special question of technique, it has been said more than once that Erna used often to have outbursts of anger during the analytic hour. Her fits of anger and her sadistic impulses would not seldom assume threatening forms towards me. It is a familiar fact that analysis releases strong affects in obsessional neurotics; and in children these find a much more direct and ungoverned outlet than in adults. From the very beginning I made Erna clearly understand that she must not attack me physically. But she was at liberty to abreact her affects

[1] I mean by this that her excessive masturbation and her masturbation done in the presence of other people, which had their roots in a compulsion, had stopped. I do not mean that she gave up masturbating altogether.

[2] So long as Erna was so much cut off from reality I was only able to analyse material connected with her phantasies; but I was continually on the look-out for any threads, however weak, that might connect those phantasies with reality. In this way, and by constantly diminishing her anxiety, I was able gradually to strengthen her relation to reality. In the latency period the analyst has very often to occupy himself for the most part with such phantasy material for long stretches of time before he can gain access to the child's real life and ego-interests.

in many other ways; and she used to break her toys or cut them up, knock down the little chairs, fling the cushions about, stamp her feet on the sofa, upset water, smudge paper, dirty the toys or the washing basin, break out into abuse, and so on, without the slightest hindrance on my part.[1] But at the same time I used to analyse her rage, and this always lessened it and sometimes cleared it up altogether. There are thus three ways in which analytic technique deals with a child's outbreaks of emotion during treatment (1) The child has to keep part of its affect under control, but it should only be required to do so in so far as there is a necessity for it in reality; (2) it may give vent to its affects in abuse and in the other ways mentioned above; and (3) its affects are lessened or cleared up by continuous interpretation and by tracing back the present situation to the original one.

The extent to which each of these methods is employed will, of course, greatly vary. For instance, with Erna I was early on driven to devise the following plan. At one period she used to have an outbreak of rage whenever I told her that the hour was at an end, and I used therefore to open both the double-doors of my room so as to check her, knowing that it would be extremely painful to her if the person who came to fetch her away saw anything of her outbursts. At this period, I may remark, my room used to look like a battlefield after Erna had left it. Later in the analysis she would content herself with hurriedly throwing down the cushions before she went out; while later still she used to leave the room perfectly calmly. Here is another example, taken from the analysis of Peter (aged three and three-quarters) who was also at one time subject to violent outbursts of rage. At a later period of his analysis he said quite spontaneously, pointing to a toy: 'I can just as easily *think* I've broken that'.[2]

[1] I regard it as an absolute necessity in child analysis that the room in which treatment is given shall be furnished in such a way that the child can abreact very freely. Damage to the furniture, floor, etc., must up to a certain limit be taken into the bargain.

[2] The remarks of even quite small children prove that they have fully grasped the nature of the transference-situation and understand that the lessening of their affects is brought about by interpreting the original situation together with the affects belonging to it. In such cases, for instance, Peter used often to distinguish be-

I might here point out that the insistence which the analyst must inevitably lay upon the child's exerting a partial control over its emotions—a rule which, of course, the child will not by any means always be able to respect—is in no sense to be regarded as a pedagogic measure; such demands are founded upon necessities of the real situation such as even the smallest child can understand. In the same way there are occasions on which I do not actually carry out the whole of the actions which have been allotted to me in a game, on the ground that their complete realization would be too difficult or unpleasant for me. Nevertheless, even in such cases I follow out the child's ideas as far as I possibly can. It is very important, too, that the analyst should show the least possible emotion in the face of the emotional outbursts of the child.

I propose now to make use of the data obtained from this case to illustrate the theoretical views which I have since formed. The gilded lamps of the engine, which Erna thought were 'so lovely, all red and burning' and which she sucked, represented her father's penis (*cf.* also the 'something long and golden' which held the captain up in the water) and her mother's breasts as well. That she had an intense feeling of guilt about sucking at things was shown by the fact that when I was playing the part of the child she declared that my sucking these lamps was my greatest fault. This sense of guilt can be explained by the fact that sucking also represented biting off and devouring her mother's breasts and her father's penis. I may refer here to my view that it is the process of weaning which, together with the child's wish to incorporate its father's penis, and its feelings of envy and hatred towards its mother, sets the Oedipus conflict in motion. At the base of this envy lies the child's early sexual theory that in copulating with the father the mother incorporates and retains his penis.

tween myself, who 'was like his Mummy', and his 'real Mummy'. For instance, in running his motor up and down he spat at me and wanted to beat me, and called me a 'naughty beast'. He contradicted my interpretation violently, but by and by he became quiet and affectionate again and asked: 'When Daddy's thingummy went into Mummy like that, did I want to say "Beast" to my *real* Mummy?'

This envy proved to be the central point of Erna's neurosis. The attacks which she made at the beginning of her analysis as the 'third person' on the house which was occupied only by a man and a woman turned out to be a portrayal of her destructive impulses against her mother's body and her father's penis imagined to be inside it. These impulses, stimulated by the little girl's oral envy, found expression in her game in which she sank the ship (her mother) and tore away from the captain (her father) the 'long, golden thing' and his head that kept him afloat, *i.e.* castrated him as he was copulating with her mother. The details of her phantasies of assault show to what heights of sadistic ingenuity these attacks upon her mother's body went. She would, for instance, transform her excrements into combustible and explosive substances so as to wreck it from within. This was depicted by the burning down and destruction of the house and the 'bursting' of the people inside it. The cutting-out of paper (making 'hash' and 'eye-salad') represented a complete destruction of the parents in the act of coition. Erna's wish to bite off my nose and to make 'fringes' in it was not only an attack directed against myself by symbolized an assault upon the incorporated penis of her father, as was proved by the material she produced in connection with it.[1]

That Erna made her attacks on her mother's body with an eye to seizing and destroying not only her father's penis but also that faeces and children there is shown by the variety of fish round which there revolved that desperatate struggle, in which every resource was employed, between the 'fishwife' (her mother) and me as the child (herself). She furthermore imagined, as we saw, that I, after looking on while she and the policeman 'wurled' money, or fish, together, tried to gain possession of the fish at all costs. The sight of her parents in sexual intercourse had induced a desire to steal her father's penis and whatever else might be inside her

---

[1] In other analyses, too, I have found that attacks upon my nose, feet, head, etc., never referred simply to those parts of my body as such; they were also directed against them as symbolic representations of the father's penis, attached to, or incorporated by me, that is, the mother.

mother's body. It will be remembered that Erna's re-action against this intention of robbing and completely destroying her mother's body was expressed in the fear she had, after her struggles with the fishwife, that a robber woman would take out everything inside her. It is this fear that I have described as belonging to the ear-liest danger-situation of the girl-child and as being equiv-alent to the castration anxiety of boys. I may here men-tion the connection between this early anxiety-situation of Erna's and her extraordinary inhibition in learning, a connection which I have since met with in other analyses. I have already pointed out that in Erna it was only the analysis of the deepest layers of her sadism and of her earliest Oedipus situation that brought about any change in that inhibition. Her strongly developed epistemophilic (fear of knowledge [Ed.]) instinct was so closely linked up with her intense sadism that the defense against the latter led to a complete inhibition of a number of activities which were based upon her desire for knowledge. Arith-metic and writing represented violent sadistic attacks upon her mother's body and her father's penis to her unconscious. They meant tearing, cutting up or burning her mother's body, together with her children it con-tained, and castrating her father. Reading, too, in con-sequence of the symbolical equation of her mother's body with books, had come to mean a violent removal of sub-stances, children, etc., from the inside of her mother.

Finally, I shall make use of this case to bring up yet another point to which, as a result of further experience, I have come to ascribe general validity. Not only was the character of Erna's phantasies and of her relations to reality typical for cases to which paranoid traits are strongly operative, but the underlying causes of those paranoid traits in her and of the homosexuality associated with them were, I have found, fundamental factors in the aetiology of paranoia in general. I will point out briefly in this place that I have discovered strong paranoic fea-tures in a number of analyses of children, and have thus been led to the conviction that one important and prom-ising task of Child Analysis is to uncover and clear up psychotic traits in the early life of the individual.

The Unknown Murderer

(1925)

by Theodor Reik, Ph. D.

From: THE COMPULSION TO CONFESS;
Farrar, Straus & Cudahy, New York, 1959.

THEODOR REIK

In 1918, Freud had founded a *Prix d'honneur* to be given each year for the best essays, one medical and one non-medical, in the field of psychoanalysis. The first winner of the non-medical essay prize was the psychologist, Theodor Reik, a man whom Freud described as "one of our best hopes." Since then Reik, the last remaining of Freud's early close associates, has frequently concerned himself with the application of psychoanalysis to problems other than those of therapy. His interests have ranged from literature through philosophy to law. As a psychologist and president of the National Psychological Association for Psychoanalysis, Reik has played a very important role in carrying out Freud's wish to train other than physicians in the theory and practice of psychoanalysis.

In this case, *The Unknown Murderer,* Reik demonstrates the use of psychoanalysis for the understanding of the attitudes of society, judges and juries to suspected criminals. He believes that frequently an "innocent" man is sacrificed or a guilty one unpunished because of our fear of facing our own suppressed criminal tendencies.

The case also shows to good advantage Reik's unique literary style which has made him one of the best known writers on psychoanalysis.

The Unknown
Murderer
(1925)

On the morning of October 28th, 1886, the body of a domestic servant, Juliane Sandbauer, was found near the little market town of Finkbrunnen in southern Austria. It was lying in a barn which belonged to a certain Andreas Ulrich. The head was terribly injured; the skull was quite battered in. The whole village was convinced that a tanner, Gregor Adamsberger, was the murderer. Juliane Sandbauer had been in his service several years. He had not been married long and had two young children, but he had started at once to make love to the girl who was eight years his junior, and in the course of four years they had had four children. Though she left his service she came to see him practically every day. Both had a bad reputation; she was said to be unsteady, he brutal, revengeful and hotheaded. Talk went round that they pilfered fields at night. There had been violent scenes between them because the woman kept asking her former lover for money. The Sunday before the murder a witness, Hans Berger, had seen Juliane leaving Gregor's house and had heard her exclaim, shaking her fist at the house, "I'll report you to the police." The circumstances to which this referred were well-known. On September 30th, 1879, one of Gregor's outhouses had been burnt down, and he had received 3,000 florins from the insurance company. In 1882, Juliane told several people that she had set fire to the outhouse at the instigation of her employer, who wanted the money. One evening in 1881 she had called out to Gregor in the marketplace, where everyone could hear her: "You made me set fire to that outhouse; I have stolen more than 200 gulden for you." Later she said she was drunk when she told such stories, and had only done so to get her own back on Gregor who ill-treated her. It was known that he

95

used to beat her; he had been seen driving her out of his house with a stick. Another neighbor deposed that Juliane had often threatened to report Gregor for arson. Only the week before the murder she had said that if she did not get money from Gregor for herself and her children she would go to the police. Gregor himself used to threaten to "kill that devilish woman."

Gregor had to admit that Juliane had spent the last hours before her death in his house. His mother-in-law, a woman respected in the village, had not much good to say of him. She told the court that on the evening of October 27th Gregor's two children had rushed into her room and said their mother had sent them away because their father was quarrelling violently with Juliane. She seemed almost to have heard the quarrel, for she continued: "Soon after, I heard a sudden scream in Gregor's house. I thought it was Juliane's voice. Then all was quiet." Nobody had seen Juliane alive after that. Next morning her body was found.

When Gregor was confronted with these facts, he protested his innocence in the strongest terms. He admitted that Juliane had been to see him on the evening in question, but she had not stayed long. She said she was going to her lover, the son of Anton Kunz, the baker, and he had not seen her since then. The first examination ended here; he had no more to say.

Nevertheless, some days later, he added a few details before the examining magistrate. He said that Juliane had often told him that she was in the habit of meeting young Franz Kunz in his parents' garden house. On these occasions he had given her food and drink, and that evening she had promised to meet him secretly in the garden house. He, Gregor, had lent her an old coat as she had said she was cold. Indeed, an old coat, later identified as Gregor's had been found on the corpse. But why had he not mentioned this before? Why had he waited till the coat was recognized as his? If this looked suspicious, what about his story of Franz Kunz? Franz was a weakly adolescent of sixteen, who was known in the village as a modest and virtuous youth. A love affair between him and an ugly woman twice his age, who stood in bad repute, was most unlikely, and the more so because nobody in the little town had any inkling of it. Gregor's story, to which he stuck obstinately as stupid liars will, was obviously untrue; that was proved by what Franz Kunz's mother said in respect to the fatal evening. Her son, who was apprenticed to the father's business, had, she declared, retired at 6 p.m. that evening and gone upstairs with her and his brothers and sisters. He had gone to bed at once and had only got up at midnight to go down to the bakery. Franz himself, in the quietest and most convincing way, denied having any connection with Juliane. He said that the story of the meeting at night was "of course" invented. He also mentioned the well-known fact that Juliane expected another child by Gregor. He finished by saying: "I should like to say that everybody knows how cruelly Gregor treated the woman. I know myself that she came crying to our house with injuries to her head, saying that they were inflicted by him."

Later on, Gregor tried to strengthen the suspicion against Franz, but what he said was shown to be quite untrue and made his own case worse. He said that Juliane had told him she had sent a letter to Franz on October 27th by her thirteen-year-old son, asking him to keep money handy for her. This letter the boy had given inadvertently to the errand boy, Valentin Pirgauer, and Franz had scolded her soundly for being so careless. Juliane's son declared the story to be untrue, and Valentin Pirgauer said it was a pure fabrication, adding: "I don't believe a word of this love story, because Franz is too young and inexperienced, and such a story would not be likely to remain a secret in a little village like Finkbrunnen." This strengthened the official view that Gregor had invented the story to save his own skin by incriminating Franz Kunz.

Gregor's subsequent behavior made this seem even more probable. Seeing that his story had not had the desired effect he tried to incriminate another neighbor who had, so he said, lived in enmity with Juliane. A search of the man's house produced nothing.

The whole village voiced the conviction that Gregor was the murderer. When the dead woman was found on October 28th, she was lying on her back with her face turned sideways. The barn was in a field near the hamlet. The body had twelve injuries, mostly on the head, some of them very serious. The inquest proved another important fact. Juliane was in the seventh month of pregnancy. Franz Kunz had mentioned this. Was this not the true motive of the crime? The doctors declared the injuries had been inflicted with a sharp axe and the murder had been deliberately planned.

The owner of the barn, Ulrich, made a strange statement. When he found the dead woman her clothes were pulled up round her body, and he and the man who joined him had therefore concluded that she had been murdered during or just after sexual intercourse. They pulled down her skirts for the sake of propriety, so that when the body was examined by the police it was no longer in its original condition.

Counsel for the prosecution moved that the corpse should be exhumed, as several points in the post mortem report were not quite clear. This was done; the corpse was re-examined and a second report made, stating that Ulrich's suspicion did not correspond with the facts. The experts further declared that the murder could not have been committed in the place where the corpse was found. There was only a little blood on the ground and the clothes had very few bloodstains in spite of the terrible injuries inflicted on the body. They also said that the blade of an axe found in Gregor's house fitted exactly into one of the victim's head wounds. A wound in the shoulder of a crescent shape had obviously been inflicted with a knife with a curved blade, such as tanners use to cut soles. Since it was improbable that the murderer had carried the corpse alone to the place where it was found, the assumption was that Juliane had been murdered in Gregor's house and that he and his wife had carried her to the barn where she was found. Now Gregor's wicked story appeared in a new light. He had arranged the girl's clothes in such a way that the suspicion he threw upon Kunz would appear more likely.

Gregor's wife must have helped him. She must have hated her rival. Her behavior on the day after the murder had been suspicious. A neighbor made the following deposition: "I went to the Adamsbergers when I heard of the murder and asked Mrs. Adamsberger, 'Where is Julie? She has been found killed.' 'Killed,' Mrs. Adamsberger repeated, without showing any emotion. Then Adamsberger, who must have heard my words through the open door, came in and I saw that his face, which was very red, changed to a remarkable pallor. 'How is that possible?' he said. 'Last night she was still here. I lent her a coat and she went through the cutting which leads into the field to fetch milk.' I know that Juliane was very timid and never went out alone at night. I then left their house, and I learned that Maria Adamsberger followed me very soon after, down to the brook, where she was said to have washed something in a great hurry."

This witness, a peasant woman, who, according to the record, spoke such correct official language, added that Gregor always ill-treated Juliane when she was pregnant by him. At such times she used to come to the witness, show her her injuries and complain that Gregor meant to kill her. Two other women deposed that Mrs. Adamsberger had indeed secretly hurried down to the brook. What was more likely than that she had washed the bloodstained clothes, as she had to reckon with a search in her house?

The motive was clear. Gregor wanted to get rid of his inconvenient mistress, and the increased responsibility of another child. She also shared the secret of his arson and was always greedy for money. He was accused of murder and convicted. Such a conviction should have entailed death. But there were formal difficulties in the law which limited the punishment to imprisonment for life.

At first Gregor lodged an appeal but he changed his mind and began his prison life on July 30th, 1887. And so a serious crime seemed to have found its expiation. No official connected with the case appears to have had the slightest doubt about Gregor's guilt, and he seemed to admit it himself, since he did not appeal against the verdict. In such a case where all the evidence, material and psychological, testified to the man's guilt a confession was unnecessary.

Two years after Gregor had begun to serve his sentence a decisive change in the situation occurred. Since the spring of 1889, a baker in Seefeld called Georg Halter had had an assistant with whom he was highly satisfied. He was cheerful and had a good character, avoided the company of women and spent his leisure hours in doing fretsaw work and playing on the zither. This assistant was Franz Kunz who Gregor had, for such obvious motives, accused of murdering Juliane. On January 20th, 1890, Franz Kunz handed two letters to his master's son, saying: "Deliver these letters at their addresses. I have been an unhappy creature for the last four years." He then locked himself in his room; and when the door was broken in he was found with his arteries cut open. The doctor was able to stop the bleeding. The two letters, one directed to the law court at Marburg and the other to his own parents, gave his reason for suicide. They contained a detailed confession of his murder of Juliane. He had been unable to bear the reproaches of his conscience any longer. Later he repeated this confession before the court. He said he had been seduced by Juliane when she came to buy pastries and found herself alone with him. Since then they had often met secretly in his parent's garden house, but nobody in the village had an inkling of their relations as they kept them very quiet. After some time Juliane told him she was with child by him, and began to frighten him with threats and blackmail. He had to steal food, liquor and money from his parents and give them to her. She threatened to put the baby on his parents' doorstep. Two days before the murder she had again asked him for eight gulden which he was unable to give her. His life had become such a burden to him that he had decided to rid himself of her at all costs.

He described exactly how he had proceeded. When Juliane asked him for money in the afternoon of October 27th, he arranged to meet her late that evening in the garden. At six o'clock he went to bed in the same room as his brother Victor. About seven he tiptoed downstairs into the garden. The woman was waiting and he asked her to come with him into the field because he felt safer there. He took with him secretly the short wood axe which he had hidden near the garden house on the previous day. When they reached Ulrich's barn Juliane lay down and, without being asked to do so, lifted her skirts to have sexual intercourse. "Without a word I knelt between her legs. She begged me to hurry, but with my right hand I felt for her head, holding the axe in my left, for I am left-handed. Then I brought the axe down on her head with all my strength." He went on to tell how he had hurried home, sawed the axe to bits and thrown them

100

into the privy. And there, in fact, the rusty weapon was found.

The case was tried again and Gregor Adamsberger was acquitted. Franz Kunz, being under twenty years of age when he committed the murder, was sentenced to seven years' penal servitude. If the functionaries of the law had impartially considered the question whether it was proved that Gregor Adamsberger had murdered Juliane they would have had to arrive at a negative answer in view of all the known facts. For even if the facts point to a certain person as the perpetrator of the deed, the answer must be negative, unless those facts are of such a nature as to put the event beyond a doubt. If the judge were to follow any other principle he would be convicting "on suspicion." He would condemn a person because "he *might* be guilty, not because he *must* be guilty and could not be innocent." Hellwig, himself a judge, also holds that the judge was to blame. In his opinion, if great caution had been exercised a false conviction must and would have been avoided. Public opinion, he thinks, had exerted undue influence, with the result that experts and judges carried out their examination without the necessary care. Gregor Adamsberger would never have been found guilty if the examining magistrate and counsel for the prosecution had regarded the case objectively, uninfluenced by public opinion. The case merely shows how important it is to be very critical in the evaluation of evidence.

It is not my intention to make a psychoanalytical investigation into judicial errors, the sources of which are many. I will show only a few of those factors which work unconsciously and affect conscious and rational thinking.

In the case of Gregor Adamsberger, it is not to discuss the question of clue and counter-clue, but to enquire into what made the judge and jury arrive at their decision besides rational considerations. What made them overestimate the value of the evidence against the accused and underestimate or even overlook the contrary possibilities?

Let us focus our attention first on the victim of the miscarriage of justice, Gregor Adamsberger. Was it only a mischievous accident that made him the object of that judicial error? Is any kind of person liable to such a fate?

101

This question does not concern the judge, the counsel for the prosecution or the jury. It does not concern the functionaries of the law today, but nobody can tell whether it will not do so tomorrow. And even today this point of view cannot be ignominiously dismissed if we can show that it is important for the finding of the truth and that a hitherto unknown or unrecognized psychological factor can upset investigations designed to discover the truth.

It would, of course, be ridiculous to try to find in the personality of the victim an explanation for every judicial error based on circumstantial evidence. In a great number of such errors, the personality of the victim plays no part at all; they arise out of a combination of external circumstances and chance events and have nothing whatever to do with the psychology of the accused. But among those avoidable errors there are certain cases which, on closer investigation, encourage the psychologist to point out in the behavior of the accused certain psychological factors that play an essential part in bringing about his judicial conviction.

All the witnesses agreed that Gregor Adamsberger was a brutal and fierce-tempered man who had often ill-treated his former mistress and had sometimes even threatened to kill her. These threats were without doubt of great importance as psychological evidence. It is true they were only the expression of his hatred against a mistress who had become inconvenient, but they assumed importance in the establishment of his judicial conviction.

Behind the conscious evaluation of the man's hatred lies an unknown realm—the unconscious realization of the intensity and direction of that hatred. At first sight this seems grotesque, because his hatred was not unconscious; it had been amply displayed. It cannot be said that his threats and insults were not taken seriously and that blows among people of that class need not imply violent hatred. But, if we admit that he cordially hated his former mistress, was this conscious hatred strong enough to bring about a murder? We do not know. All we know is that Gregor did *not* commit the murder. What I wish to emphasize here is that it was the echoes of this hatred in the man's unconscious, and its intensity there, that influenced the court and led to the mistaken verdict. But is it not absurd to suppose that Gregor's hatred against

Juliane, though intense enough to make him contemplate murder, should be the decisive factor in his conviction? How could the judge and jury have taken cognizance of what happened in Gregor's unconscious mind? The answer is, that their unconscious minds recognized the unconscious, or only partly conscious, processes in the accused by certain signs and reacted to those signs as if they were manifestations of his guilt. It is as if the judge and jury regarded secret thoughts, wishes and impulses as real deeds. They react to the expression of the prisoner's hatred by equating psychical and material reality. I maintain quite seriously that the mistaking of unconsciously perceived psychical actual reality constitutes an important etiological factor in judicial errors. The precise nature of the communication between the two unconscious minds, a phenomenon most readily comparable to the instinctive knowledge possessed by animals, remains as inexplicable as before.

The case of Gregor Adamsberger, the tanner, has been more instructive than we thought, since, viewed analytically, it can enlighten us about more than one of the dangers connected with circumstantial evidence. In this case there were a number of clues against the accused whose evidential value was dependent on time, opportunity and motive. We know that their importance was increased by a hidden circumstance, i.e., the perception of an unconscious tendency in Gregor to kill Juliane. No one who has followed the case can fail to ask, "But did not Adamsberger himself say that on the evening of the murder Juliane told him that she was going to her lover, the son of the baker, Kunz?" Gregor also deposed later that Juliane told him of frequent meetings with Kunz in his parents' garden house. On that evening, too, she was to meet him secretly. These were definite and unequivocal pieces of information. What use was made of them? The judge, the counsel for the prosecution and the jury could not possibly say later on that they had never been told them. It would be truer to say that they had taken no notice of them. They might say, to be sure, that Adamsberger's story sounded incredible. What a suspected person says is usually discredited and this time it seemed particularly fantastic. In view of young Kunz's youth and good reputation and of the fact that no one knew of his relations with the woman, who incidentally was more than twice his age, Gregor's suspicions would have been disbelieved even if the young baker had not had a good alibi. Kunz's own quiet denial made those strange sexual relations still more unlikely. When Gregor was found to have told a lie, his suspicions about Juliane and Kunz were "proved" to be entirely untrue. He had talked about a letter which Juliane's son had given Kunz in which she asked him for money; and he had added that Kunz had scolded her for her carelessness. Obviously it was all invented.

What Gregor had said about Kunz was clear and definite. It is true it did not accord with other facts and nobody thought Kunz capable of such a deed. Every rational consideration spoke in favor of Kunz and against Gregor; but also in the innermost soul of judge and jury there must have been a strong prejudice in favor of Kunz. I think that we can apprehend what it was if we are able to realize the secret meaning of those apparently rational arguments, if we will listen to what they want to say, not to what they actually do say. We may think it incredible that the shy, sixteen-year-old boy should have had sexual relations with a woman of bad repute and twice his age. He might have been her son. It seems to me that it is from this point that the unconscious motives sprang for refusing to credit Adamsberger's statements. Does it not sound like the denial of an accusation of incest? And another circumstance, too, strengthened this unconscious, affective idea of incest. Juliane's son, who, according to Gregor, had acted as an intermediary, was thirteen years old and her lover sixteen. The power of repression that showed itself here by ignoring a well-founded suspicion will also have the same effect in other cases, perhaps by overlooking important clues, separating certain connections, etc. Such an ignoring of suspicions is often combined with the construction of a very different picture of how the thing happened—a procedure which we have called a "system." A set of ideas of this kind, which is comparable to delusions, is made to seem still more convincing through the effect of the mechanisms of repression. The existing clues become more weighty because those pointing in another direction are ignored. The omis-

104

sion of clues pointing in the opposite direction can sometimes lead to calamitous results.

The criminal history of the last few decades exhibits a large number of cases in which certain possibilities which turned out later to be facts have been ignored by judge, jury and prosecution simply because there were other more likely possibilities. This cannot be explained by negligence or carelessness, nor can the intellectual qualities or the personal integrity of the functionaries concerned be doubted. Something irresistible, because hidden and intangible, must have prevented them from seeing a certain fact; at a certain point repression must have diverted their thoughts. Nietzsche hints at this barrier of repression when he says: "Even the most courageous man has rarely the courage to recognize what he knows." It is nonsense to brand all the judges, witnesses and experts in the Dreyfus case as idiots, scoundrels and fanatics, as is sometimes done. Some of them must have revolted against seeing in a French officer, one of themselves, a traitor; for that meant the deterioration of the army, of national honor, of the glory of the army. If such a thing were possible there was the possibility that similar impulses lived in them, too. It was simpler to assume that the stranger, the Jew, had committed the fell deed. Clearly one aim of repression is to save pain, because the discovery of the real culprit in these cases is apt to injure the narcissism of the individual and the masses.

The unconscious factors traceable in the psychopathology of judicial error may follow two courses. They may cause the deed to be ascribed to an innocent person (innocent in the material sense), or, on the other hand, they may prevent the real culprit from being found. In regard to circumstantial evidence, that is, they may smother the seemingly guilty man with weighty clues or else overlook existing clues against the real author of the deed. An unconscious attraction to the one course is assisted by the work of defensive repression belonging to the other. A larger proportion of the false judgments arrived at in such cases is due to the combination of these two unconscious tendencies, which are supported by sound, rational arguments and a strong chain of circumstantial evidence.

I cannot in this place give specific examples to show how the psychological components interact. I must be content to illustrate the effectiveness of unconscious factors in a single typical instance. The lessons that can be learned by exploring the depths of the mind may not be pleasant for judges and juries who pride themselves on their shrewdness; but let us hope that they will quickly get over such a narcissistic injury and realize that even their intellect may sometimes be dimmed by the irruption of unconscious impulses. How stupid is the man who thinks he is always clever!

The Girl
Who Couldn't
Stop Eating

(1954)

Robert Lindner, Ph.D.

Solitaire

From: THE FIFTY-MINUTE HOUR
Rinehart & Co., Inc., New York: 1955.

ROBERT LINDNER

Robert Lindner is one of the American psychologists who was strongly influenced by Theodor Reik in following the psychoanalytic path. While Lindner may not have made contributions to psychoanalysis on the same scale as Abraham, Ferenczi or Reik, his book, *The Fifty-Minute Hour,* because of the dramatic force of its style, helped introduce many thousands to psychoanalysis who would otherwise have found the more scientific style of other writers too difficult or perhaps too uninteresting to follow. In addition, Lindner did valuable work in applying psychoanalysis to the treatment of the criminal and the delinquent.

This particular case deals with a problem frequently seen in psychoanalytic practice—the problem of compulsive eating. The unconscious reason Lindner felt he had tracked down in the case of *The Girl Who Couldn't Stop Eating* is not the only possible reason for compulsive eating. Most analysts find overeating to be overdetermined, i.e., a product of many factors.

More important than the theoretical construction of the case is the difference in attitude shown between Lindner's reporting of the case and some of the earlier histories. Rather than being the remote and anonymous figure behind the couch, Lindner, like many modern psychoanalysts, took a more active and human part in the treatment situation. He was willing to reveal himself as a living, breathing human being with feelings and emotions of his own. This willingness to share in the human condition has recently received considerable emphasis in the writings of analysts of many different theoretical backgrounds.

The Girl
Who Couldn't
Stop Eating
(1954)

"Sooner murder an infant in its cradle than nurse unacted desires."
—Wm. Blake, *Marriage of Heaven and Hell.*

Laura had two faces. The one I saw that morning was hideous. Swollen like a balloon at the point of bursting, it was a caricature of a face, the eyes lost in pockets of sallow flesh and shining feverishly with a sick glow, the nose buried between bulging cheeks splattered with blemishes, the chin an oily shadow mocking human contour; and somewhere in this mass of fat a crazy-angled carmined hole was her mouth.

Her appearance astonished and disgusted me. The revulsion I felt could not be hidden. Observing it, she screamed her agonized self-loathing.

"Look at me, you son-of-a-bitch!" she cried. "Look at me and vomit! Yes—it's me—Laura. Don't you recognize me? Now you see, don't you? Now you see what I've been talking about all these weeks—while you've been sitting back there doing nothing, saying nothing. Not even listening when I've begged and begged you for help. Look at me!"

"Lie down, please," I said, "and tell me about it."

A cracked laugh, short and rasping, came from her hidden mouth. The piglike eyes raised to some unseen auditor above, while clenched fists went up in a gesture of wrath.

"Tell him about it! Tell him about it! What the hell do you think I've been telling you about all this time!"

"Laura," I said more firmly, "stop yelling and lie down" —and I turned away from her toward the chair behind the couch. But before I could move she grabbed my arms and swung me around to face her. I felt her nails bite through my coat and dig into the skin beneath. Her grip was like a vise.

She thrust her face toward mine. Close up, it was a huge, rotting wart. Her breath was foul as she expelled it in a hoarse, passionate whisper.

"No," she said, "I'm not going to lie down. I'm going to stand here in front of you and make you look at me— make you look at me as I have to look at myself. You want me to lie down so you won't have to see me. Well, I won't do it. I'm going to stand here forever!" She shook me. "Well," she said. "Say something! Go on, tell me what you're thinking. I'm loathsome, aren't I? Disgusting. Say it! Say it!" Then suddenly her grasp loosened. Collapsing, she fell to the floor. "O, God," she whimpered, "please help me. Please . . . please. . . ."

I had never met anyone like Laura before, nor had I encountered the strange symptoms she presented. In the literature of morbidity occasional reference was made to a disorder called bulimia, or pathological craving for food; and I had of course met with numerous instances of related oral disturbances, such as perverted appetite or addiction to a specific food. As a matter of fact, one of the most amusing incidents of my career concerned a case in this category. It happened at the Federal Penitentiary in Atlanta, where I had been sent on a special assignment during the first years of the war. One day I received a note from an inmate requesting an answer to the engaging question, "Do you think I will get ptomaine poisoning from eating tomatoes on top of razor blades?" I showed this provocative communication to my colleagues in the Clinic who thought, as I did, that someone was pulling my leg. In reply, therefore, I wrote the questioner that the outcome of such a meal depended on whether the razor blades were used or new. Much to my chagrin, a few days later the X-ray technician called me into his office and exhibited two pictures on the stereoscopic viewer, inviting me to look at the "damnedest thing you ever saw." I looked. In the area of the stomach

1 saw a number of clearly defined, oblong shadows. "What the heck are those?" I asked. "What do they look like to you?" he responded. I looked again. "To me," I said, "they look like—well, I'll be damned! Razor blades!"

We called the inmate from the hall where he had been sitting hunched over on a bench, moaning with pain. When he saw me, he complained, "I did what you said. I only ate new blades like you told me. . . . Now look what's happened!"

"Musta been the tomatoes, then," was the technician's dry comment.

When the surgeons went to work on this man they discovered him to be a veritable walking hardware store. I was present in the operating room when they opened him up, and my eyes bulged with amazement as they carefully removed piece after piece of the junk he later told us he had been swallowing for many years. Somewhere in my private collection of psychological curiosa, I have a photograph of the debris collected from this man's interior. It shows not only numerous fragments of razor blades, but also two spoons, a coil of wire, some bottle caps, a small screw driver, a few bolts, about five screws, some nails, many bits of colored glass and a couple of twisted metallic objects no one can identify.

Laura's difficulty, however, did not involve the perversion of appetite but something far more distressing psychologically. She was subject to episodes of depression during which she would be seized by an overwhelming compulsion to gorge herself, to eat almost continuously. A victim of forces beyond her ken or control, when this strange urge came upon her she was ravenous—insatiable. Until she reached a stage of utter exhaustion, until her muscles no longer responded, until her distended insides protested with violent pain, until her strained senses succumbed to total intoxication, she would cram herself with every available kind of food and drink.

The torment Laura suffered before, during and after these fits (as she called them) is really beyond description, if not beyond belief. Articulate as she was, I could not appreciate the absolute horror, the degradation, the insensate passion of these wild episodes until, with my own eyes, I saw her in the midst of one. Her own report

111

of the onset and course of these experiences, a report I heard many times, is as follows:

"It seems to come out of nowhere. I've tried to discover what touches it off, what leads up to it, but I can't. Suddenly, it hits me. . . . It seems I can be doing anything at the time—painting, working at the Gallery, cleaning the apartment, reading, or talking to someone. It doesn't matter where I am or what's going on. One minute I'm fine, feeling gay, busy, loving life and people. The next minute I'm on an express highway to hell.

"I think it begins with a feeling of emptiness inside. Something, I don't know what to call it, starts to ache; something right in the center of me feels as if it's opening up, spreading apart maybe. It's like a hole in my vitals appears. Then the emptiness starts to throb—at first softly like a fluttering pulse. For a little while, that's all that happens. But then the pulsing turns into a regular beat; and the beat gets stronger and stronger. The hole gets bigger. Soon I feel as if there's nothing to me but a vast, yawning space surrounded by skin that grabs convulsively at nothingness. The beating gets louder. The sensation changes from an ache to a hurt, a pounding hurt. The feeling of emptiness becomes agony. In a short while there's nothing of me, of Laura, but an immense, drumming vacuum."

I remember asking her, when she reached this point in her description, where the hunger started, at what place in the course of this weird, crescendoing compound of emptiness and pain the compulsion to eat entered.

"It's there from the first," she would say. "The moment I become aware of the hole opening inside I'm terrified. I want to fill it. I have to. So I start to eat. I eat and eat—everything, anything I can find to put in my mouth. It doesn't matter what it is, so long as it's food and can be swallowed. It's as if I'm in a race with the emptiness. As it grows, so does my hunger. But it's not really hunger, you see. It's a frenzy, a fit, something automatic and uncontrollable. I want to stop it, but I can't. If I try to, the hole gets bigger, I become idiotic with terror, I feel as if I'm going to *become* nothing, become the emptiness—get swallowed up by it. So I've got to eat."

I tried to find out, in the early days of her analysis, if

there was any pattern to her eating, any design, any specificity.

"No," Laura told me. "It's just a crazy, formless thing. There's nothing I *want* to eat, nothing in the world that will satisfy me—because, you see, it's the emptiness that has to be filled. So it doesn't matter what I swallow. The main thing, the only thing, is to get it inside of me. So I stuff anything I can find into my mouth, loathing myself while I do it, and swallowing without tasting. I eat. I eat until my jaws get numb with chewing. I eat until my body swells. I swill like an animal—a pig. I get sick with eating and still I eat—fighting the sickness with swallowing, retching, vomiting—but always eating more and more. And if my supply of food runs out, I send for more. Before it comes I go mad with the growing emptiness, I shiver with fear. And when it arrives I fall on it like someone who's been starved for weeks."

I would ask her how the frenzy ended.

"Most of the time I eat myself into unconsciousness. I think I reach a state of drunkenness, or something very like it. Anyhow, I pass out. This is what usually happens. Once or twice I've been stopped by exhaustion. I couldn't open my mouth any more, couldn't lift my arms. And there've been times, too, when my body just revolted, refused to take in any more food.

"But the very worst is the aftermath. No matter how the fit ends, it's followed by a long sleep, sometimes for as much as two whole days and nights. A sleep of sick dreams that go on and on, terrible dreams I can hardly recall on awakening—thank goodness. And when I awaken I have to face myself, the mess I've made of Laura. That's even more horrible than what's gone before. I look at myself and can hardly believe the loathsome thing I see in the mirror is human, let alone me. I'm all swollen, everywhere. My body is out of shape. My face is a nightmare. I have no features. I've become a creature from hell with rottenness oozing from every pore. And I want to destroy this disgusting thing I've become."

Three months of intensive analytic work had passed before the morning Laura confronted me with her tragically distorted body and insisted I look at it. They had

113

been stormy months for both of us, each analytic hour tearful and dramatic as Laura recited the story of her life. In the recounting she could find no relief, as many other patients do, since it was a tale of almost endless sorrow in which one dismal incident was piled upon another. Used as I am to hearing the woeful stories of abuse, neglect and unhappiness that people bring to an analyst, I was nevertheless moved by Laura's narrative and could hardly help expressing my sympathy. By this I do not mean that I verbalized the feelings she aroused in me, for the discipline of these long years of practice and the experience gained through the many errors I have made safeguard against such a gross tactical blunder; but in small ways of which I was largely unaware I communicated my compassion to her. With Laura, this turned out to be a serious mistake. Typically misreading my attitude for one of pity, hardly had the analysis begun than she set out to exploit this quality and to demand more and more of it. Paradoxically, just because I somehow betrayed sympathy for her, she charged me increasingly with a total lack of warmth, and upbraided me almost daily for my "coldness," my "stonelike impassivity," my "heartless indifference" to her suffering. Our meetings, therefore, followed a curious pattern after the first few weeks. They would begin with one of her moving chronicles, to the telling of which she brought a remarkable histrionic talent; then she would wait for some response from me: when this was not forthcoming in the manner she desired, she would attack me viciously.

I recall one such hour quite clearly, not only because of its content but also, perhaps, because it preceded by a few days the episode I described earlier; and the contrast between the way Laura looked on the day I have in mind and her appearance only a short while thereafter remains vivid in my memory. For Laura between seizures was nothing like the piteous wreck she made of herself at those times. Although poor, she always dressed becomingly, with a quiet good taste that never failed to emphasize her best features. The ascetic regime she imposed on herself between bouts of abnormal eating kept her fashionably thin. Her face, set off in a frame of hair so black that it reflected deep, purple lights, was not pretty in the ordinary sense, but striking, compelling attention because of its exotic cast. It conveyed an almost Oriental flavor by the juxtaposition of exceptionally high cheekbones, heavy-lidded brown eyes, a moderately small, thin nose with widely flaring nostrils, and an ovoid mouth. On the day I wish to tell about, one could hardly imagine the ruin that was even then creeping up on her.

She began the hour with her usual complaint of fantastic nightmares populated by grotesque forms whose exact description and activities always eluded her. These dreams occurred every night, she said, and interfered with her rest. She would awaken in terror from one, often aroused by her own frightened screams, only to have another of the same kind as soon as she fell asleep again. They were weird dreams, she claimed, and left her with only vague memories in the morning of surrealistic scenes, faceless figures, and nameless obscenities just beyond the perimeters of recall. Water—endless, slow-moving stretches of it, or torrential cascades that beat upon her with the fury of whips; footsteps—the haunting, inexorable beat of a disembodied pair of shoes mercilessly following her through empty corridors, or the mad staccato of an angry mob of pursuers; and laughter—the echoing hysteria of a lone madwoman's howl of mockery, or the shrieking, derisive chorus of countless lunatics: these three elements were never absent from her nighttime gallery of horrors.

"But you can't remember anything more?" I asked.

"Nothing definite—only water again, and being chased, and the sound of laughter."

"Yet you speak of odd shapes, rooms, landscapes, action of some sort, scenes. . . . Describe them."

"I can't," she said, covering her eyes with her hands. "Please don't keep after me so. I'm telling you everything I remember. Maybe they're so terrible I have to forget them—my dreams, I mean."

"What else could you mean?" I entered quickly.

She shrugged. "I don't know. My memories, I guess."

"Any particular memory?"

"They're all terrible. . . ."

I waited for her to continue, observing meanwhile that her hands were no longer over her eyes but interlocked tightly over her forehead, the knuckles slowly whitening

115

and the fingers flushing as she increased their pressure against each other.

"I'm thinking," she began, "about the night my father left. Have I ever told you about it?"

. . . It was raining outside. The supper dishes had just been cleared away; Laura and her brother were sitting at the dining-room table doing their homework. In the kitchen Freda, the oldest child, was washing up. Their mother had moved her wheel chair into the front bedroom, where she was listening to the radio. The apartment, a railroad flat on the edge of the factory district, was cold and damp. A chill wind from the river penetrated the windows, whistling through newspapers that had been stuffed into cracks around the frames. Laura's hands were stiff with cold. From time to time she would put her pencil down and blow on her fingers or cross her arms, inserting her hands beneath the two sweaters she wore and pressing them into her armpits. Sometimes, just for fun and out of boredom with her sixth-grade geography lesson, she would expel her breath toward the lamp in the middle of the table, pretending the cloud it made was smoke from an invisible cigarette. Across from her Little Mike, intent on forming fat letters according to the copybook models before him, seemed unaware of the cold as he labored. Laura could tell which letter of the alphabet he was practicing from watching his mouth as lips and tongue traced familiar patterns.

When the door opened, Little Mike glanced up at her. Their eyes met in a secret communication of recognition and fear as heavy footsteps came down the hall. Bending again to their lessons, they now only pretended to work. In the kitchen Freda closed the tap so that she, too, could listen.

In a moment, they heard their father's grunting hello and a mumbled reply in kind from their mother. Then there was a creak of the springs as he sat heavily on the bed, followed by the sharp noise of his big shoes falling to the floor when he kicked them off. The bedsprings groaned again as he stood up.

"Peasant," they heard their mother say over the music from the radio, "if you're not going to bed, wear your shoes. It's cold in here."

"Let me alone," he replied. "I'm not cold."

"'I'm not cold,'" their mother mimicked. "Of course you're not cold. Why should you be? If I had a bellyful of whisky I wouldn't be cold either."

"Don't start that again, Anna," he said. "I'm tired."

"Tired," she mocked. "And from what are you tired? — Not from working, that's for sure."

"Oh, shut up, Anna," he said wearily over his shoulder as he walked through the doorway. Behind him there was the click of the dial as their mother shut off the radio, then the rasping sound of her wheel chair following him into the dining room.

Laura looked up at her father and smiled. He bent to brush his lips against the cheek she offered. The stiff hairs of his thick mustache scraped her skin and the smell of whisky made her slightly dizzy. Straightening, he ruffled Little Mike's hair with one huge hand, while with the other he pulled a chair away from the table.

"Freda!" he called as he sat down.

The older girl came to the door, smoothing her hair with both hands. "Yes, Papa," she answered.

"Get the old man something to eat, huh?" he asked.

Anna wheeled herself into the space between the table and the open kitchen door where Freda stood. "There's nothing here for you," she said. "You want to eat, come home when supper's ready. This ain't a restaurant."

Ignoring her, he spoke over her head to Freda. "Do like I said, get me some supper."

As Freda turned to obey, Anna shouted at her. "Wait! Don't listen to him!" She glared balefully at her husband, her thin face twisted with hate. When she spoke, the veins in her long neck stood out and her whole shrunken body trembled. "Bum! You come home to eat when you've spent all the money on those tramps. You think I don't know. Where've you been since yesterday? Don't you know you've got a family?"

"Anna," he said, "I told you to shut up."

"I'm not shutting up. . . . You don't care what happens to us. You don't care if we're cold or starving or what. All you think about is the lousy whores you give your money to. Your wife and children can rot for all it matters to you."

"Anna," he started to say, "the kids . . ."

"The kids," she screamed. "You think they don't know

117

what kind of a rotten father they've got? You think they don't know where you go when you don't come home?"

He slammed his palm down on the table and stood up. "Enough!" he yelled. "I don't have to listen to that. Now keep quiet!"

He started for the kitchen. Anticipating him, Anna whirled her chair across the entrance. "Where're you going?" she asked.

"If you won't get me something to eat I'll get it myself."

"No you won't," she said. "There nothing in there for you."

"Get out of my way, Anna," he said menacingly, "I want to go in the kitchen."

"When you bring home money for food you can go in the kitchen," she said.

His face darkened and his hands clenched into fists. "Cripple!" he spat. "Move away or I'll——"

Her laugh was short and bitter. "You'll what? Hit me? Go ahead—hit the cripple! What're you waiting for?"

Framed in the doorway they faced each other, frozen in a tableau of mutual hatred. Behind the father Laura and Little Mike sat stiffly, eyes wide and bodies rigid. In the silence that followed Anna's challenge they heard the rain slap against the windows.

Their father's hands relaxed slowly. "If you don't move out of the way," he said evenly, "I'm getting out of this house and I'm never coming back."

"So go," Anna said, leering up at him. "Who wants you here anyway?"

Like a statue, he stood still for a long minute; then he turned and walked swiftly toward the bedroom, followed by their eyes. Now the tense quiet was broken by the noises he made as he moved around the next room, and shadows, cast by his tall figure, crossed and recrossed the threshold.

On Anna's face, when she became aware of what he was doing, the look of triumph gave place to alarm. Her bony fingers clutched the wheels of her chair. Hastily, she propelled herself around the table. In the doorway, she stopped.

"Mike," she said, "what're you doing?"

There was no answer—only the sound of the bed-

118

springs, twice, and the firm stamp of his shoes against the naked floorboards.

"Mike"—her voice was louder this time and tremulous with fright—"where're you going?— Wait!"

The wheel chair raced into the bedroom, beyond sight of the children. They listened, their chests aching with terror.

She clutched at his coat. "Mike. Wait, Mike," she cried. "Please don't go. I didn't mean it. Please. . . . Come back. Come into the kitchen. I was only fooling, Mike. Don't go."

He pulled away from her, lifting her body from the chair. Her hands broke the fall as useless legs collapsed. The outer door slammed. Then there was the slapping sound of rain again between her heavy sobs. . . .

"—He meant it," Laura said. "I guess she went too far that time. He never did come back. Once in a while he'd send a few dollars in a plain envelope. On my next birthday I got a box of salt-water taffy from Atlantic City. . . . But we never saw him again."

She fumbled with the catch on her purse and groped inside for a handkerchief. Tears were streaming from the corners of her eyes. Some caught on the lobes of her ears and hung there like brilliant pendants. Idly, I wondered if they tickled.

She dabbed at her eyes, then blew her nose noisily. Her bosom rose and fell unevenly. The room was quiet. I glanced at my watch.

"Well?" she said.

"Well what?" I asked.

"Why don't you say something?"

"What should I say?"

"You might at least express some sympathy."

"For whom?"

"For me, of course!"

"Why only you?" I asked. "What about Freda, or Little Mike, or your mother? Or even your father?"

"But I'm the one who's been hurt most by it," she said petulantly. "You know that. You should feel sorry for me."

"Is that why you told me this story . . . so that I'd feel sorry for you?"

She turned on the couch and looked at me, her face

119

drawn in a grimace of absolute malice.

"You don't give an inch, do you?" she said.

"You don't want an inch, **Laura**," I responded quietly. "You want it all . . . from me, from everybody."

"What d'you mean?" she asked.

"Well, for example, the story you just told. Of course it's a dreadful one, and anyone hearing it would be moved, but——"

"—But you're not," she almost spat. "Not you. Because you're not human. You're a stone—a cold stone. You give nothing. You just sit there like a goddam' block of wood while I tear my guts out!" Her voice, loaded with odium, rose to a trembling scream. "Look at you!" she cried. "I wish you could see yourself like I see you. You and your lousy objectivity! Objectivity, my eye! Are you a man or a machine? Don't you ever *feel* anything? Do you have blood or ice water in your veins? Answer me! Goddam' you, answer me!"

I remained silent.

"You see?" she shouted. "You say nothing. Must I die to get a word out of you? What d'you want from me?"

She stood up. "All right," she said. "Don't say anything. . . . Don't give anything. I'm going. I can see you don't want me here. I'm going—and I'm not coming back." With a swirl of her skirt she rushed from the room.

Curious, I reflected, how well she enacted the story she had just told. I wondered if she knew it too?

Laura came back, of course—four times each week for the next two years. During the first year she made only few—and those very minor—advances so far as her symptoms were concerned, particularly the symptoms of depression and sporadic overeating. These persisted: indeed, for several months following the "honeymoon" period of psychoanalysis—when, as usual, there was a total remission of all symptoms and Laura, like so many patients during this pleasant time, believed herself "cured" —her distress increased. The seizures of abnormal appetite became more frequent, and the acute depressions not only occurred closer to each other in time but were of greater intensity. So, on the surface, it seemed that treatment was not helping my patient very much, even that it might be making her worse. But I knew—and so did Laura—that subtle processes had been initiated by her therapy, and that these were slowly, but secretly, advancing against her neurosis.

This is a commonplace of treatment, known only to those who have undergone the experience of psychoanalysis and those who practice the art. Externally, all appears to be the same as it was before therapy, often rather worse; but in the mental underground, unseen by any observer and inaccessible to the most probing investigation, the substructure of the personality is being affected. Insensibly but deliberately the foundations of neurosis are being weakened while, at the same time, there are being erected new and more durable supports on which, eventually, the altered personality can rest. Were this understood by the critics of psychoanalysis (or better still, by friends and relatives of analysands who understandably complain of the lack of evident progress), many current confusions about the process would disappear, and a more rational discussion of its merits as a form of therapy would be made possible.

For a year, then, Laura seemed to be standing still or losing ground. Chiefly, as in the episode I have already related, she reviewed her past and, in her sessions with me, either immediately or soon after, acted out their crucial or formative aspects. My consulting room became a stage on which she dramatized her life: my person became the target against which she directed the sad effects of her experience. In this manner she sought compensation for past frustrations, utilizing the permissive climate of therapy to obtain benefits she had missed, satisfactions that had been denied, and comforts she had lacked. Since the total effect of this pattern of emotional damming had been to cut her off from the many real satisfactions life offered, and to force her energies and talents into unproductive and even self-destructive channels, I allowed her, for that first year, almost endless opportunity for the "drainage" she required. The idea behind my attitude of complete permissiveness in therapy was to hold up to her a mirror of her behavior and to let her see not only the extravagance of the methods she used to obtain neurotic gratification, but also the essential hollowness, the futility and the infantilism of the desires she had been pursuing

121

by such outlandish methods all of her life. Finally, the procedure was designed to illustrate, in sharpest perspective, the impossibility of securing basic, long-lasting and solid satisfactions from her accustomed modes of behavior. The latter aim, of course, set definite limits on my responsiveness to her conduct: I had to be careful to measure out to her, at the proper time and in correct amounts, the rewards she deserved when these were due her as a consequence of mature behavior toward mature goals.

Yes, this first year with Laura was a trying one, not only for her but for her analyst. I often wished she had chosen someone else to take her troubles to, and could hardly help hoping, on those many occasions when she threatened to break off treatment, that I would never see her again.

One episode from this time haunts me. I set it down here to show the strain she placed me under as much as to illustrate my technique with her and the weird dynamics of her neurosis that were uncovered by this technique.

According to my notes, what I am about to tell took place in the eleventh month of psychoanalysis. By that time the pattern of treatment had stabilized, I was in possession of most of the accessible facts of Laura's life, and the more obvious psychodynamics of her personality disorder were known to us. She, meanwhile, was in a period of relative quiet and contentment. It had been a month or more since her last attack, her job at the Gallery was going well, and she had recently formed a promising relationship with an eligible young man. It was on the theme of this affair that the first of these two crucial hours began, for Laura was deeply concerned about it and wished ardently that it might develop into something more rewarding and more lasting than her many previous romances.

"I don't want to foul this one up," she said, "but I'm afraid I'm going to. I need your help desperately."

"In what way d'you think you might foul it up?" I asked.

"Oh," she replied airily, "by being my usual bitchy self. You know—you ought to since you pointed it out; you know how possessive I get, how demanding I become.

122

But I'd like, just for a change, not to be that way. For once I'd like to have a love affair work out well for me."

"You mean you're thinking of matrimony?" I asked.

She laughed brightly. "Well," she said, "if you must know, I've had a few choice daydreams—fantasies, you'd probably call them—about marrying Ben. But that's not what I've got my heart set on now. What I want is love— I want to give it and I want to get it."

"If that attitude is genuine," I said, "you don't need my help in your affair."

She ground out the cigarette she was smoking against the bottom of the ash tray with short, angry jabs.

"You're horrible," she complained, "just horrible. Here I tell you something that I think shows real progress, and right away you throw cold water on it."

"What d'you think shows progress?"

"Why my recognition of giving, of course. I hope you noticed that I put it first."

"I did."

"And doesn't that mean something to you? Doesn't that show how far I've come?"

"It does," I said, "if it's genuine."

"Goddammit!" she flared. "You call *me* insatiable; *you're* the one who's never satisfied. But I'll show you yet."

She lit another cigarette and for the next few moments smoked in silence. Quite naturally my skepticism had shaken her confidence somewhat, as I had meant it to do, since I knew from experience how much she was given to these pat, semianalytical formulations that were consciously designed to impress as well as mislead me. I was just considering the wisdom of pursuing the topic she had opened and getting her somehow to explore her real goals in this new relationship when she began talking again.

"Anyhow," she said, "that's not what I wanted to talk about today. I had a dream. . . . Shall I tell you about it?"

I have found that when a patient uses this way of presenting a dream—announcing it first, then withholding until the analyst asks for it; actually dangling it like some tantalizing fruit before the analyst's eyes but insisting he reach out for it—the analyst had better listen closely. For this particular mode of dream presentation signifies

123

the special importance of the dream, and it can be anticipated that it holds some extraordinarily meaningful clue to the patient's neurosis. Unconsciously, the patient, too, "knows" this, and by the use of the peculiar formula communicates his inarticulate but nonetheless high estimate of the dream's value. More than this, he is offering the dream, when he invites attention to it this way, as a gift to the analyst, a gift that has implications extending far beyond the dream itself and including the possibility of surrendering an entire area of neurotic functioning. His reservations about giving up a piece of his neurosis and the gratifications he has been receiving from it are betrayed by his use of the "shall I tell you about it?": he wants assurance, in advance, that the sacrifice will be worth while, that the analyst will appreciate (and love him for) it, and that he (the patient) will experience an equal amount of gratification from the newer, healthier processes which will henceforth replace the old. For this reason the analyst must be wary of reaching for the tempting fruit being offered him; to grasp at it would be to rob his patient of the painful but necessary first steps toward responsible selfhood, and to commit himself to bargains and promises he has no right to make.

Therefore, when Laura held out the gift of her dream, although I was most eager to hear it, I responded with the evasive but always handy reminder of the "basic rule": "Your instructions have always been to say what comes to you during your hours here. If you're thinking of a dream, tell it."

"Well," she said, "this is what I dreamed. . . . I was in what appeared to be a ballroom or dance hall, but I knew it was really a hospital. A man came up to me and told me to undress, take all my clothes off. He was going to give me a gynecological examination. I did as I was told but I was very frightened. While I was undressing, I noticed that he was doing something to a woman at the other end of the room. She was sitting or lying in a funny kind of contraption with all kinds of levers and gears and pulleys attached to it. I knew that I was supposed to be next, that I would have to sit in that thing while he examined me. Suddenly he called my name and I found myself running to him. The chair or table—whatever it was—was now empty, and he told me to get on it. I re-

124

fused and began to cry. It started to rain—great big drops of rain. He pushed me to the floor and spread my legs for the examination. I turned over on my stomach and began to scream. I woke myself up screaming."

Following the recital Laura lay quietly on the couch, her eyes closed, her arms crossed over her bosom.

"Well," she said after a brief, expectant silence, "what does it mean?"

"Laura," I admonished, "you know better than that. Associate, and we'll find out."

"The first thing I think of is Ben," she began. "He's an interne at University, you know. I guess that's the doctor in the dream—or maybe it was you. Anyhow, whoever it was, I wouldn't let him examine me."

"Why not?"

"I've always been afraid of doctors . . . afraid they might hurt me."

"How will they hurt you?"

"I don't know. By jabbing me with a needle, I guess. That's funny. I never thought of it before. When I go to the dentist I don't mind getting a needle; but with a doctor it's different. . . ." Here I noticed how the fingers of both hands clutched her arms at the elbows while her thumbs nervously smoothed the inner surfaces of the joints. "I shudder when I think of having my veins punctured. I'm always afraid that's what a doctor will do to me."

"Has it ever been done?"

She nodded. "Once, in college, for a blood test. I passed out cold."

"What about gynecological examinations?"

"I've never had one. I can't even bear to think of someone poking around inside me." Again silence; then, "Oh," she said, "I see it now. It's sex I'm afraid of. The doctor in the dream *is* Ben. He wants me to have intercourse, but it scares me and I turn away from him. That's true. . . . The other night after the concert he came to my apartment. I made coffee for us and we sat there talking. It was wonderful—so peaceful, just the two of us. Then he started to make love to me. I loved it—until it came to having intercourse. I stopped him there: I had to; I became terrified. He probably thinks I'm a virgin—or that I don't care for him enough. But it isn't

125

that. I do—and I want him to love me. Oh, Dr. Lindner, that's why I need your help so much now. . . ."

"But other men have made love to you," I reminded her.

"Yes," she said, sobbing now, "but I only let them as a last resort, as a way of holding on to them a little longer. And if you'll remember, I've only had the real thing a few times. Mostly I've made love to the man—satisfied him somehow. I'd do anything to keep them from getting inside me—poking into me . . . like the needle, I guess."

"But why, Laura?"

"I don't know," she cried, "I don't know. Tell me."

"I think the dream tells you," I said.

"The dream I just told you?"

"Yes. . . . There's a part of it you haven't considered. What comes to your mind when you think of the other woman in the dream, the woman the doctor was examining before you?"

"The contraption she was sitting in," Laura exclaimed. "It was like a—like a wheel chair—my mother's wheel chair! Is that right?"

"Very likely," I said.

"But why would he be examining *her?* What would that mean?"

"Well, think of what that kind of examination signifies for you."

"Sex," she said. "Intercourse—that's what it means. So that's what it is—that's what it means! Intercourse put my mother in the wheel chair. It paralyzed her. And I'm afraid that's what it will do to me. So I avoid it—because I'm scared it will do the same thing to me. . . . Where did I ever get such a crazy idea?"

—Like so many such "ideas" all of us have, this one was born in Laura long before the age when she could think for herself. It arose out of sensations of terror when she would awaken during the night, shocked from sleep by the mysterious noises her parents made in their passion, and incapable yet of assembling these sounds into a design purporting the tender uses of love. The heavy climate of hate, the living antagonism between her parents, made this impossible; so the sounds in the night—the "Mike, you're hurting me," the moans and cries, the protestations, even the laughter—impressed upon her the

126

darker side of their sex, the brutish animality of it and the pain. And when the disease struck her mother a natural bridge of associations was formed between the secret drama that played itself out while Laura slept—or sometimes awakened her to fright—and the final horror of the body imprisoned on the chair.

I explained this to Laura, documenting my explanation with material the analysis had already brought out. For her, the interpretation worked a wonder of insight. Obvious as it may seem to us, to Laura, from whom it had been withheld by many resistances and defenses, it came as a complete surprise. Almost immediately, even before she quit the couch at the end of that hour, she felt a vast relief from the pressure of many feelings that had tormented her until that very day. The idea that sexual love was impossible for her, the idea that she was so constructed physically that the joys of love would forever be denied her, feelings of self-dissatisfaction, and numerous other thoughts and emotions collected around the central theme of sex—these vanished as if suddenly atomized.

"I feel free," Laura said as she rose from the couch when time was called. "I think this has been the most important hour of my analysis." At the door she paused and turned to me with moist, shining eyes. "I knew I could count on you," she said. "And I'm very grateful—believe me."

When she left, in the ten-minute interval between patients during which I ordinarily make notes, attend to messages or read, I reviewed the hour just ended. I, too, had a feeling of satisfaction and relief from it. And while I did not consider it to have been her most important hour—for the analyst's standards are markedly different from the patient's—nevertheless I did not underestimate its potential for the eventual solution of Laura's difficulties. I therefore looked forward to her next hour with pleasurable anticipation, thinking that the mood in which she had departed would continue and hoping she would employ it to stabilize her gains.

The session I have just described took place on a Saturday. On Monday, Laura appeared at the appointed time. The moment I saw her in the anteroom I knew something had gone wrong. She sat dejectedly, chin cupped in her hands, a light coat carelessly draped about her shoulders. When I greeted her, she raised her eyes listlessly.

"Ready for me?" she asked in a toneless voice.

I nodded and motioned her into the next room. She stood up wearily, dropping the coat on the chair, and preceded me slowly. As I closed the door behind us, she flopped on the couch sideways, her feet remaining on the floor. In the same moment she raised one arm to her head and covered her brow with the back of her hand. The other arm dangled over the side of the couch.

"I don't know why we bother," she said in the same flat voice.

I lit a cigarette and settled back in my chair to listen.

She sighed. "Aren't you going to ask me what's wrong?"

"There's no need to ask," I said. "You'll tell me in due time."

"I guess I will," she said, sighing again.

She lifted her feet from the floor, then squirmed to find a more comfortable position. Her skirt wrinkled under her and for some moments she was busy with the tugging and pulling women usually go through in their first minutes of each session. Under her breath she muttered impatient curses. At last she was settled.

"I don't have to tell you I went to bed with Ben, do I?" she asked.

"If that's what you're thinking of," I said.

"I think you must be a voyeur," she commented acidly after another pause. "That's probably the way you get your kicks."

I said nothing.

"Probably why you're an analyst, too," she continued. "Sublimating . . . isn't that the word? Playing Peeping Tom with your ears. . . ."

"Laura," I asked, "why are you being so aggressive?"

"Because I hate you," she said. "I hate your guts."

"Go on."

She shrugged. "That's all. I've got nothing more to say. I only came here today to tell you how much I despise you. I've said it and I'm finished. . . . Can I go now?" She sat up and reached for her purse.

"If that's what you want to do," I said.

"You don't care?" she asked.

128

"Care isn't the right word," I said. "Of course I'll be sorry to see you leave. But, as I said, if that's what you want to do . . ."

"More double talk," she sighed. "All right. The hell with it. I'm here and I may as well finish out the hour— after all, I'm paying for it." She fell back on the couch and lapsed into silence again.

"Laura," I said, "you seem very anxious to get me to reject you today. Why?"

"I told you—because I hate you."

"I understand that. But why are you trying to make *me* reject *you?*"

"Do we have to go through that again?" she asked. "Because that's my pattern—according to you. I try to push people to the point where they reject me, then I feel worthless and sorry for myself, and find a good excuse to punish myself. Isn't that it?"

"Approximately. But why are you doing it here today?"

"You must be a glutton for punishment, too," she said. "How many times must I say it?—I hate you, I loathe you, I despise you. Isn't that sufficient?"

"But why?"

"Because of what you made me do over the weekend."

"With Ben?"

"Ben!" she said contemptuously. "Of course not. What's that got to do with it? All that happened was that I went to bed with him. We slept together. It was good . . . wonderful. For the first time in my life I felt like a woman."

"Then what . . . ?" I started to say.

"—Keep quiet!" she interrupted. "You wanted to know why I hate you and I'm telling you. It's got nothing to do with Ben or what happened Saturday night. It's about my mother. What we talked about last time . . . that's why I hate you so. She's haunted me all weekend. Since Saturday I can't get her out of my mind. I keep thinking about her—the awful life she had. And the way I treated her. Because you forced me to, I remembered things, terrible things I did to her . . . That's why I hate you—for making me remember." She turned on her side and looked at me over her shoulder. "And you," she

129

continued, "you bastard . . . you did it purposely. You fixed it so I'd remember how rotten I was to her. I've spent half my life trying to forget her and that goddam' wheel chair. But no; you won't let me. You brought her back from the grave to haunt me. That's why I hate you so!"

This outburst exhausted Laura. Averting her head once more, she lay quietly for some minutes. Then she reached an arm behind her.

"Give me the Kleenex," she commanded.

I gave her the box of tissues from the table by my chair. Removing one, she dabbed at her eyes.

"Let me have a cigarette," she said, reaching behind her again.

I put my cigarettes and a box of matches in her hand. She lit up and smoked.

"It's funny," she said. "Funny how I've clung to everything I could find to keep on hating her. You see, I always blamed her for what happened. I always thought it was her fault my father left us. I made it out that she drove him away with her nagging and complaining. I've tried to hide from myself the fact that he was just no good—a lazy, chicken-chasing, selfish son-of-a-bitch. I excused him for his drinking and his neglect of us all those years. I thought, 'Why not? Why shouldn't he run around, stay out all night, have other women? After all, what good was she to him with those useless legs and dried-up body?' I pushed out of my head the way he was before . . . before she got sick. The truth is he was never any different, always a bum. Even when I was small he was no good, no good to her and no good to us. But I loved him—God! how I loved that man. I could hardly wait for him to come home. Drunk, sober—it didn't matter to me. He made a fuss over me and that's why I loved him. She said I was his favorite: I guess I was. At least he made over me more than the others.

"When I'd hear them fighting, I always blamed her. 'What's she picking on him for?' I'd think. 'Why doesn't she let him alone?' And when he went away, I thought it was her fault. Ever since then, until Saturday, I thought it was her fault. And I made her suffer for it. I did mean things to her, things I never told you about, things I tried to forget—did forget—until this weekend. I did them to

130

punish her for kicking him out, for depriving me of his love. His love!

"Would you like to hear one of the things I did? I've thought this one over for two days. . . . Maybe if I tell you I can get rid of it."

. . . Every day on the way home from school she played the same game with herself. That was the reason she preferred to walk home alone. Because what if it happened when the other kids were around? How would she explain it to them? As far as they were concerned she didn't have a father. Even on the high-school admission blank, where it said: "Father—living or dead—check one," she had marked a big X over "dead." So what would she say if, suddenly, he stepped out of a doorway, or came around a corner, or ran over from across the street—and grabbed her and kissed her like he used to? Could she say, "Girls, this is my father?" Of course not! It was better to walk home alone, like this, pretending he was in that alley near the bottom of the hill, or standing behind the coal truck, or hiding behind the newsstand by the subway entrance . . . or that those footsteps behind her—the ones she kept hearing but there was no one there when she turned around—were his footsteps.

The game was over. It ended in the hallway of the tenement house, the same house they had lived in all of her life. If he wasn't here, in the smelly vestibule, on the sagging stairs, on standing expectantly on the first-floor landing in front of their door, the game had to end. And he wasn't: he never was. . . .

She heard the radio as she climbed the stairs, and her insides contracted in a spasm of disgust. "The same thing," she thought, "the same darned thing. Why can't it be different for once, just for once?" With her shoulder she pushed open the door. It closed behind her with a bang; but Anna, sleeping in her chair as usual, hardly stirred.

Laura put her books down on the dresser, then switched the dial of the radio to "off" with a hard, vicious twist of her fingers. Crossing the room she opened the closet, hung up her coat, and slammed the door hard, thinking, "So what if it wakes her? I hope it does!" But it didn't.

On the way to the rear of the apartment she glanced

131

briefly at her mother. In the wheel chair Anna slumped like an abandoned rag doll. Her peroxided hair, showing gray and brown at the roots where it was parted, fell over her forehead. Her chin was on her breast, and from one corner of her mouth a trickle of spittle trailed to the collar of the shabby brown dress. The green sweater she wore was open; it hung about her thin shoulders in rumpled folds, and from its sleeves her skinny wrists and the fingers tipped with bright red nails protruded like claws of a chicken, clutching the worn arms of the chair. Passing her, Laura repressed an exclamation of contempt.

In the kitchen Laura poured herself a glass of milk and stood drinking it by the drain. When she had finished, she rinsed the glass under the tap. It fell from her hand and shattered against the floor.

"Is that you, Laura?" Anna called.

"Yeah."

"Come here. I want you to do something for me."

Laura sighed. "O.K. As soon as I clean up this mess." She dried her hands and walked into the front room. "What is it?" she asked.

Anna motioned with her head. "Over there, on the dresser," she said. "The check from the relief came. I wrote out the store order. You can stop on your way back and give the janitor the rent."

"All right," Laura said wearily. She took her coat from the closet. At the door to the hall she paused and turned to face Anna, who was already fumbling with the radio dial. "Anything else?" she asked, playing out their bimonthly game.

Anna smiled. "Yes," she said. "I didn't put it on the store list, but if they have some of those chocolate-covered caramels I like . . ."

Laura nodded and closed the door. Music from the radio chased her downstairs.

When she returned, laden with packages, she stopped in the bedroom only momentarily to turn down the volume of the radio. "The least you can do is play it quietly," she muttered. "I could hear it a block away."

In the kitchen, still wearing her coat, she disposed of the groceries.

"Did you get everything, Laura?" Anna called.

132

"Yeah."

"Pay the rent?"

"Uh-huh."

"Did they have any of those caramels?"

This time Laura didn't answer. Somewhere, deep inside, the low-burning flame of hate flickered to a new height.

"Laura!" Anna called.

"What d'you want?" the girl shouted angrily.

"I asked if you got my candy."

About to reply, Laura's gaze fell to the remaining package on the porcelain-topped kitchen table. It seemed to hypnotize her, holding her eyes fast and drawing her hand toward its curled neck. Slowly her fingers untwisted the bag and plunged inside. When they emerged, they carried two squares of candy to her mouth. Without tasting, she chewed and swallowed rapidly.

Behind her Laura heard the shuffle of wheels. She turned to find Anna crossing the threshold of the bedroom. Snatching up the bag, the girl hurried into the dining room and faced her mother across the oval table.

"D'you have the candy?" Anna asked.

Laura nodded and held up the sack.

"Give it here," Anna said, extending her hand.

Laura shook her head and put the hand with the paper bag behind her back. Puzzled, Anna sent her chair around the table toward the girl, who waited until her mother came near, then moved quickly to the opposite side, placing the table between them again.

"What kind of nonsense is this?" Anna asked. In reply, Laura put another piece of candy in her mouth.

"Laura!" Anna demanded. "Give me my candy!" She gripped the wheels of her chair and spun them forward. It raced around the table after the girl, who skipped lightly before it. Three times Anna circled the table, chasing the elusive figure that regarded her with narrowed eyes. Exhausted, finally, she stopped. Across from her, Laura stuffed more candy into her mouth and chewed violently.

"Laura," Anna panted, "what's got into you? Why are you doing this?"

Laura took the bag from behind her back and held it temptingly over the table. "If you want it so bad," she said, breathing hard, "come get it." She shook the bag triumphantly. "See," she said, "it's almost all gone. You'd better hurry."

Inside, at the very core of her being, the flame was leaping. A warm glow of exultation swept through her, filling her body with a sense of power and setting her nerves on fire. She felt like laughing, like screaming, like dancing madly. In her mouth the taste of chocolate was intoxicating.

Her mother whimpered. "Give me the candy. . . . Please, Laura."

Laura held the bag high. "Come and get it!" she screamed, and backed away slowly toward the front room.

Anna spun her chair in pursuit. By the time she reached the bedroom, Laura was at the door. She waited until her mother's chair came close, then she whirled and ran through, pulling the door behind her with a loud crash.

Leaning against the banister, Laura listened to the thud of Anna's fists against the wood and her sobs of angry frustration. The wild exhilaration mounted. Hardly conscious of her actions, she crammed the remaining candies into her mouth. Then, from deep in her body, a wave of laughter surged upward. She tried to stop it, but it broke through in a crazy tide of hilarity. The sound of this joyless mirth rebounded from the stair well and echoed from the ceiling of the narrow hallway—as it was to echo, thereafter, along with the sound of footsteps and falling rain, in her dreams. . . .

The weeks following the crucial hours I have just described were very difficult ones for Laura. As she worked through the guilt-laden memories now released from repression, her self-regard, never at any time very high, fell lower and lower. Bitterly, she told the ugly rosary of her pathetic past, not sparing herself (or me) the slightest detail. In a confessional mood, she recited all her faults of behavior—toward her family, her friends, her teachers, her associates—throughout the years. Under the influence of newly acquired but undigested insights the pattern of her sessions with me changed. No longer did she find it necessary to pour out the acid of her hate and contempt, to vilify and condemn me and the world for our lack of love for her. Now she swung the pendulum to the other side: everyone had been too nice to her, too tolerant; she didn't deserve anyone's good opinion, particularly mine.

In keeping with her new mood, Laura also changed the style of her life. She became rigidly ascetic in her dress, adopted a strict diet, gave up smoking, drinking, cosmetics, dancing and all other ordinary amusements. The decision to surrender the novel joys of sex with her lover, Ben, was hard to make, but, tight-lipped and grim with determination, she declared her intention to him and stuck by her word.

For my part, in these weeks of confession and penitential repentance I remained silent and still permissive, revealing nothing of my own thoughts or feelings. I neither commented on the "sins" Laura recounted nor the expiatory measures she employed to discharge them. Instead, as I listened, I tried to reformulate her neurosis in terms of the dynamic information available to us at that point. Naturally, I saw through the recent shift in analytic content and behavior: it was, of course, but a variant of the old design, only implemented by conscious, deliberate techniques. Fundamentally, Laura was still Laura. That she now chose to destroy herself and her relationships in a more circumspect and less obvious fashion; that the weapons she now turned upon herself were regarded—at least by the world outside the analytic chamber—in the highest terms, altered not one whit the basic fact that the core of her neurosis, despite our work, remained intact. Laura, in short, was still profoundly disturbed, still a martyr to secret desires that had not been plumbed.

She did not think so—nor did her friends. As a matter of fact, they were astonished at what they called her "progress," and word reached me that my reputation in Baltimore—an intimate city where who is going to which analyst is always a lively topic at parties—had soared to new heights. And, indeed, to the casual observer Laura seemed improved. In the curious jargon of the analytic sophisticate, she was "making an adjustment." Her rigorous diet, her severity of manner and dress, her renunciation of all fleshly joys and amusements, her sobriety and devotion to "serious" pursuits, above all her maintenance of a "good" relationship with the eligible

Ben (*without sex,* it was whispered)—these were taken as tokens of far-reaching and permanent alterations in personality due to the "miracle" of psychoanalysis. Those with whom she came in contact during this time of course never bothered to peer beneath the mask of public personality she wore. They were content to take her at face value. Because she no longer disrupted their gatherings with demonstrations of her well-known "bitchiness," because she no longer thrust her problems on them or called for their help in times of distress, they felt relieved in their consciences about her. In brief, without laboring the point, so long as Laura disturbed no one else and kept her misery to herself; and so long as she represented to her associates the passive surrender to the mass ideal each one of them so desperately but fruitlessly sought, just so long were they impressed by the "new look" that Laura wore.

But we knew, Laura and I, that the battle had yet to be joined, for only we knew what went on behind the closed doors of 907 in the Latrobe Building. In this room the masks fell away: either they were discarded because here they could not hide the truth, or they were taken from her by the soft persuasion of continuous self-examination with insight. The first to go was the last she had assumed: the defensive mask of self-abnegation.

The time came when I found it necessary to call a halt to Laura's daily *mea culpas,* to put a stop to the marathon of confession she had entered at the beginning of her second year with me. Three factors influenced my decision to force her, at last, off the new course her analysis had taken. The first and most important of these was my perception of the danger implicit in this program of never-ending self-denunciation. As she searched her memory for fresh evidence of guilt, I could see how overwhelmed she was becoming by the enormity of her past behavior. Try as she might, I knew she could never salve her conscience by the penitential acts and renunciations she invented, and I feared the outcome of a prolonged contest between contrition and atonement; it could only lead to the further debility of her ego, to a progressive lowering of self-esteem which might wind up at a point I dared not think about.

The second and hardly less important reason why I felt

136

I had to urge Laura away from this attempt to shrive herself in the manner she chose was the simple fact of its unproductiveness for therapy. As I have already said, this psychic gambit of self-abnegation only substituted one set of neurotic symptoms for another and left the basic pathological structure untouched. Moreover, it provided precisely the same kind of neurotic satisfaction she had been securing all along by her old techniques. The martyrdom she now suffered by her own hand was equivalent to the self-pity formerly induced by the rejection she had unconsciously arranged to obtain from others. And while it is true that she no longer exercised hate, hostility and aggressive contempt outwardly, it was only the direction in which these negative elements were discharged that had been altered: they remained.

Finally, my decision was also influenced by sheer fatigue and boredom with what I knew to be only an act, a disguise of behavior and attitude adopted to squeeze the last ounce of neurotic gratification from me and the entire world which, by psychic extension from love-withholding parents, she viewed as rejective and denying. To tell the truth, I became tired of the "new" Laura, weary of her pious pretenses, and a trifle nauseated with the holier-than-thou manner she assumed. And while this was the least of my reasons for doing what I did, I hold it chiefly responsible for the almost fatal error in timing I committed when I finally acted on an otherwise carefully weighed decision to eject my patient from the analytic rut in which she was, literally, wallowing.

The session that precipitated the near catastrophe took place on a Thursday afternoon. Laura was the last patient I was to see that day, since I was taking the Congressional Limited to New York where I was scheduled to conduct a seminar that night and give a lecture on Friday. I was looking forward to the trip which, for me, represented a holiday from work and the first break in routine in many months. Something of this mood of impatience to get going and pleasurable anticipation must have been communicated to Laura, for she began her hour with a hardly disguised criticism of my manner and appearance.

"Somehow," she said after composing herself on the couch, "somehow you seem different today."

"I do?"

"Yes." She turned to look at me. "Maybe it's because of the way you're dressed. . . . That's a new suit, isn't it?"

"No," I said, "I've worn it before."

"I don't remember ever seeing it." She resumed her usual position. "Anyway, you look nice."

"Thank you."

"I like to see people look nice," she continued. "When a person gets all dressed up, it makes them feel better. I think it's because they think other people will judge them on the basis of their outer appearance—and if the outer appearance is pleasing and nice, people will think what's behind is pleasing and nice, too—and being thought of that way makes you feel better. Don't you think so?"

I was lost in the convolutions of this platitude, but its inference was pretty clear.

"What exactly are you getting at?" I asked.

She shrugged. "It's not important," she said. "Just a thought . . ." There was a moment of silence, then, "Oh!" she exclaimed. "I know why you're all dressed up. . . . Today's the day you go to New York, isn't it?"

"That's right," I said.

"That means I won't see you on Saturday, doesn't it?"

"Yes. I won't be back until Monday."

"Is the lecture on Saturday?"

"No, the lecture's tomorrow, Friday."

"—But you're going to stay over until Monday. . . . Well, I think the rest will do you good. You need it. I think everyone needs to kick up his heels once in a while, just get away, have some fun and forget everything—if he can."

The dig at my irresponsibility toward my patients, particularly Laura, and the implication that I was going to New York to participate in some kind of orgy, were not lost on me.

"I hate to miss an hour," Laura continued in the same melancholy tone she had been using since this meeting began. "Especially now. I feel I really need to come here now. There's so much to talk about."

"In that case," I said, "you should take more advantage of the time you're here. For example, you're not using this hour very well, are you?"

"Perhaps not," she said. "It's just that I feel this is the wrong time for you to be going away."

"Now look here, Laura," I said. "You've known about missing the Saturday hour for more than a week. Please don't pretend it's a surprise to you. And, besides, it's only one hour."

"I know," she sighed. "I know. But it feels like you're going away forever. . . . What if I should need you?"

"I don't think you will. . . . But if you should, you can call my home or the office here and they'll put you in touch with me."

I lit a cigarette and waited for her to go on. With the first inhalation, however, I began to cough. Laura again turned around.

"Can I get you something?" she asked. "A glass of water?"

"No, thank you," I answered.

"That cough of yours worries me," she said when the spasm had passed and I was once more quiet. "You should give up smoking. I did, you know. It's been two months since I had a cigarette. And my cough's all gone. I think that's the best of it—no more coughing. I feel fine. You should really try it."

I continued to smoke in silence, wondering where she would take this theme. Before long, I found out.

"It wasn't easy. The first two weeks were agony, but I determined not to give in. After all, I had a reason. . . ."

"To stop coughing?" I suggested, permitting myself the small satisfaction of retaliating for her deliberate provocation of the past half hour.

"Of course not!" she exclaimed. "You know very well I had good reasons for giving up smoking—and other things too."

"What were they?" I asked.

"You of all people should know," she said.

"Tell me."

"Well—it's just that I want to be a better person. If you've been listening to everything I've said these past weeks you know how I used to behave. Now I want to make amends for it, to be different, better. . . ."

"And you think giving up smoking and so on will make you a better person?"

She fell silent. Glancing over at her, I noticed the

139

rigidity of her body. Her hands, until now held loosely on her lap, were clenched into fists. I looked at my watch and cursed myself for a fool. Only ten minutes left and a train to catch! Why had I let myself rise to the bait? Why had I permitted this to come up now, when it couldn't be handled? Was there any way out, any way to avoid the storm I had assisted her to brew? I put my trust in the gods that care for idiots and took a deep breath.

"Well?" I asked.

"Nothing I do is right," she said hollowly. "There's no use trying. I just make it worse."

"What are you talking about?"

"Myself," she said. "Myself and the mess I make of everything. I try to do what's right—but I never can. I think I'm working it all out—but I'm not. I'm just getting in deeper and deeper. It's too much for me, too much. . . ."

When the hour ended, I rose and held the door open for her.

"I'll see you Monday," I said.

Her eyes were glistening. "Have a good time," she sighed.

On the train to New York I thought about Laura and the hour just ended, reviewing it word for word and wondering just where I had made my mistake. That I had committed a serious error I had no doubt, and it hardly needed Laura's abrupt change of mood to bring this to my attention. To mobilize guilt and anxiety just prior to a recess in therapy is in itself unwise. In this instance I had compounded the blunder by losing control over myself and responding, as I seldom do in the treatment situation, to criticism and provocation. I asked myself—had she touched some peculiarly sensitive chord in me? Am I so susceptible to faultfinding? Have I, all unaware, become especially tender on the subject of my incessant smoking? my cough? my responsibility to my patients? my appearance? Or was it, as I suspected then and am sure of now, that I had made the decision to contrive a directional change in Laura's analysis but had been incited to violate the timetable of therapy by an unexpected display of the fatuousness that had become her prevailing defense?

That evening I had dinner with friends and conducted the scheduled seminar, after which many of us gathered for a series of nightcaps and further discussion in a colleague's home. I had forgotten all about Laura by the time I returned to my hotel, and when the desk clerk gave me a message to call a certain long-distance operator in Baltimore, I thought it would concern only something personal at home or a communication from my office. I was surprised when Laura's voice came over the wire.

"Dr. Lindner?"

"Yes, Laura. What is it?"

"I've been trying to get you for hours."

"I'm sorry. Is something wrong?"

"I don't know. I just wanted to talk with you."

"What about?"

"About the way I feel. . . ."

"How do you feel?"

"Scared."

"Scared of what?"

"I don't know. Just scared, I guess. Of nothing in particular—just everything. . . . I don't like being alone."

"But you're alone most other nights, aren't you?" I asked.

"Yes . . . but somehow it's different tonight."

"Why?"

"Well, for one thing, you're not in Baltimore."

The line was silent as I waited for her to continue.

"And then," she said, "I think you're angry with me."

"Why do you think that?"

"The way I acted this afternoon. It was mean of me, I know. But I couldn't help it. Something was egging me on."

"What was it?"

"I don't know. I haven't figured it out. Something . . ."

"We'll talk about it Monday," I said.

More silence. I thought I heard noises as if she were crying.

"Do you forgive me?" she sobbed.

"We'll review the whole hour on Monday," I said, seeking a way out of this awkward situation. "Right now you'd better get to bed."

"All right," she said meekly. "I'm sorry I bothered you."

141

"No bother at all," I said. "Good night, Laura"—and hung up with relief.

I gave the lecture on Friday afternoon, and when it was over returned to my room for a nap before beginning my holiday with dinner in a favorite restaurant and a long-anticipated evening at the theater. In the quiet room, I bathed and lay down for a peaceful interlude of sleep. Hardly had I begun to doze when the phone rang. It was my wife, calling from Baltimore. Laura, she said, had slashed her wrists: I had better come home—quick. . . .

The doctor and I sat in the corner of the room, talking in whispers. On the bed, heavily sedated, Laura breathed noisily. Even in the dim light the pallor of her face was discernible, and I could see a faint white line edging her lips. On the blanket her hands lay limply. The white bandages at her wrists forced themselves accusingly on my attention. From time to time her hands twitched.

"I doubt that it was a serious attempt," the physician was saying, "although of course you never know. It's harder than you think, trying to get out that way. You've really got to mean it—you've got to mean it enough to saw away hard to get down where it counts. I don't think she tried very hard. The cut on the left wrist is fairly deep, but not deep enough, and the ones on the right wrist are superficial. There wasn't a hell of a lot of blood, either."

"I understand you got there awfully fast," I said.

"Pretty fast," he replied. "What happened was this: Right after she slashed herself she began screaming. A neighbor ran in and had the good sense to call me immediately. My office is in the same building, on the first floor, and I happened to be there at the time. I rushed upstairs, took a look at the cuts and saw they weren't too bad——"

"They were made with a razor blade, weren't they?" I interrupted.

"Yes," he said, and then continued, "so I slapped a couple of tourniquets on, phoned the hospital that I was sending her in, then called the ambulance. I followed it here to Sinai. In the Accident Room they cleaned her up and had her wrists sutured by the time I arrived. She was still quite excited, so I decided to put her in for a day or two. I gave her a shot of morphine and sent her upstairs."

142

"Who called my home?" I asked.

He shrugged. "I don't know. Before the ambulance came, her neighbor called Laura's sister and told her what happened and what I was going to do. I think the sister tried to get hold of you."

"I guess so," I said. "She knows Laura's in treatment with me."

"I don't envy you," he said. "She's a lulu."

"What did she do?"

He shrugged and motioned toward the bed with a wave of his hand. "This kind of business, for one thing. Then the way she carried on until the shot took effect."

"What did she do?"

"Oh," he said vaguely, "she kept screaming and throwing herself around. Pretty wild." He stood up. "I don't think you've got anything to worry about as far as her physical condition goes, though. She'll be fine in the morning. Maybe a little groggy, that's all."

"I'm very grateful to you," I said.

"Not at all," he said on his way from the room. "There'll be some business with the police tomorrow. If you need me, just call."

Laura had her hour on Saturday—in the hospital. During it and many subsequent sessions we worked out the reasons for her extravagant, self-destructive gesture. As the physician had observed, her act was hardly more than a dramatic demonstration without serious intent, although in the way of such things it could well have miscarried to a less fortunate conclusion. Its immediate purpose was to recall me from my holiday and to reawaken the sympathetic attention she believed herself to have prejudiced by her hostile provocativeness on Thursday. But the whole affair, we learned subsequently, had much deeper roots.

The motivation behind Laura's attempt at suicide was twofold. Unconsciously, it represented an effort to re-enact, with a more satisfying outcome, the desertion of her father; and, at the same time, it served the function of providing extreme penance for so-called "sins" of behavior and thought-crimes between the ages of twelve and twenty-four. So far as the first of these strange motivations is concerned, it is understandable how Laura interpreted my brief interruption of therapy as an abandonment similar to that abrupt and permanent earlier departure of her father. This time, however, as indicated by the phone call to my hotel on the night I left, she believed herself to have been at least in part responsible for it, to have driven him (in the person of the analyst) away. To call him back, her distraught mind conceived the suicidal act, which was nothing less than a frenzied effort—planned, so it appeared, but not executed, more than a decade before—to repeat the original drama but insure a different and more cordial ending.

The mad act was also powered dynamically by the fantastic arithmetic of confession and penance that Laura, like some demented accountant, had invented to discharge her guilty memories. As I had feared when the pattern became clear to me, the mental balance sheet she was keeping with her hourly testaments of culpability and the increasing asceticism of her life could never be stabilized. Self-abnegation had to lead to a martyrdom of some kind. My effort to prevent this miscarried—not because it was misconceived, but because it was so sloppily executed. My own unconscious needs—the residual infantilisms and immaturities within me—in this case subverted judgment and betrayed me into the commission of a timing error that could have cost Laura's life.

We both profited from this terrible experience and, in the end, it proved to have been something of a boon to each of us. I, of course, would have preferred to learn my lesson otherwise. As for Laura, she made a rapid recovery and returned to the analysis much sobered by her encounter with death. Apart from all else, the episode provided her with many genuine and useful insights, not the least of which were those that led her to abandon her false asceticism and to stop playing the role of the "well-analyzed," "adjusted" paragon among her friends.

The events just described furnished us with vast quantities of material for analysis in subsequent months. Particularly as it referred directly to the situation in psychoanalysis known technically as the "transference neurosis" —or the reflection in therapy of former patterns of relationship with early, significant figures in the life of the patient—the suicidal gesture Laura made led to an even deeper investigation of her existing neurotic attitudes and

144

behavior. And as we dealt with this topic of transference —the organic core of every therapeutic enterprise; as we followed its meandering course through our sessions together, Laura rapidly made new and substantial gains. With every increase in her understanding another rich facet of personality was disclosed, and the burden of distress she had borne for so long became lighter and lighter.

The metamorphosis of Laura was a fascinating thing to observe. I, as the human instrument of changes that were taking place in her, was immensely gratified. Nevertheless, my pleasure and pride were incomplete, for I remained annoyingly aware that we had yet to find the explanation for the single remaining symptom that had so far evaded the influence of therapy. No progress at all had been made against the strange complaint which brought her into treatment: the seizures of uncontrollable hunger, the furious eating, and their dreadful effects.

I had my own theory about this stubborn symptom and was often tempted to follow the suggestion of a certain "school" of psychoanalysis and communicate my ideas to Laura. However, because I felt—and still feel—that such technique is theoretically unjustified—a reflection of the therapist's insecurity and impatience rather than a well-reasoned approach to the problems of psychotherapy— because I felt this way, I determined to curb my eagerness to bring Laura's chief symptom into focus by testing my interpretations on her. In adherence to methods in which I have been trained, therefore, I held my tongue and waited developments. Fortunately, they were not long in appearing; and when they did arrive, in one mighty tide of insight my patient's being was purged of the mental debris that had made her existence a purgatory.

Laura was seldom late for appointments, nor had she ever missed one without canceling for good cause well in advance. On this day, therefore, when she failed to appear at the appointed time I grew somewhat anxious. As the minutes passed, my concern mounted. Finally, after a half hour had sped and there was still no sign of Laura, I asked my secretary to call her apartment. There was no answer.

During the afternoon, caught up in work with other patients, I gave only a few passing thoughts to Laura's

145

neglect to keep her hour or to inform me she would be absent. When I reminded myself of it at the close of the day, I tried, in a casual way, to recall her previous session and examine it for some clue to this unusual delinquency. Since none came readily, I pushed the matter from my mind and prepared to leave the office.

We were in the corridor awaiting the elevator when we heard the telephone. I was minded to let it ring, but Jeanne, more compulsive in such matters than I, insisted on returning to answer. While I held the elevator, she re-entered the office. A few moments later she reappeared, shrugging her shoulders in answer to my question.

"Must have been a wrong number," she said. "When I answered all I heard was a funny noise and then the line went dead."

I arrived home shortly after six o'clock and dressed to receive the guests who were coming for dinner. While in the shower, I heard the ringing of the telephone, which my wife answered. On emerging from the bathroom, I asked her who had called.

"That was the queerest thing," she said. "The party on the other end sounded like a drunk and I couldn't make out a word."

During dinner I was haunted by a sense of unease. While attending to the lively conversation going on around me, and participating in it as usual, near the edges of consciousness something nagged uncomfortably. I cannot say that I connected the two mysterious calls with Laura and her absence from the hour that day, but I am sure they contributed to the vague and fitful feelings I experienced. In any case, when the telephone again rang while we were having our coffee, I sprang from my place and rushed to answer it myself.

I lifted the receiver and said, "Hello?" Over the wire, in response, came a gurgling, throaty noise which, even in retrospect defies comparison with any sound I have ever heard. Unmistakably produced by the human voice, it had a gasping, breathless quality, yet somehow seemed animal in nature. It produced a series of meaningless syllables, urgent in tone but unidentifiable.

"Who is this?" I demanded.

There was a pause, then, laboriously, I heard the first long-drawn syllable of her name.

146

"Laura!" I said. "Where are you?"

Again the pause, followed by an effortful intake of breath and its expiration as if through a hollow tube: "Home . . ."

"Is something wrong?"

It seemed to come easier this time.

"Eat-ing."

"Since when?"

". . . Don't—know."

"How d'you feel?" I asked, aware of the absurdity of the question but desperately at a loss to know what else to say.

"Aw-ful . . . No—more—food . . . Hun-gry . . ."

My mind raced. What could I do? What was there to do?

"Help—me," she said—and I heard the click of the instrument as it fell into its cradle.

"Laura," I said. "Wait!"—But the connection had been broken and my words echoed in my own ears. Hastily, I hung up and searched through the telephone directory for her number. My fingers spun the dial. After an interval, I heard the shrill buzz of her phone. Insistently, it repeated itself, over and over. There was no answer.

I knew, then, what I had to do. Excusing myself from our guests, I got my car and drove to where Laura lived. On the way there, I thought about what some of my colleagues would say of what I was doing. No doubt they would be appalled by such a breach of orthodoxy and speak pontifically of "counter-transference," my "anxiety" at Laura's "acting out," and other violations of strict procedure. Well, let them. To me, psychoanalysis is a vital art that demands more of its practitioners than the clever exercise of their brains. Into its practice also goes the heart, and there are occasions when genuine human feelings take precedence over the rituals and dogmas of the craft.

I searched the mailboxes in the vestibule for Laura's name, then ran up the stairs to the second floor. In front of her door I paused and put my ear against the metal frame to listen. I heard nothing.

I pushed the button. Somewhere inside a chime sounded. A minute passed while I waited impatiently. I rang again, depressing the button forcefully time after time. Still no one came to the door. Finally, I turned the knob with one hand and pounded the panel with the flat of the other. In the silence that followed, I heard the noise of something heavy crashing to the floor, then the sibilant shuffling of feet.

I put my mouth close to the crack where door met frame.

"Laura!" I called. "Open the door!"

Listening closely, I heard what sounded like sobs and faint moaning, then a voice that slowly pronounced the words, "Go—away."

I shook the knob violently. "Open up!" I commanded. "Let me in!"

The knob turned in my hand and the door opened. I pushed against it, but a chain on the jamb caught and held. In the dim light of the hallway, against the darkness inside, something white shone. It was Laura's face, but she withdrew it quickly.

"Go—away," she said in a thick voice.

"No."

"Please!"

She leaned against the door, trying to close it again. I put my foot in the opening.

"Take that chain off," I said with all the authority I could muster. "At once!"

The chain slid away and I walked into the room. It was dark, and I could make out only vague shapes of lamps and furniture. I fumbled along the wall for the light switch. Before my fingers found it, Laura, who was hardly more than an indistinguishable blur of whiteness by my side, ran past me into the room beyond.

I discovered the switch and turned on the light. In its sudden, harsh glare I surveyed the room. The sight was shocking. Everywhere I looked there was a litter of stained papers, torn boxes, empty bottles, open cans, broken crockery and dirty dishes. On the floor and on the tables large puddles gleamed wetly. Bits of food—crumbs, gnawed bones, fish-heads, sodden chunks of unknown stuffs—were strewn all about. The place looked as if the contents of a garbage can had been emptied in it, and the stench was sickening.

I swallowed hard against a rising wave of nausea and

148

hurried into the room where Laura had disappeared. In the shaft of light that came through an archway, I saw a rumpled bed, similarly piled with rubbish. In a corner, I made out the crouching figure of Laura.

By the entrance I found the switch and pressed it. As the light went on, Laura covered her face and shrank against the wall. I went over to her, extending my hands.

"Come," I said. "Stand up."

She shook her head violently. I bent down and lifted her to her feet. When she stood up, her fingers still hid her face. As gently as I could, I pulled them away. Then I stepped back and looked at Laura. What I saw, I will never forget.

The worst of it was her face. It was like a ceremonial mask on which some inspired maniac had depicted every corruption of the flesh. Vice was there, and gluttony; lust also, and greed. Depravity and abomination seemed to ooze from great pores that the puffed tautness of skin revealed.

I closed my eyes momentarily against this apparition of incarnate degradation. When I opened them, I saw the tears welling from holes where her eyes should have been. Hypnotized, I watched them course in thin streams down the bloated cheeks and fall on her nightgown. And then, for the first time, I saw it!

Laura was wearing a night robe of some sheer stuff that fell loosely from straps at her shoulders. Originally white, it was now soiled and stained with the evidences of her orgy. But my brain hardly registered the begrimed garment, except where it bulged below her middle in a sweeping arc, ballooning outward from her body as if she were pregnant.

I gasped with disbelief—and my hand went out automatically to touch the place where her nightgown swelled. My fingers encountered a softness that yielded to their pressure. Questioning, I raised my eyes to that caricature of a human face. It twisted into what I took for a smile. The mouth opened and closed to form a word that it labored to pronounce.

"Ba-by," Laura said.

"Baby?" I repeated. "Whose baby?"

"Lau-ra's ba-by. . . . Lo-ok."

She bent forward drunkenly and grasped her gown by

149

the hem. Slowly she raised the garment, lifting it until her hands were high above her head. I stared at her exposed body. There, where my fingers had probed, a pillow was strapped to her skin with long bands of adhesive.

Laura let the nightgown fall. Swaying, she smoothed it where it bulged.

"See?" she said. "Looks—real—this way."

Her hands went up to cover her face again. Now great sobs shook her, and tears poured through her fingers as she cried. I led her to the bed and sat on its edge with her, trying to order the turmoil of my thoughts while she wept. Soon the crying ceased, and she bared her face again. Once more the lost mouth worked to make words.

"I—want—a—baby," she said, and fell over on the bed—asleep. . . .

I covered Laura with a blanket and went into the other room, where I remembered seeing a telephone. There, I called a practical nurse who had worked with me previously and whom I knew would be available. Within a half hour, she arrived. I briefed her quickly: the apartment was to be cleaned and aired: when Laura awakened, the doctor who lived downstairs was to be called to examine her and advise on treatment and diet: she was to report to me regularly, and in two days she was to bring Laura to my office. Then I left.

Although the night was cold I lowered the top on my car. I drove home slowly, breathing deeply of the clean air.

Two days later, while her nurse sat in the outer room, Laura and I began to put together the final pieces in the puzzle of her neurosis. As always, she had only a vague, confused memory of events during her seizure, recollecting them hazily through a fog of total intoxication. Until I recounted the episode, she had no clear remembrance of my visit and thought she had dreamed my presence in her rooms. Of the portion that concerned her pitiful imitation of pregnancy, not the slightest memorial trace remained.

It was clear that Laura's compelling desire was to have a child, that her feelings of emptiness arose from this desire, and that her convulsions of ravenous appetite were unconsciously designed to produce its illusory satisfaction.

150

What was not immediately apparent, however, was why this natural feminine wish underwent such extravagant distortion in Laura's case, why it had become so intense, and why it had to express itself in a manner at once monstrous, occult and self-destructive.

My patient herself provided the clue to these focal enigmas when, in reconstructing the episode I had witnessed, she made a slip of the tongue so obvious in view of the facts that it hardly required interpretation.

It was about a week after the incident I have recorded. Laura and I were reviewing it again, looking for further clues. I was intrigued by the contrivance she wore that night to simulate the appearance of a pregnant woman, and asked for details about its construction. Laura could supply none. Apparently, she said, she had fashioned it in an advanced stage of her intoxication from food.

"Was this the first time you made anything like that?" I asked.

"I don't know," she said, somewhat hesitantly. "I can't be sure. Maybe I did and destroyed the thing before I came out of the fog. It seems to me I remember finding something like you describe a couple of years ago after an attack, but I didn't know—or didn't want to know—what it was, so I just took it apart and forgot about it."

"You'd better look around the apartment carefully," I said, half joking. "Perhaps there's a spare hidden away someplace."

"I doubt it," she replied in the same mood. "I guess I have to mike a new baby every . . ." Her hand went over her mouth. "My God!" she exclaimed. "Did you hear what I just said?"

Mike was her father's name; and of course it was his baby she wanted. It was for this impossible fulfillment that Laura hungered—and now was starved no more. . . .

PART II

THE DISSENTERS
FROM
FREUD'S THEORIES

This section of the book will include cases by therapists who differed from Freud's theories to the point where they set up independent schools. While Adler, Jung and Rogers have felt their differences to be great enough to consider themselves non-Freudian, Karen Horney and her followers considered themselves neo-Freudian, or as having reinterpreted Freud's findings in the light of later developments.

Sullivan falls halfway between these camps, as much of his theory was influenced by the work of Adolf Meyer, the American psychiatrist, and by the discipline of the social sciences, specifically social psychology.

The Anxious
Young Woman and
The Retired
Business Man

Carl Gustave Jung, M.D.
translated by R. F. C. Hull

From: Two Essays on Analytical
Psychology
Meridian Books, New York, 1956

155

CARL GUSTAVE JUNG

Carl Gustave Jung (1875–) met Freud in 1906, after having corresponded with him for some time. In 1909, he came to America with Freud and Ferenczi to lecture on psychoanalysis. When he returned to middle-class Switzerland he became increasingly uneasy about Freud's emphasis on sexual matters and broke with him in 1913, to establish his own school of thought, generally referred to as "Analytical Psychology."

While formally breaking with Freud, Jung has granted that the problems of the neurotic patient under forty years old can well be helped by utilizing the techniques of Freud or Adler. However, Jung believes that older patients require a different approach because they are suffering from the senselessness and aimlessness of their lives rather than from a definite neurosis (an idea currently emphasized by the "existential" analysts). In his technique, Jung appears to stress the uniqueness of the individual and the desirability of the individual's acceptance and full development of all sides of his personality.

Jung is responsible for the popularity of the terms "introvert" and "extravert" which he saw as one-sided developments of the personality.

In the following material, Jung illustrates first the Freudian, and second the Jungian theory, and in doing so, demonstrates how his theory both resembles and differs from Freudian psychoanalysis.

156

The Anxious Young Woman

and

The Retired Business Man

I remember a young woman who suffered from acute hysteria following a sudden fright. She had been to an evening party and was on her way home about midnight in the company of several acquaintances, when a cab came up behind them at full trot. The others got out of the way, but she, as though spellbound with terror, kept to the middle of the road and ran along in front of the horses. The cabman cracked his whip and swore; it was no good, she ran down the whole length of the road, which led across a bridge. There her strength deserted her, and to avoid being trampled on by the horses she would in her desperation have leapt into the river had not the passers-by prevented her. Now, this same lady had happened to be in St. Petersburg on the bloody twenty-second of January, in the very street which was cleared by the volleys of the soldiers. All round her people were falling to the ground dead or wounded; she, however, quite calm and clear-headed, espied a gate leading into a yard through which she made her escape into another street. These dreadful moments caused her no further agitation. She felt perfectly well afterwards—indeed, rather better than usual.

Essentially similar reactions can frequently be observed. Hence it necessarily follows that the intensity of a trauma has very little pathogenic significance in itself, but it must have a special significance for the patient. That is to say, it is not the shock as such that has a pathogenic effect under all circumstances, but, in order to have an effect, it must impinge on a special psychic disposition, which may, in certain circumstances, consist in the patient's unconsciously attributing a specific sig-

157

nificance to the shock. Here we have a possible key to the "predisposition." We have therefore to ask ourselves: what are the special circumstances of the scene with the cab? The patient's fear began with the sound of the trotting horses; for an instant it seemed to her that this portended some terrible doom—her death, or something as dreadful; the next moment she lost all sense of what she was doing.

The real effect evidently comes from the horses. The patient's predisposition to react in so unaccountable a way to this unremarkable incident might therefore consist in the fact that horses have some special significance for her. We might conjecture, for instance, that she once had a dangerous accident with horses. This was actually found to be the case. As a child of about seven she was out for a drive with her coachman, when suddenly the horses took fright and at a wild gallop made for the precipitous bank of a deep river-gorge. The coachman jumped down and shouted to her to do likewise, but she was in such deadly fear that she could hardly make up her mind. Nevertheless she jumped in the nick of time, while the horses crashed with the carriage into the depths below. That such an event would leave a very deep impression scarcely needs proof. Yet it does not explain why at a later date such an insensate reaction should follow the perfectly harmless hint of a similar situation. So far we only know that the later symptom had a prelude in childhood, but the pathological aspect of it still remains in the dark. In order to penetrate this mystery, further knowledge is needed. For it had become clear with increasing experience that in all the cases analysed so far, there existed, apart from the traumatic experiences, another, special class of disturbances which lie in the province of love. Admittedly "love" is an elastic concept that stretches from heaven to hell and combines in itself good and evil, high and low. With this discovery Freud's views underwent a considerable change. He had formerly sought the cause of the neurosis in traumatic experiences, now the center of gravity of the problem shifted to an entirely different point. This is best illustrated by our case: we can understand well enough why horses should play a special part in the life of the patient, but we do not understand the later reaction, so exaggerated and uncalled for. The pathological peculiarity of this story lies in the fact that she is frightened of quite harmless horses. Remembering the discovery that apart from the traumatic experience there is often a disturbance in the province of love, we might inquire whether perhaps there is some peculiarity in this connection.

The lady knows a young man to whom she thinks of becoming engaged; she loves him and hopes to be happy with him. At first nothing more is discoverable. But it would never do to be deterred from investigation by the negative results of the preliminary questioning. There are indirect ways of reaching the goal when the direct way fails. We therefore return to that singular moment when the lady ran headlong in front of the horses. We inquire about her companions and what sort of festive occasion it was in which she had just taken part. It had been a farewell party for her best friend, who was going abroad to a health resort on account of her nerves. This friend is married and, we are told, happily; she is also the mother of a child. We may take leave to doubt the statement that she is happy; for, were she really so, she would presumably have no reason to be "nervous" and in need of a cure. Shifting my angle of approach, I learned that after her friends had rescued her they brought the patient back to the house of her host—her best friend's husband—as this was the nearest shelter at that late hour of night. There she was hospitably received in her exhausted state. At this point the patient broke off her narrative, became embarrassed, fidgeted, and tried to change the subject. Evidently some disagreeable reminiscence had suddenly bobbed up. After the most obstinate resistance had been overcome, it appeared that yet another very remarkable incident had occurred that night: the amiable host had made her a fiery declaration of love, thus precipitating a situation which, in the absence of the lady of the house, might well be considered both difficult and distressing. Ostensibly this declaration of love came to her like a bolt from the blue, but these things usually have their history. It was now the task of the next few weeks to dig out bit by bit a long love story, until at last a complete picture emerged which I attempt to outline somewhat as follows:

159

As a child the patient had been a regular tomboy, caring only for wild boys' games, scorning her own sex, and avoiding all feminine ways and occupations. After puberty, when the erotic problem might have come too close, she began to shun all society, hated and despised everything that even remotely reminded her of the biological destiny of man, and lived in a world of fantasies which had nothing in common with rude reality. Thus, until about her twenty-fourth year, she evaded all those little adventures, hopes, and expectations which ordinarily move a girl's heart at this age. Then she got to know two men who were destined to break through the thorny hedge that had grown up around her. Mr. A was her best friend's husband, and Mr. B was his bachelor friend. She liked them both. Nevertheless it soon began to look as though she liked Mr. B a vast deal better. An intimacy quickly sprang up between them and before long there was talk of a possible engagement. Through her relations with Mr. B and through her friends she often came into contact with Mr. A, whose presence sometimes disturbed her in the most unaccountable way and made her nervous. About this time the patient went to a large party. Her friends were also present. She became lost in thought and was dreamily playing with her ring when it suddenly slipped off her finger and rolled under the table. Both gentlemen looked for it and Mr. B succeeded in finding it. He placed the ring on her finger with an arch smile and said, "You know what that means!" Overcome by a strange and irresistible feeling, she tore the ring from her finger and flung it through the open window. A painful moment ensued, as may be imagined, and soon she left the party in deep dejection. Not long after this, so-called chance brought it about that she should spend her summer holidays in a health resort where Mr. and Mrs. A were also staying. Mrs. A then began to grow visibly nervous, and frequently remained indoors because she felt out of sorts. The patient was thus in a position to go out for walks alone with Mr. A. On one occasion they went boating. So boisterous was she in her merriment that she suddenly fell overboard. She could not swim, and it was only with great difficulty that Mr. A pulled her half-unconscious into the boat. And then it was that he kissed her. With this romantic episode the

160

bonds were tied fast. But the patient would not allow the depths of this passion to come to consciousness, evidently because she had long habituated herself to pass over such things or, better, to run away from them. To excuse herself in her own eyes she pursued her engagement to Mr. B all the more energetically, telling herself every day that it was Mr. B whom she loved. Naturally this curious little game had not escaped the keen glances of wifely jealousy. Mrs. A, her friend, had guessed the secret and fretted accordingly, so that her nerves only got worse. Hence it became necessary for Mrs. A to go abroad for a cure. At the farewell party the evil spirit stepped up to our patient and whispered in her ear, "Tonight he is alone. Something must happen to you so that you can go to his house." And so indeed it happened: through her own strange behavior she came back to his house, and thus she attained her desire.

After this explanation everyone will probably be inclined to assume that only a devilish subtlety could devise such a chain of circumstances and set it to work. There is no doubt about the subtlety, but its moral evaluation remains a doubtful matter, because I must emphasize that the motives leading to this dramatic dénouement were in no sense conscious. To the patient, the whole story seemed to happen of itself, without her being conscious of any motive. But the previous history makes it perfectly clear that everything was unconsciously directed to this end, while the conscious mind was struggling to bring about the engagement to Mr. B. The unconscious drive in the other direction was stronger.

So once more we return to our original question, namely, whence comes the pathological (i.e., peculiar or exaggerated) nature of the reaction to the trauma? On the basis of a conclusion drawn from analogous experiences, we conjectured that in this case too there must be, in addition to the trauma, a disturbance in the erotic sphere. This conjecture has been entirely confirmed, and we have learnt that the trauma, the ostensible cause of the illness, is no more than an occasion for something previously not conscious to manifest itself, i.e., an important erotic conflict. Accordingly the trauma loses its exclusive significance, and is replaced by a much deeper

161

and more comprehensive conception which sees the pathogenic agent as an erotic conflict.

One often hears the question: why should the erotic conflict be the cause of the neurosis rather than any other conflict? To this we can only answer: no one asserts that it must be so, but in point of fact it frequently is so. In spite of all indignant protestations to the contrary, the fact remains that love, its problems and its conflicts, is of fundamental importance in human life and, as careful inquiry consistently shows, is of far greater significance than the individual suspects.

The trauma theory has therefore been abandoned as antiquated; for with the discovery that not the trauma but a hidden erotic conflict is the root of the neurosis, the trauma loses its causal significance.

Once, in America, I was consulted by a business man of about forty-five. He was a typical American self-made man who had worked his way up from the bottom. He had been very successful and had founded an immense business. He had also succeeded in organizing it in such a way that he was able to think of retiring. Two years before I saw him he had in fact taken his farewell. Until then he had lived entirely for his business and concentrated all his energies on it with the incredible intensity and one-sidedness peculiar to successful American business men. He had purchased a splendid estate where he thought of "living," by which he meant horses, automobiles, golf, tennis, parties and what not. But he had reckoned without his host. The energy which should have been at his disposal would not enter into these alluring prospects, but went capering off in quite another direction. A few weeks after the initiation of the longed-for life of bliss, he began brooding over peculiar, vague sensations in his body, and a few weeks more sufficed to plunge him into a state of extreme hypochondria. He had a complete nervous collapse. From a healthy man, of uncommon physical strength and abounding energy, he became a peevish child. That was the end of all his glories. He fell from one state of anxiety to the next and worried himself almost to death with hypochondriacal mopings. He then consulted a famous specialist, who recognized at once that there was nothing wrong with the man but lack of work. The patient saw the sense of this,

162

and returned to his former position. But, to his immense disappointment, no interest in the business could be aroused. Neither patience nor resolution was of any use. His energy could not by any means be forced back into the business. His condition naturally became worse than before. All that had formerly been living, creative energy in him now turned against him with terrible destroying force. His creative genius rose up, as it were, in revolt against him; and just as before he had built up great organizations in the world, so now his dæmon spun equally subtle systems of hypochondriacal delusion that completely annihilated him. When I saw him he was already a hopeless moral ruin. Nevertheless I tried to make clear to him that though such a gigantic energy might be withdrawn from the business, the question remained, where should it go? The finest horses, the fastest cars, and the most amusing parties may very likely fail to allure the energy, although it would be rational enough to think that a man who had devoted his whole life to serious work had a sort of natural right to enjoy himself. Yes, if fate behaved in a humanly rational way, it would certainly be so: first work, then well-earned rest. But fate behaves irrationally, and the energy of life inconveniently demands a gradient agreeable to itself; otherwise it simply gets dammed up and turns destructive. It regresses to former situations—in the case of this man, to the memory of a syphilitic infection contracted twenty-five years before. Yet even this was only a stage on the way to the resuscitation of infantile reminiscences which had all but vanished in the meantime. It was the original relation to his mother that mapped the course of his symptoms: they were an "arrangement" whose purpose it was to compel the attention and interest of his long-dead mother. Nor was this stage the last; for the ultimate goal was to drive him back, as it were, into his own body. After he had lived since his youth only in his head. He had differentiated one side of his being; the other side remained in an inert physical state. He would have needed this other side in order to "live." The hypochondriacal "depression" pushed him down into the body he had always overlooked. Had he been able to follow the direction indicated by his depression and hypochondriacal illusion, and make himself conscious of the fan-

163

tasies which proceed from such a condition, that would have been the road to salvation. My arguments naturally met with no response, as was to be expected. A case so far advanced can only be cared for until death; it can hardly be cured.

This example clearly shows that it does not lie in our power to transfer "disposable" energy at will to a rationally chosen object. The same is true in general of the apparently disposable energy which is disengaged when we have destroyed its unserviceable forms through the corrosive of reductive analysis. This energy, as we have said, can at best be applied voluntarily for only a short time. But in most cases it refuses to seize hold, for any length of time, of the possibilities rationally presented to it. Psychic energy is a very fastidious thing which insists on fulfilment of its own conditions. However much energy may be present, we cannot make it serviceable until we have succeeded in finding the right gradient.

This question of the gradient is an eminently practical problem which crops up in most analyses. For instance, when in a favorable case the disposable energy, the so-called libido, does seize hold of a rational object, we think we have brought about the transformation through conscious exertion of the will. But in that we are deluded, because even the most strenuous exertions would not have sufficed had there not been present at the same time a gradient in that direction. How important the gradient is can be seen in cases when, despite the most desperate exertions, and despite the fact that the object chosen or the form desired impresses everybody with its reasonableness, the transformation still refuses to take place, and all that happens is a new repression.

It has become abundantly clear to me that life can flow forward only along the path of the gradient. But there is no energy unless there is a tension of opposites; hence it is necessary to discover the opposite to the attitude of the conscious mind. It is interesting to see how this compensation by opposites also plays its part in the historical theories of neurosis: Freud's theory espoused Eros, Adler's the will to power. Logically, the opposite of love is hate, and of Eros, Phobos (fear); but psychologically it is the will to power. Where love reigns, there is no will to power; and where the will to power is paramount, love is lacking. The one is but the shadow of the other: the man who adopts the standpoint of Eros finds his compensatory opposite in the will to power, and that of the man who puts the accent on power is Eros. Seen from the one-sided point of view of the conscious attitude, the shadow is an inferior component of the personality and is consequently repressed through intensive resistance. But the repressed content must be made conscious so as to produce a tension of opposites, without which no forward movement is possible. The conscious mind is on top, the shadow underneath, and just as high always longs for low and hot for cold, so all consciousness, perhaps without being aware of it, seeks its unconscious opposite, lacking which it is doomed to stagnation, congestion, and ossification. Life is born only of the spark of opposites.

It was a concession to intellectual logic on the one hand and to psychological prejudice on the other that impelled Freud to name the opposite of Eros the destructive or death instinct. For in the first place, Eros is not equivalent to life; but for anyone who thinks it is, the opposite of Eros will naturally appear to be death. And in the second place, we all feel that the opposite of our own highest principle must be purely destructive, deadly, and evil. We refuse to endow it with any positive life-force; hence we avoid and fear it.

As I have already indicated, there are many highest principles both of life and of philosophy, and accordingly there are just as many different forms of compensation by opposition. Earlier on I singled out the two—as it seems to me—main opposite types, which I have called introverted and extraverted. William James had already been struck by the existence of both these types among thinkers. He distinguished them as "tender-minded" and "tough-minded." Similarly Ostwald found an analogous division into "classical" and "romantic" types among men of learning. So I am not alone in my idea of types, to mention only these two well-known names among many others. Inquiries into history have shown me that not a few of the great spiritual controversies rest upon the opposition of the two types. The most significant case of this kind is the opposition between nominalism and realism which, beginning with the difference between the Platonic and Megaric schools, became the heritage of scholastic philosophy, where it is Abelard's great merit to have hazarded at least the attempt to unite the two opposed standpoints in his "conceptualism." This controversy has continued right into our own day, as is shown in the opposition between idealism and materialism. And again, not only the human mind in general, but each individual has a share in this opposition of types. It has come to light on closer investigation that either type has a predilection to marry its opposite, each being unconsciously complementary to the other. The reflective nature of the introvert causes him always to think and consider before acting. This naturally makes him slow to act. His shyness and distrust of things induces hesitation, and so he always has difficulty in adapting to the external world. Conversely the extravert has a positive relation to things. He is, so to speak, attracted by them. New, unknown situations fascinate him. In order to make closer acquaintance with the unknown he will jump into it with both feet. As a rule he acts first and thinks afterwards. Thus his action is swift, subject to no misgivings and hesitations. The two types therefore seem created for a symbiosis. The one takes care of reflection and the other sees to the initiative and practical action. When the two types marry they may effect an ideal union. So long as they are fully occupied with their adaptation to the manifold external needs of life they fit together admirably. But when the man has made enough money, or if a fine legacy should drop from the skies and external necessity no longer presses, then they have time to occupy themselves with one another. Hitherto they stood back to back and defended themselves against necessity. But now they turn face to face and look for understanding—only to discover that they have never understood one another. Each speaks a different language. Then the conflict between the two types begins. This struggle is envenomed, brutal, full of mutual depreciation, even when conducted quietly and in the greatest intimacy. For the value of the one is the negation of value for the other. It might reasonably be supposed that each, conscious of his own value, could peaceably recognize the other's value, and that in this way any conflict would be superfluous. I have seen a good number of cases where this line of argument

166

was adopted, without, however, arriving at a satisfactory goal. Where it is a question of normal people, such critical periods of transition will be overcome fairly smoothly. By "normal" I mean a person who can somehow exist under all circumstances which afford him the minimum needs of life. But many people cannot do this; therefore not so very many people are normal. What we commonly mean by a "normal person" is actually an ideal person whose happy blend of character is a rare occurrence. By far the greater number of more or less differentiated persons demand conditions of life which afford considerably more than the certainty of food and sleep. For these the ending of a symbiotic (mutually dependent [Ed.]) relationship comes as a severe shock.

It is not easy to understand why this should be so. Yet if we consider that no man is simply introverted or simply extraverted, but has both attitudes potentially in him— although he has developed only one of them as a function of adaptation—we shall immediately conjecture that with the introvert extraversion lies dormant and undeveloped somewhere in the background, and that introversion leads a similar shadowy existence in the extravert. And this is indeed the case. The introvert does possess an extraverted attitude, but it is unconscious, because his conscious gaze is always turned to the subject. He sees the object, of course, but has false or inhibiting ideas about it, so that he keeps his distance as much as possible, as though the object were something formidable and dangerous. I will make my meaning clear by a simple illustration:

Let us suppose two youths rambling in the country. They come to a fine castle; both want to see inside it. The introvert says, "I'd like to know what it's like inside." The extravert answers, "Right, let's go in," and makes for the gateway. The introvert draws back—"Perhaps we aren't allowed in," says he, with visions of policemen, fines, and fierce dogs in the background. Whereupon the extravert answers, "Well, we can ask. They'll let us in all right"—with visions of kindly old watchmen, hospitable seigneurs, and the possibility of romantic adventures. On the strength of extraverted optimism they at length find themselves in the castle. But now comes the dénouement. The castle has been rebuilt inside, and contains nothing but a couple of rooms with a collection of old manuscripts. As it happens, old manuscripts are the chief joy of the introverted youth. Hardly has he caught sight of them when he becomes as one transformed. He loses himself in contemplation of the treasures, uttering cries of enthusiasm. He engages the keeper in conversation so as to extract from him as much information as possible, and when the result is meagre the youth asks to see the curator in order to propound his questions to him. His shyness has vanished, objects have taken on a seductive glamour, and the world wears a new face. But meanwhile the spirits of the extraverted youth are ebbing lower and lower. His face grows longer and he begins to yawn. No kindly watchmen are forthcoming here, no knightly hospitality, not a trace of romantic adventure—only a castle made over into a museum. These are manuscripts enough to be seen at home. While the enthusiasm of the one rises, the spirits of the other fall, the castle bores him, the manuscripts remind him of a library, library is associated with university, university with studies and menacing examinations. Gradually a veil of gloom descends over the once so interesting and enticing castle. The object becomes negative. "Isn't it marvellous," cries the introvert, "to have stumbled on this wonderful collection?" "The place bores me to extinction," replies the other with undisguised ill humor. This annoys the introvert, who secretly vows never again to go rambling with an extravert. The latter is annoyed with the other's annoyance, and he thinks to himself that he always knew the fellow was an inconsiderate egotist who would, in his own selfish interest, waste all the lovely spring day that could be enjoyed so much better out of doors.

What has happened? Both were wandering together in happy symbiosis until they discovered the fatal castle. Then the forethinking, or Promethean, introvert said it might be seen from the inside, and the after-thinking, or Epimethean, extravert opened the door. At this point the types invert themselves: the introvert, who at first resisted the idea of going in, cannot now be induced to go out, and the extravert curses the moment when he set foot inside the castle. The former is now fascinated by the object, the latter by his negative thoughts. When the introvert spotted the manuscripts, it was all up with him. His shyness vanished, the object took possession of him, and he yielded himself willingly. The extravert, however, felt a growing resistance to the object and was eventually made the prisoner of his own ill-humored subjectivity. The introvert became extraverted, the extravert introverted. But the extraversion of the introvert is different from the extraversion of the extravert, and vice versa. So long as both were wandering along in joyous harmony, neither fell foul of the other, because each was in his natural character. Each was positive to the other, because their attitudes were complementary. They were complementary, however, only because the attitude of the one included the other. We can see this from the short conversation at the gateway. Both wanted to enter the castle. The doubt of the introvert as to whether an entry were possible also held good for the other. The initiative of the extravert likewise held good for the other. Thus the attitude of the one included the other, and this is always in some degree true if a person happens to be in the attitude natural to him, for this attitude has some degree of collective adaptation. The same is true of the introvert's attitude, although this always comes from the subject. It simply goes from subject to object, while the extravert's attitude goes from object to subject.

But the moment when, in the case of the introvert, the object overpowers and attracts the subject, his attitude loses its social character. He forgets the presence of his friend, he no longer includes him, he becomes absorbed into the object and does not see how very bored his friend is. In the same way the extravert loses all consideration for the other as soon as his expectations are disappointed and he withdraws into subjectivity and moodiness.

We can therefore formulate the occurrence as follows: in the introvert the influence of the object produces an inferior extraversion, while in the extravert an inferior introversion takes the place of his social attitude. And so we come back to the proposition from which we started: "The value of the one is the negation of value for the other."

Positive as well as negative occurrences can constellate the inferior counter-function. When this happens, sensitiveness appears. Sensitiveness is a sure sign of the presence of inferiority. This provides the psychological basis for discord and misunderstanding, not only as between two people, but also in ourselves. The essence of the inferior function is autonomy: it is independent, it attacks, it fascinates and so spins us about that we are no longer masters of ourselves and can no longer rightly distinguish between ourselves and others.

And yet it is necessary for the development of character that we should allow the other side, the inferior function, to find expression. We cannot in the long run allow one part of our personality to be cared for symbiotically by another; for the moment when we might have need of the other function may come at any time and find us unprepared, as the above example shows. And the consequences may be bad: the extravert loses his indispensable relation to the object, and the introvert loses his to the subject. Conversely, it is equally indispensable for the introvert to arrive at some form of action not constantly bedevilled by doubts and hesitations, and for the extravert to reflect upon himself, yet without endangering his relationships.

In extraversion and introversion it is clearly a matter of two antithetical, natural attitudes or trends, which Goethe once referred to as diastole and systole. They ought, in their harmonious alternation, to give life a rhythm, but it seems to require a high degree of art to achieve such a rhythm. Either one must do it quite unconsciously, so that the natural law is not disturbed by any conscious act, or one must be conscious in a much higher sense, to be capable of willing and carrying out the antithetical movements. Since we cannot develop backwards into animal unconsciousness, there remains only the more strenuous way forwards into higher consciousness. Certainly that consciousness, which would enable us to live the great Yea and Nay of our own free will and purpose, is an altogether superhuman ideal. Still, it is a goal. Perhaps our present mentality only allows us consciously to will the Yea and to bear with the Nay. When that is the case, much is already achieved.

The problem of opposites, as an inherent principle of human nature, forms a further stage in our process of realization. As a rule it is one of the problems of maturity. The practical treatment of a patient will hardly ever begin with this problem, especially not in the case of young people. The neuroses of the young generally come from a collision between the forces of reality and an inadequate, infantile attitude, which from the casual point of view is characterized by an abnormal dependence on the real or imaginary parents, and from the teleological point of view by unrealizable fictions, plans, and aspirations. Here the reductive methods of Freud and Adler are entirely in place. But there are many neuroses which either appear only at maturity or else deteriorate to such a degree that the patients become incapable of work. Naturally one can point out in these cases that an unusual dependence on the parents existed even in youth, and that all kinds of infantile illusions were present; but all that did not prevent them from taking up a profession, from practising it successfully, from keeping up a marriage of sorts until that moment in riper years when the previous attitude suddenly failed. In such cases it is of little help to make them conscious of their childhood fantasies, dependence on the parents, etc., although this is a necessary part of the procedure and often has a not unfavorable result. But the real therapy only begins when the patient sees that it is no longer father and mother who are standing in this way, but himself—i.e., an unconscious part of his personality which carries on the role of father and mother. Even this realization, helpful as it is, is still negative; it simply says, "I realize that it is not father and mother who are against me, but I myself." But *who* is it in him that is against him? What is this mysterious part of his personality that hides under the father- and mother-imagos, making him believe for years that the cause of his trouble must somehow have got into him from outside? This part is the counterpart to his conscious attitude; and it will leave him no peace and will continue to plague him until it has been accepted. For young people a liberation from the past may be enough: a beckoning future lies ahead, rich in possibilities. It is sufficient to break a few bonds; the life-urge will do the rest. But we are faced with another task in the case of people who have left a large part of their life behind them, for whom the future no longer beckons with marvellous possibilities, and nothing is to be expected

171

but the endless round of familiar duties and the doubtful pleasures of old age.

If ever we succeed in liberating young people from the past, we see that they always transfer the imagos of their parents to more suitable substitute figures. For instance, the feeling that clung to the mother now passes to the wife, and the father's authority passes to respected teachers and superiors or to institutions. Although this is not a fundamental solution, it is yet a practical road which the normal man treads unconsciously and therefore with no notable inhibitions and resistances.

The problem for the adult is very different. He has put this part of the road behind him with or without difficulty. He has cut loose from his parents, long since dead perhaps, and has sought and found the mother in the wife, or, in the case of a woman, the father in the husband. He has duly honored his fathers and their institutions, has himself become a father, and, with all this in the past, has possibly come to realize that what originally meant advancement and satisfaction has now become a boring mistake, part of the illusion of youth, upon which he looks back with mingled regret and envy, because nothing now awaits him but old age and the end of all illusions. Here there are no more fathers and mothers; all the illusions he projected upon the world and upon things gradually come back to him, jaded and way-worn. The energy streaming back from these manifold relationships falls into the unconscious and activates all the things he had neglected to develop.

In a young man, the instinctual forces tied up in the neurosis give him, when released, buoyancy and hope and the chance to extend the scope of his life. To the man in the second half of life the development of the function of opposites lying dormant in the unconscious means a renewal; but this development no longer proceeds via the solution of infantile ties, the destruction of infantile illusions and the transference of old imagos to new figures: it proceeds via the problem of opposites.

The principle of opposition is, of course, fundamental even in adolescence, and a psychological theory of the adolescent psyche is bound to recognize this fact. Hence the Freudian and Alderian viewpoints contradict each other only when they claim to be generally applicable

172

theories. But so long as they are content to be technical, auxiliary concepts, they do not contradict or exclude one another. A psychological theory, if it is to be more than a technical makeshift, must base itself on the principle of opposition; for without this it could only reestablish a neurotically unbalanced psyche. There is no balance, no system of self-regulation, without opposition. The psyche is just such a self-regulating system.

If at this point we take up the thread we let fall earlier, we shall now see clearly why it is that the values which the individual lacks are to be found in the neurosis itself. At this point, too, we can return to the case of the young woman and apply the insight we have gained. Let us suppose that this patient is "analysed," i.e., she has, through the treatment, come to understand the nature of the unconscious thoughts lurking behind her symptoms, and has thus regained possession of the unconscious energy which constituted the strength of those symptoms. The question then arises: what to do with the so-called disposable energy? In accordance with the psychological type of the patient, it would be rational to transfer this energy to an object—to philanthropic work, for example, or some useful activity. With exceptionally energetic natures that are not afraid of wearing themselves to the bone, if need be, or with people who delight in the toil and moil of such activities, this way is possible, but mostly it is impossible. For—do not forget—the libido, as this psychic energy is technically called, already possesses its object unconsciously, in the form of the young Italian or some equally real human substitute. In these circumstances a sublimation is as impossible as it is desirable, because the real object generally offers the energy a much better gradient than do the most admirable ethical activities. Unfortunately far too many of us talk about a man only as it would be desirable for him to be, never about the man as he really is. But the doctor has always to do with the real man, who remains obstinately himself until all sides of his reality are recognized. True education can only start from naked reality, not from a delusive ideal.

It is unhappily the case that no man can direct the so-called disposable energy at will. It follows its own gradient. Indeed, it had already found that gradient even before we set the energy free from the unserviceable form to which it was linked. For we discover that the patient's fantasies, previously occupied with the young Italian, have now transferred themselves to the doctor. The doctor has himself become the object of the unconscious libido. If the patient altogether refuses to recognize the fact of the transference, or if the doctor fails to understand it, or interprets it falsely, vigorous resistances supervene, directed towards making the relation with the doctor completely impossible. Then the patient goes away and looks for another doctor, or for some one who understands; or, if he gives up the search, he gets stuck in his problem.

If, however, the transference to the doctor takes place, and is accepted, a natural form is found which supplants the earlier one and at the same time provides the energy with an outlet relatively free from conflict. Hence if the libido is allowed to run its natural course, it will find its own way to the destined object. Where this does not happen, it is always a question of wilful defiance of the laws of nature, or of some disturbing influence.

In the transference all kinds of infantile fantasies are projected. They must be cauterized, i.e., resolved by reductive analysis, and this used to be called "severing the transference." Thereby the energy is again released from an unserviceable form, and again we are faced by the problem of its disposability. Once more we shall put our trust in nature, hoping that, even before it is sought, an object will have been chosen which will provide a favorable gradient.

The Drive
for
Superiority

Alfred Adler, M.D.

From: *Chapter VI,* THE PROBLEMS OF NEU-
ROSIS, Cosmopolitan Book Co., 1939.

ALFRED ADLER

Alfred Adler (1870–1937) was one of the founding members of the Vienna Psychoanalytic Society and was later its president. Even during the period from 1902 to 1911 when he worked with Freud he began to develop ideas which were different from those of Freud and others in the Vienna Society. When these differences became too wide, he presented his view to the Society and as a result of the criticism and denunciation his position was accorded by other members of the Society, he resigned to develop his own school of psychotherapy under the name of Individual Psychology.

Adler de-emphasised Freud's finding in sexual matters. A term which has passed into general usage as "inferiority complex" was coined by Adler and is the one thing most people think of in connection with his name. However, Adler actually contributed many other ideas and had great influence outside the field of psychoanalysis—in education, criminology and medicine, for instance, as well as on the development of American psychoanalysis in particular. His emphasis on social factors probably influenced American therapists like Erich Fromm, Carl Rogers, Karen Horney and Harry Stack Sullivan.

Adler saw the inevitable result of feelings of inferiority would be strivings for superiority. He later developed the theory that social interest rather than striving for superiority is the only true and natural compensation for feelings of inferiority.

In the cases described in the succeeding chapter, Adler stresses some of the neurotic ways in which striving for superiority is sometimes carried out. The cases also illustrate Adler's emphasis on the life style, that is, the way in which the individual organizes his life to compensate for his feelings of inferiority.

The Drive
for
Superiority

A curious case of depression which I once treated illustrates very clearly how sadness may be used to heighten the feeling of superiority. This was the case of a man of fifty, who said he felt perfectly healthy except when he was in a notably comfortable situation. It was when he was at a concert or theatre with his family, for instance, that a fit of melancholy would descend upon him: and in such depression he always remembered an intimate friend who had died when he was twenty-five. This friend had been his rival, not only in business but as a suitor for the hand of his wife—an unsuccessful rival, however, for by the time he contracted his fatal illness, my patient already had the advantage over him both in love and in business.

Success had been his lot, both before and after the friend's death; he was the favorite of his parents, unsurpassed by brothers and sisters, and prosperous in the world. His wife, however, was an ambitious character who strove to solve every domestic problem by a personal triumph or conquest, moral or otherwise: and between two such persons, the struggle was naturally continuous and severe. The wife sometimes gained the ascendency very cleverly, not by quarrelling or domineering in any way, but by becoming very nervous in disadvantageous situations, and conquering him by her painful condition. She never expressed her excessive jealousies, but sought to shackle him as required by her fits of anxiety. Thus, successful as he was in all but one relation of life, the man felt uncertain of having reached his goal of superiority, and his excessive ambition was demanding compensation.

I know that many psychologists would seek for a "guilt complex" to explain this depression. They would investigate the patient's childhood to find out a very early desire to kill someone—probably the father. This patient, however, had been the favorite of his father, and there was not the least reason why he should ever have desired his death, as he had always been able to manage him in his own interest. Such a mistaken search for a "guilt complex" might also lead a psychologist to think that the patient had secretly wished to murder his friend and rival: and that after having triumphed over him and having had the death-wish granted by fate, he remained still unsatisfied. If that were so, the guilt complex might be developed by the striving of the patient to see himself in an intenser light. He would want to express his good feeling and liking for his former rival with the highest sincerity and honesty; and at the same time he would be shaken by the memory of his rival's fatal end and the thoughts which he had been unable wholly to dismiss before it happened. This would amount to the complicated state of self-accusation and repentance at the same time, which we call a guilt complex, which is always a superiority-striving on the useless side of life. As I have already observed, it means: "I have reached the summit of error" or "My virtue is so lofty that this slight stain upon it is killing me."

However, in this case I found no indications of the kind, and the man's valuation of honesty as a virtue was not abnormally developed. His depressions were an attempt to show himself superior to his wife. To be depressed in very favorable situations called attention to his good fortune much more than if he had allowed himself to enjoy them. Everyone was surprised at his depression, and he constantly asked himself, "You happy being, *why* are you depressed when you have everything you want?" The unmanageable wife was the one sorrow in his comfortable life, and he compensated for this by *remembering his victory* in the most difficult phase of his history —when he outstripped his friend and won the woman from him. Loyalty forbade him to rejoice in the memory of his dead friend: but he could nevertheless feed upon this ancient triumph by being depressed in the box of the theatre. The more melancholy he was and upon the

178

brighter the occasion, the more he was able to think of his past conquest and to elevate the consciousness of his estate. Deeper enquiries confirmed my conclusion. His friend had died from paralysis after syphilis, a disease which they had both contracted at the same time. My patient was cured, however; and now, surrounded by his healthy wife and six children, could not but recall, to-gether with the triumph over his friend, his conquest of the disease.

Such, then, were his consolations. In his marriage this man did not feel superior; but at least his wife was the woman his friend had desired, and she had chosen him instead. By contemplating his friend's disaster in a dis-creet gloom he heightened the sense of victory. Consola-tion of this nature is on the useless side, however, and tends, as we see, towards disease.

A man of thirty-six came to me for advice about sexual impotence after having tried various treatments. He was a self-made man, in a good position, and physically healthy, but not very well educated: and he had a love relation with a well-educated girl. He was a second child between two girls, and had lost both parents at the age of five. He remembered that his family had been very poor, but that he had been a spoilt child, very pretty and quiet, to whom the neighbors liked to give presents: and that he exploited their generosity, behaving like a beggar. One of his earliest remembrances was of walk-ing the streets on Christmas Eve and looking into the shop windows at the Christmas trees destined *for others*. In the orphanage, to which he was transferred at the age of five, he was strictly treated, but his habitual docility and the striving nature he possessed as a second child enabled him to surpass others. His servility stood him in good stead, for he was promoted to be the principal servant of the institution. In this occupation he had some-times to wait for a long time at an old and deserted rail-way station in the country; and at these times, when only the humming of the telegraph wires relieved the dead stillness of the night, he felt utterly isolated and alone in a friendless world. He preserved strong memories of this experience.

Often, in later life, he complained of buzzing in the ears, for which no aurist could find the cause. It proved,

179

however, to be quite coherent with his style of life. When he felt isolated, which happened very often, the memory of the humming wires returned with all the liveliness of a hallucination. After this had been explained to him, and he had been a little more socially reconciled and encouraged to marry his sweetheart, the humming ceased.

It is quite usual for children who are brought up in an orphanage to make the strongest efforts to hide the fact, as though it were a disgrace. This man justified his concealment by asserting that many orphans do not succeed in later life. He regarded failure in life as the inexorable fate of orphans, which gave him his tense and striving attitude in business. For the same reason he halted before the problem of love and marriage, and his neurotic impotence was the immediate result of this profound hesitation.

This man's style of life, as we have seen, was to be a beggar. In business, however (as previously in the orphanage), begging had paved the way to domination. In business he enjoyed nothing more than a begging attitude on the part of his subordinates. He was only a beggar until he could be a conqueror, and he played the second role as heartily as the first. There is no need to drag in the idea of "ambivalent" characteristics, as some psychologists would do immediately. Rightly understood, the whole of this mental process—working from below to above, expressing an inferiority but compensating with a superiority—is not ambivalence but a dynamic unity. Only if it is not understood as a whole do we see it as two contradictory and warring entities. In his business we find the man with a "superiority complex": but if he were to lose his position and have to start again he would promptly go back to the expression of inferiority and make capital out of it. In his love-problem he was, for the time being, upon the submissive line of action, begging for love, but trying to reach domination. His sweetheart liked him and wanted to marry him, so she responded to his hesitancy by taking up more and more of a begging attitude towards him! He was well on the way, in fact, towards getting the upper hand with her, and frequently did so in minor matters.

He had still not overcome his hesitant attitude: but after having had his style of life explained to him and having been encouraged, his state improved and his impotence disappeared. He then set up a second resistance, which was that every woman attracted him, and these polygamous desires were an escape from marriage. At this time he dreamt that he was lying upon a couch in my room, and he became sexually excited and had a pollution.

There is no couch in my consulting room. My patients sit, stand, or move about as they please; but the couch in this dream was in the room of a doctor who had formerly treated him for a few months. This dream extracted a confession which he had never made before. He believed that both the other doctor and I belonged to a secret society, the object of which was to cure patients such as himself by providing sexual intercourse for them. For this reason he had been trying to find out which of my woman patients would be chosen for him. The fact that he missed the couch in my room was like an accusation against me. I was not the right doctor. He had come to me *begging,* expecting me to settle his difficulties, take over his responsibilities, and to assist him to escape from marriage. My collusion in stopping his marriage was to go to the length of being his procurer, a fantasy to which his fright, his impotence and his polygamous tendencies were all contributory. Failing that, he would solve his sexual problem by pollutions, as others might resort to masturbation or perversion.

He married, but it was difficult to prevent him from developing a tyrannical attitude towards his conciliatory wife.

Another case of the begging attitude was brought to me by a man fifty years old, the youngest of a very poor family. He had been indulged by his mother and the neighbors because of an apparent weakness, and early developed a very timid manner. He always tried to lean upon his mother and to appeal to the sympathies of weak persons, especially in difficult times when he exhibited great depression and cried until help came. We have already seen the use which is made of crying by both children and adults. This man's earliest memory was that he had fallen down and hurt himself. The choice of this incident to treasure in the memory out of all possible

181

recollections is explained only by his desire to impress himself with the danger of life. His technique of life was to perfect himself in the role of a beggar, to attract support, consolation and favor by calling attention to his infirmities. Every incident was made into a matter for tears.

As a child the man had been very backward in learning to talk, and his mother, as always happens in such cases, had to attend all the more carefully to him to find out what he wanted. In this way he was able to feel like a little king. As Lessing said, "The real beggar is the only real king." He became a master of the begging art, expressing his inferiority in the power of his plight over others. "How can I make the poor weak child a king?" was the problem of life as he saw it, and he answered it by elaborating his own individual and essentially mendicant style.

This is one way of living, and so early an apprentice becomes a past master of its technique. He will not change it, unless the cost becomes clearly too great, when he may be brought to see that his childish method is inadequate for present problems. Otherwise change is impossible for him, because he has all his life ascribed every success to the begging art and every failure to lack of proficiency in it. Such a goal as this is not calculable from the inheritance or the environmental stimuli, for the child's individual conception of the future is the dominant causal factor, and this patient's conception was such that whenever he wanted to attain superiority he had to make a mistake or get himself into a mess of some kind. All his feelings were appropriately ordered towards the goal of thus getting something for nothing.

After a few days' treatment this man was very much impressed by what I told him; and he sent me a pamphlet he had written some years before. It was entitled "An Association of Beggars."

Habitual criticism, anger, and envy are indications of a useless striving for superiority: they are motions towards the suppression of others, either in reality or fancy, so as to be supreme. Useful criticism of a constructive tendency is always in some comprehensible relation with social feeling, but where the motive is merely relative self-elevation by lowering or degrading others the tendency is

182

neurotic. Neurotics often make use of the truth in order to undervalue others, and it is important, when checking a neurotic criticism, not to overlook the element of truth in the observation.

Anger is usually a sign that the person who is angry feels at a disadvantage—at least temporarily. Neurotics use it freely as a weapon to intimidate those who are responsible for them. Although occasional anger is an understandable attitude in certain critical relations, when it is habitual it is a sign of anxiety, of impatience, or of feelings of helplessness or suppression. Patients of this habit are often very clever in the selection of vulnerable points to attack in others, and are also great strategists in preparing such situations that they put others slightly in the wrong before they begin a fight.

Envy is universally an expression of inferiority, though it may sometimes be a stimulus to useful action. In neurosis, however, envy of another's good does not go so far as practical emulation. It stops like a tram before the journey's end, leaving the patient irritable and depressed.

In a certain popular music-hall turn the "strong man" comes on and lifts an enormous weight with care and immense difficulty, and then, during the hearty applause of the audience, a child comes in and gives away the fraud by carrying the dummy weight off with one hand. There are plenty of neurotics who swindle us with such weights, and who are adepts in the art of appearing overburdened. They could really dance with the load under which they stagger like Atlas bearing the world on his shoulders. Yet it cannot be denied that neurotics feel their burden very keenly. They may be continually tired. They may sometimes perspire very freely, and their symptoms may suggest the possibility of tuberculosis. Every movement is very tiring, and they often suffer from palpitation of the heart. Usually depressed, they continually demand more zealous care from others, and yet find it continually insufficient.

I had a case of agoraphobia (fear of open places [Ed.]) in a man of fifty-three, who found that he could not breathe properly when he was in company with others. He was living with his sister, and had a son whose characteristics were very much like his own.

When I investigated the cause of this man's unusual concentration of interest upon himself, I found that he had been orphaned at ten years of age, and there were two elder brothers in the home. It was when they quarrelled that he had had his first attack. This indicates the tendency to meet a difficult situation by breakdown. The man was the youngest of a family of eight, and educated by his grandfather. A grandparent is almost invariably a spoiling foster-parent. The patient's father and mother had been happily married; the father was superior and the mother rather cold, so the boy was attracted to his father.

A child's first good-fellowship in life is always with the mother if she is present, so that if it inclines more towards the father we may assume that the mother does not give the child sufficient attention: she is probably unkind, otherwise occupied, or more attentive to a younger child. In such circumstances the child turns to the father if possible, and in this case the resistance to the mother was very marked.

People are often unable correctly to remember their earliest situations, but experience enables us to reconstruct their circumstances from comparatively slight indications. One man said he could only remember three incidents from early childhood which had deeply impressed his memory. The first of these occurred at the age of three, when his brother died. He was with his grandfather on the day of the funeral, when his mother returned from the cemetery, sorrowful and sobbing, and when the grandfather kissed her, whispering some words of kindness and consolation, the boy saw that his mother smiled a little. He was very much upset by this, and for long afterwards resented his mother's smile on the day that her child was buried. A second memory that he had preserved was of a friendly reproof from his uncle, who had asked him, "Why are you always so rough towards your mother?" A third remembrance from the same period of his life related to a quarrel between his parents, after which he turned to his father, saying, "You were brave, daddy, like a soldier!" He depended much upon his father, and was pampered by him: and he always admired his father more than his mother, although he realized that his mother's character was of a better type.

184

All these memories, which appeared to date from his third or fourth year, showed the fighting attitude towards the mother. The first and the third remembrances were clearly ruled by his goal, which was to criticize the mother and to justify him in turning towards the father. His reason for turning away from the mother is easy to guess: he had been too much spoilt by her to be able to put up with the younger brother's appearance upon the scene,—that same younger brother who figures in an apparently innocent manner in the first recollection.

This patient had married at the age of twenty-four, and marriage had disappointed him, because of his wife's demands upon him. Marriage between two spoilt children is always unhappy, because both remain in the expectant attitude and neither begins to give. This man went through varied experiences and tried different occupations without success. His wife was not sympathetic, and complained that she would rather be the mistress of a rich man than the wife of a poor one, and the union ended in a divorce. Although the man was not really poor, he was very stingy towards his wife, and she divorced him by way of revenge.

After his divorce he turned misogynistic, and developed homosexual tendencies; he had no actual relationships with men, but felt a desire to embrace men. This homosexual trend was as usual a kind of cowardliness. He had been twice defeated and baulked by women—first by his mother and afterwards by his wife—and he was now trying to divert his sexuality towards men so as to evade women and further possibilities of humiliation. To confirm himself in such a tendency a man can easily falsify the past by recollecting and magnifying the importance of certain common experiences which are then taken by him as proofs of inborn homosexual tendencies. Thus, this patient remembered that he had been in love with a schoolmaster, and that in his youth a boy friend had seduced him into mutual masturbation.

The determining factor in this man's behavior was that he was a spoiled child who wanted everything for nothing. His agoraphobia resulted from the fear of meeting women on the one hand, and on the other hand it was also dangerous to meet men, because of possible erotic inclination towards them. In this tension of feel-

185

ings about going out of doors he developed stomach and respiratory troubles. Many nervous people begin to swallow air when they get into a state of tension, which causes flatulence, stomach trouble, anxiety and palpitation, besides affecting the breathing. When I made him realize that this was his condition he asked the usual question: "What shall I do not to swallow air?" Sometimes I reply: "I can tell you how to mount a horse, but I can't tell you how *not* to mount a horse." Or sometimes I advise: "If you want to go out, and feel in a conflict about it, swallow some air quickly." This man, like some other patients, swallowed air even in sleep, but after my advice he began to control himself, and discontinued the habit. Air-swallowing at night and vomiting upon waking occur in these patients who suffer from stomach trouble and anxiety when they are bothered by a difficulty which must be confronted upon the following day. The patient in question began to recuperate when he came to understand that, as a pampered child, he expected continually to take without giving. He now realized that he had first stopped his normal sexual life, looking for something easier, and afterwards adopted a fictitious homosexuality in which he also stopped short of danger, the whole process being an elaborate way of coming to a standstill. The last obstacle to be removed was his fear of mixing with strangers who did not care for him, such as the people in the streets. This fear is produced by the deeper motive of agoraphobia, which is to exclude all situations in which one is not the center of attention.

The Ever-Tired Editor

Karen Horney, M.D.

From: SELF-ANALYSIS
W. W. Norton & Co., Inc., New York: 1942

187

KAREN HORNEY

Karen Horney (1885–1952) first practiced psychoanalysis in Germany and came to the United States after the rise of Nazism. She became dissatisfied with "orthodox" Freudian psychoanalysis and joined with others to found the Association for the Advancement of Psychoanalysis and The American Institute of Psychoanalysis. While she felt her ideas were within the framework of Freudian psychology, she did establish, because of her emphasis on what she considered the falacies in Freud's thinking, an independent school which had considerable influence on the American scene while she was alive.

Her chief difference with Freud was that she believed his orientation was too mechanical and biological and without emphasis on social factors. She also objected strongly to Freud's description of female psychology. She differed specifically with Freud's attitude that female conflicts grew out of the woman's feeling of inferiority and jealousy toward the male because of his possession of a penis. Her primary concept was that all of us have basic anxiety, and that this basic anxiety is a result of anything that disturbs the security of the child in his relationship first to his parents and later to society.

Karen Horney believed further that the insecure, anxious child develops a variety of methods by which to cope with his feelings of insecurity and isolation. She classified these methods under three headings: moving towards people as exemplified in the need for love; moving away from people as exemplified in the need for independence; and moving against people as exemplified in the need for power. She believed that neurotic difficulties came when the individual could not accept all three of these aspects within his own personality and therefore developed one-sidedly. She felt that such difficulties were avoidable if a child is raised in a home where there is security, trust, love, respect and warmth. Unlike Freud and Jung, she did not believe that conflict is instinctive in man and therefore inevitable, but instead believed that conflict was the result of social conditions.

The case that follows illustrates how Karen Horney analyzed some of the neurotic trends that interfered with her patients' ability to work and to love.

Utilizing the method of "character analysis" as Wilhelm Reich called it, or discovering the "life-style" as Alfred Adler called it, Karen Horney concentrated on the way her patient characteristically functioned (i.e., her compulsive modesty, her dependency and her need to excel), rather than concentrating on the search for early traumatic factors which cause these patterns, as the early Freudians might have done. This emphasis on the patient's way of living is frequently followed by modern analysts of all schools.

The Ever-Tired Editor

Clare was an unwanted child. The marriage was unhappy. After having one child, a boy, the mother did not want any more children. Clare was born after several unsuccessful attempts at an abortion. She was not badly treated or neglected in any coarse sense: she was sent to schools as good as those the brother attended, she received as many gifts as he did, she had music lessons with the same teacher, and in all material ways was treated as well. But in less tangible matters she received less than the brother, less tenderness, less interest in school marks and in the thousand little daily experiences of a child, less concern when she was ill, less solicitude to have her around, less willingness to treat her as a confidante, less admiration for looks and accomplishments. There was a strong, though for a child intangible, community between the mother and brother from which she was excluded. The father was no help. He was absent most of the time, being a country doctor. Clare made some pathetic attempts to get close to him but he was not interested in either of the children. His affection was entirely focused on the mother in a kind of helpless admiration. Finally, he was no help because he was openly despised by the mother, who was sophisticated and attractive and beyond doubt the dominating spirit in the family. The undisguised hatred and contempt the mother felt

189

for the father, including open death wishes against him, contributed much to Clare's feeling that it was much safer to be on the powerful side.

As a consequence of this situation Clare never had a good chance to develop self-confidence. There was not enough of open injustice to provoke sustained rebellion, but she became discontented and cross and complaining. As a result she was teased for always feeling herself a martyr. It never remotely occurred to either mother or brother that she might be right in feeling unfairly treated. They took it for granted that her attitude was a sign of an ugly disposition. And Clare, never having felt secure, easily yielded to the majority opinion about herself and began to feel that everything was her fault. Compared with the mother, whom everyone admired for her beauty and charm, and with the brother, who was cheerful and intelligent, she was an ugly duckling. She became deeply convinced that she was unlikable.

This shift from essentially true and warranted accusations of others to essentially untrue and unwarranted self-accusations had far-reaching consequences, as we shall see presently. And the shift entailed more than an acceptance of the majority estimate of herself. It meant also that she repressed all grievances against the mother. If everything was her own fault the grounds for bearing a grudge against the mother were pulled away from under her. From such repression of hostility it was merely a short step to join the group of those who admired the mother. In this further yielding to majority opinion she had a strong incentive in the mother's antagonism toward everything short of complete admiration: it was much safer to find shortcomings within herself than in the mother. If she, too, admired the mother she need no longer feel isolated and excluded but could hope to receive some affection, or at least be accepted. The hope for affection did not materialize, but she obtained instead a gift of doubtful value. The mother, like all those who thrive on the admiration of others, was generous in giving admiration in turn to those who adored her. Clare was no longer the disregarded ugly duckling, but became the wonderful daughter of a wonderful mother. Thus, in place of a badly shattered self-confidence, she built up

190

the spurious pride that is founded on outside admiration.

Through this shift from true rebellion to untrue admiration Clare lost the feeble vestiges of self-confidence she had. To use a somewhat vague term, she lost herself. By admiring what in reality she resented, she became alienated from her own feelings. She no longer knew what she herself liked or wished or feared or resented. She lost all capacity to assert her wishes for love, or even any wishes. Despite a superficial pride her conviction of being unlovable was actually deepened. Hence later on, when one or another person was fond of her, she could not take the affection at its face value but discarded it in various ways. Sometimes she would think that such a person misjudged her for something she was not; sometimes she would attribute the affection to gratitude for having been useful or to expectations of her future usefulness. This distrust deeply disturbed every human relationship she entered into. She lost, too, her capacity for critical judgment, acting on the unconscious maxim that it is safer to admire others than to be critical. This attitude shackled her intelligence, which was actually of a high order, and greatly contributed to her feeling stupid.

In consequence of all these factors three neurotic trends developed. One was a compulsive modesty as to her own wishes and demands. This entailed a compulsive tendency to put herself into second place, to think less of herself than of others, to think that others were right and she was wrong. But even in this restricted scope she could not feel safe unless there was someone on whom she could depend, someone who would protect and defend her, advise her, stimulate her, approve of her, be responsible for her, give her everything she needed. She needed all this because she had lost the capacity to take her life into her own hands. Thus she developed the need for a "partner"—friend, lover, husband—on whom she could depend. She would subordinate herself to him as she had toward the mother. But at the same time, by his undivided devotion to her, he would restore her crushed dignity. A third neurotic trend —a compulsive need to excel others and to triumph over them—likewise aimed at restoration of self-regard, but in addition absorbed all the vindictiveness accumulated through hurts and humiliations.

191

Clare came for analytic treatment at the age of thirty, for various reasons. She was easily overcome by a paralyzing fatigue that interfered with her work and her social life. Also, she complained about having remarkably little self-confidence. She was the editor of a magazine, and though her professional career and her present position were satisfactory her ambition to write plays and stories was checked by insurmountable inhibitions. She could do her routine work but was unable to do productive work, though she was inclined to account for this latter inability by pointing out her probable lack of talent. She had been married at the age of twenty-three, but the husband had died after three years. After the marriage she had had a relationship with another man which continued during the analysis. According to her initial presentation both relationships were satisfactory sexually as well as otherwise.

The analysis stretched over a period of four and a half years. She was analyzed for one year and a half. This time was followed by an interruption of two years, in which she did a good deal of self-analysis, afterward returning to analysis for another year at irregular intervals.

Clare's analysis could be roughly divided into three phases: the discovery of her compulsive modesty; the discovery of her compulsive dependence on a partner; and finally, the discovery of her compulsive need to force others to recognize her superiority. None of these trends was apparent to herself or to others.

In the first period the data that suggested compulsive elements were as follows. She tended to minimize her own value and capacities: not only was she insecure about her assets but she tenaciously denied their existence, insisting that she was not intelligent, attractive, or gifted and tending to discard evidence to the contrary. Also, she tended to regard others as superior to herself. If there was a dissension of opinion she automatically believed that the others were right. She recalled that when her husband had started an affair with another woman she did nothing to remonstrate against it, though the experience was extremely painful to her; she managed to consider him justified in preferring the other on the grounds that the latter was more attractive and more loving. Moreover, it was almost impossible for her to spend

192

money on herself: when she traveled with others she could enjoy living in expensive places, even though she contributed her share in the expenses, but as soon as she was on her own she could not bring herself to spend money on such things as trips, dresses, plays, books. Finally, though she was in an executive position, it was impossible for her to give orders: she would do so in an apologetic way if orders were unavoidable.

The conclusion reached from such data was that she had developed a compulsive modesty, that she felt compelled to constrict her life within narrow boundaries and to take always a second or third place. When this trend was once recognized, and its origin in childhood discussed, we began to search systematically for its manifestations and its consequences. What role did this trend actually play in her life?

She could not assert herself in any way. In discussions she was easily swayed by the opinions of others. Despite a good faculty for judging people she was incapable of taking any critical stand toward anyone or anything, except in editing, when a critical stand was expected of her. She had encountered serious difficulties, for instance, by failing to realize that a fellow worker was trying to undermine her position; when this situation was fully apparent to others she still regarded the other as her friend. Her compulsion to take second place appeared clearly in games: in tennis, for instance, she was usually too inhibited to play well, but occasionally she was able to play a good game and then, as soon as she became aware that she might win, she would begin to play badly. The wishes of others were more important than her own: she would be contented to take her holidays during the time that was least wanted by others, and she would do more work than she needed to if the others were dissatisfied with the amount of work to be done.

Most important was a general suppression of her feelings and wishes. Her inhibitions concerning expansive plans she regarded as particularly "realistic"—evidence that she never wanted things that were beyond reach. Actually she was as little "realistic" as someone with excessive expectations of life; she merely kept her wishes beneath the level of the attainable. She was unrealistic in living in every way beneath her means—socially, eco-

193

nomically, professionally, spiritually. It was attainable for her, as her later life showed, to be liked by many people, to look attractive, to write something that was valuable and original.

The most general consequences of this trend were a progressive lowering of self-confidence and a diffuse discontentment with life. Of the latter she had not been in the least aware, and could not be aware as long as everything was "good enough" for her and she was not clearly conscious of having wishes or of their not being fulfilled. The only way this general discontentment with life had shown itself was in trivial matters and in sudden spells of crying which had occurred from time to time and which had been quite beyond her understanding.

For quite a while she recognized only fragmentarily the truth of these findings; in important matters she made the silent reservation that I either overrated her or felt it to be good therapy to encourage her. Finally, however, she recognized in a rather dramatic fashion that real, intense anxiety lurked behind this façade of modesty. It was at a time when she was about to suggest an improvement in the magazine. She knew that her plan was good, that it would not meet with too much opposition, that everyone would be appreciative in the end. Before suggesting it, however, she had an intense panic which could not be rationalized in any way. At the beginning of the discussion she still felt panicky and had to leave the room because of a sudden diarrhea. But as the discussion turned increasingly in her favor the panic subsided. The plan was finally accepted and she received considerable recognition. She went home with a feeling of elation and was still in good spirits when she came to the next analytical hour.

I dropped a casual remark to the effect that this was quite a triumph for her, which she rejected with a slight annoyance. Naturally she had enjoyed the recognition but her prevailing feeling was one of having escaped from a great danger. It was only after more than two years had elapsed that she could tackle the other elements involved in this experience, which were along the lines of ambition, dread of failure, triumph. At that time her feelings, as expressed in her associations, were all concentrated on the problem of modesty. She felt that

194

she had been presumptuous to propound a new plan. Who was she to know better! But gradually she realized that this attitude was based on the fact that for her the suggesting of a different course of action meant a venturing out of the narrow artificial precincts that she had anxiously preserved. Only when she recognized the truth of this observation did she become fully convinced that her modesty was a façade to be maintained for the sake of safety. The result of this first phase of work was a beginning of faith in herself and a beginning of courage to feel and assert her wishes and opinions.

The second period was dedicated prevailingly to work on her dependency on a "partner." The majority of the problems involved she worked through by herself, as will be reported later on in greater detail. This dependency, despite its overwhelming strength, was still more deeply repressed than the previous trend. It had never occurred to her that anything was wrong in her relationships with men. On the contrary, she had believed them to be particularly good. The analysis gradually changed this picture.

There were three main factors that suggested compulsive dependence. The first was that she felt completely lost, like a small child in a strange wood, when a relationship ended or when she was temporarily separated from a person who was important to her. The first experience of this kind occurred after she left home at the age of twenty. She then felt like a feather blown around in the universe, and she wrote desperate letters to her mother, declaring that she could not live without her. This homesickness stopped when she developed a kind of crush on an older man, a successful writer who was interested in her work and furthered her in a patronizing way. Of course, this first experience of feeling lost when alone could be understood on the basis of her youth and the sheltered life she had lived. But later reactions were intrinsically the same, and formed a strange contrast to the rather successful professional career that she was achieving despite the difficulties mentioned before.

The second striking fact was that in any of these relationships the whole world around her became submerged and only the beloved had any importance. Thoughts and feelings centered around a call or a letter or a visit from him; hours that she spent without him were empty, filled only with waiting for him, with a pondering about his attitude to her, and above all with feeling utterly miserable about incidents which she felt as utter neglect or humiliating rejection. At these times other human relationships, her work, and other interests lost almost every value for her.

The third factor was a fantasy of a great and masterful man whose willing slave she was and who in turn gave her everything she wanted, from an abundance of material things to an abundance of mental stimulation, and made her a famous writer.

As the implications of these factors were gradually recognized the compulsive need to lean on a "partner" appeared and was worked through in its characteristics and its consequences. Its main feature was an entirely repressed parasitic attitude, an unconscious wish to feed on the partner, to expect him to supply the content of her life, to take responsibility for her, to solve all her difficulties and to make her a great person without her having to make efforts of her own. This trend had alienated her not only from other people but also from the partner himself, because the unavoidable disappointments she felt when her secret expectations of him remained unfulfilled gave rise to a deep inner irritation; most of this irritation was repressed for fear of losing the partner, but some of it emerged in occasional explosions. Another consequence was that she could not enjoy anything except when she shared it with the partner. The most general consequence of this trend was that her relationships served only to make her more insecure and more passive and to breed self-contempt.

The interrelations of this trend with the previous one were twofold. On the one hand, her compulsive modesty was one of the reasons that accounted for her need for a partner. Since she could not take care of her own wishes she had to have someone else who took care of them. Since she could not defend herself she needed someone else to defend her. Since she could not see her own values she needed someone else to affirm her worth. On the other hand, there was a sharp conflict between the compulsive modesty and the excessive expectations of the partner. Because of this unconscious conflict she

196

had to distort the situation every time she was disappointed over unfulfilled expectations. In such situations she felt herself the victim of intolerably harsh and abusive treatment, and therefore felt miserable and hostile. Most of the hostility had to be repressed because of fear of desertion, but its existence undermined the relationship and turned her expectations into vindictive demands. The resulting upsets proved to have a great bearing on her fatigue and her inhibition toward productive work.

The result of this period of analytical work was that she overcame her parasitic helplessness and became capable of greater activity of her own. The fatigue was no longer continual but appeared only occasionally. She became capable of writing, though she still had to face strong resistances. Her relationships with people became more friendly, though they were still far from being spontaneous; she impressed others as being haughty while she herself still felt quite timid. An expression of the general change in her was contained in a dream in which she drove with her friend in a strange country and it occurred to her that she, too, might apply for a driver's license. Actually, she had a license and could drive as well as the friend. The dream symbolized a dawning insight that she had rights of her own and need not feel like a helpless appendage.

The third and last period of analytical work dealt with repressed ambitious strivings. There had been a period in her life when she had been obsessed by frantic ambition. This had lasted from her later years in grammar school up to her second year in college, and had then seemed to disappear. One could conclude only by inference that it still operated underground. This was suggested by the fact that she was elated and over-joyed at any recognition, by her dread of failure, and by the anxiety involved in any attempt at independent work.

This trend was more complicated in its structure than the two others. In contrast to the others, it constituted an attempt to master life actively, to take up a fight against adverse forces. This fact was one element in its continued existence: she felt herself that there had been a positive force in her amibition and wished repeatedly to be able to retrieve it. A second element feeding the ambition was the necessity to re-establish her lost self-

197

esteem. The third element was vindictiveness: success meant a triumph over all those who had humiliated her, while failure meant disgraceful defeat. To understand the characteristics of this ambition we must go back in her history and discover the successive changes it underwent.

The fighting spirit involved in this trend appeared quite early in life. Indeed, it preceded the development of the other two trends. At this period of the analysis early memories occurred to her of opposition, rebellion, belligerent demands, all sorts of mischief. As we know, she lost this fight for her place in the sun because the odds against her were too great. Then, after a series of unhappy experiences, this spirit re-emerged when she was about eleven, in the form of a fierce ambition at school. Now, however, it was loaded with repressed hostility: it had absorbed the piled-up vindictiveness for the unfair deal she had received and for her downtrodden dignity. It had now acquired two of the elements mentioned above: through being on top she would re-establish her sunken self-confidence, and by defeating the others she would avenge her injuries. This grammar-school ambition, with all its compulsive and destructive elements, was nevertheless realistic in comparison with later developments, for it entailed efforts to surpass others through greater actual achievements. During high school she was still successful in being unquestionably the first. But in college, where she met greater competition, she rather suddenly dropped her ambition altogether, instead of making the greater efforts that the situation would have required if she still wanted to be first. There were three main reasons why she could not muster the courage to make these greater efforts. One was that because of her compulsive modesty she had to fight against constant doubts as to her intelligence. Another was the actual impairment in the free use of her intelligence through the repression of her critical faculties. Finally, she could not take the risk of failure because the need to excel the others was too compulsive.

The abandonment of her manifest ambition did not, however, diminish the impulse to triumph over others. She had to find a compromise solution, and this, in contrast to the frank ambition at school, was devious in character. In substance it was that she would triumph

198

over the others without doing anything to bring about that triumph. She tried to achieve this impossible feat in three ways, all of which were deeply unconscious. One was to register whatever good luck she had in life as a triumph over others. This ranged from a conscious triumph at good weather on an excursion to an unconscious triumph over some "enemy" falling ill or dying. Conversely, she felt bad luck not simply as bad luck but as a disgraceful defeat. This attitude served to enhance her dread of life because it meant a reliance on factors that are beyond control. The second way was to shift the need for triumph to love relationships. To have a husband or lover was a triumph; to be alone was a shameful defeat. And the third way of achieving triumph without effort was the demand that husband or lover, like the masterful man in the fantasy, should make her great without her doing anything, possibly by merely giving her the chance to indulge vicariously in his success. These attitudes created insoluble conflicts in her personal relationships and considerably reinforced the need for a "partner," since he was to take over these all-important functions.

The consequences of this trend were worked through by recognizing the influence they had on her attitude toward life in general, toward work, toward others, and toward herself. The outstanding result of this examination was a diminution of her inhibitions toward work.

We then tackled the interrelations of this trend with the two others. There were, on the one hand, irreconcilable conflicts and, on the other hand, mutual reinforcements, evidence of how inextricably she was caught in her neurotic structure. Conflicts existed between the compulsion to assume a humble place and to triumph over others, between ambition to excel and parasitic dependency, the two drives necessarily clashing and either arousing anxiety or paralyzing each other. This paralyzing effect proved to be one of the deepest sources of the fatigue as well as of the inhibitions toward work. No less important, however, were the ways in which the trends reinforced one another. To be modest and to put herself into a humble place became all the more necessary as it served also as a cloak for the need for triumph. The partner, as already mentioned, became

199

an all the more vital necessity as he had also to satisfy in a devious way the need for triumph. Moreover, the feelings of humiliation generated by the need to live beneath her emotional and mental capacities and by her dependency on the partner kept evoking new feelings of vindictiveness, and thus perpetuated and reinforced the need for triumph.

The analytical work consisted in disrupting step by step the vicious circles operating. The fact that her compulsive modesty had already given way to some measure of self-assertion was of great help because this progress automatically lessened also the need for triumph. Similarly, the partial solution of the dependency problem, having made her stronger and having removed many feelings of humiliation, made the need for triumph less stringent. Thus when she finally approached the issue of vindictiveness, which was deeply shocking to her, she could tackle with increased inner strength an already diminished problem. To have tackled it at the beginning would not have been feasible. In the first place we would not have understood it, and in the second place she could not have stood it.

The result of this last period was a general liberation of energies. Clare retrieved her lost ambition on a much sounder basis. It was now less compulsive and less destructive; its emphasis shifted from an interest in success to an interest in the subject matter. Her relationships with people, already improved after the second period, now lost the tenseness created by the former mixture of a false humility and a defensive haughtiness.

The Inefficient Wife

Harry Stack Sullivan, M.D.

Consultation on the Case of a Schizoid from
CLINICAL STUDIES IN PSYCHIATRY
W. W. Norton & Co. Inc., New York: 1956

HARRY STACK SULLIVAN

Harry Stack Sullivan's (1892–1949) chief emphasis in psychoanalysis was on the crucial importance of interpersonal relations. He did not believe that personality could be separated from interpersonal situations and that therefore the only thing that could be interpreted would be interpersonal behavior. Thus he did not consider the individual himself as the object of study but rather the individual's interaction with people around him. He felt that even a hermit carries with him his memories of relationships with others. Like Adler and Horney with whom he joined in de-emphasizing the rôle of instinct, Sullivan saw the field of psychoanalysis as being closely allied to social psychology. In his therapy he stressed the interview and the technique of the interview. He felt that the skill of the analyst in person to person interviews was of fundamental importance. Sullivan was the leader of the William Alanson White Psychiatric Foundation.

Like most leading practitioners, Sullivan spent a great deal of time in teaching. The case that follows then is not a case that Sullivan himself treated, but rather his advice to a student on how to deal with a specific problem which the patient had presented. The advice that Sullivan gives is focused on the interpersonal relations between the patient and her husband.

The Inefficient Wife

Sullivan commented on the therapeutic problems of eliciting and interpreting communication. The therapist's problem is to find a way to relate to what is communicative in the patient's productions. Such communications are, of course, fragmentary, and therefore Sullivan's comments on the problems presented by his colleagues are fragmentary. For this reason, we have included here, as a case illustration of his therapeutic approach, his comments on the case of a schizoid (unsocial; introverted [Ed.]) who—while relatively inarticulate—was able to communicate something of her problems to her therapist.

The case is then that of a schizoid—a young married woman who is extremely tense, apprehensive, and inarticulate. Her main difficulty, as she describes it, is that she is an inefficient housekeeper who "lazes" most of the day away. She looks upon herself as a failure. Treatment in the case has bogged down, after several months, and the question raised in the presentation of the problem is, What techniques can be used to get things moving again?

The patient is a product of an extremely traumatic childhood, during which she was deserted by her mother and later abandoned to the care of the maternal grandparents by her father, who was himself unreliable. In the grandparents' home she was treated more or less as a servant; but as she was very gifted intellectually, she managed to finish college and earn a Ph.D. in economics. She married a fellow-student in the same field and became a housewife. Her husband is extremely critical of her as a housekeeper, and has frequently told her about romantic entanglements with other women, always presenting these women to her as romantic ideals. During the ten years of marriage, in which two children have been born, the relationship has steadily worsened, with the husband threatening divorce and immersing himself in his work, and the wife leading an increasingly inactive and isolated life.

Sullivan: I have a number of considerations in mind, the first of which is to get the patient to notice that, even before her husband's recent promotion, they were perfectly able to afford at least a part-time maid. And as the patient finds herself showing, I suppose, unrecognized resentment of the burdens of her life every morning, I would start therapy by asking, "Well, why haven't you a maid?" And I want to *know*, in a fashion that makes it perfectly clear to me why they don't have a maid. If there isn't any adequate explanation, I would then ask, "How about getting one?"

I would go on by saying that her training seems to be rather exceptional for a person who has accepted a purely domestic role all these years and that, under the circumstances, her feeling of helplessness to get going in the morning rather encourages me than otherwise. Has she never heard of a woman who preferred something else to domestic preoccupations? I would ask, "Has this never occurred to you, or has it occurred to you as something morbid and strange?" (I would suppose it had actually never occurred to her at all.) Then I would want to know how it happened that she went through college and took a graduate degree in economics; since women economists are not the most common thing in the world, I would point out that it looks to me as if she must have followed some natural bent. Now of course it may come out that she did it because great-aunt Catherine recommended it, something of that kind, but that immediately excites me about great-aunt Catherine, who seems to have had ideas, you know.

What I am attempting to do here is to get her mind open a little bit to the fact that not only is she in a disagreeable situation, but she finds it disagreeable. And by sort of hounding her to prove that she is an exceptional woman with an exceptional education—and an exceptional inclination to go on suffering an impossibly silent domestic involvement—I am simply hoping to crack the shell that surrounds all her feelings. Until she raises her sights to something, I think that an attempt to get her clear on how much she resents her husband and all that would be merely an intellectual exercise. She would catch on very quickly, and nothing would happen, except possibly that she would feel that things were getting a little worse. But if I start the other way—if I get her to wondering what the hell she has been doing all this time and why she has never felt entitled to object to any of it —then I can anticipate that she will be equal to feeling some very real anger at times.

I would sort of hound her with commonplace things, not because I care too much about the facts themselves at the moment, but because I want her mind to begin to reach a little outside the magic circle of insulation in which she has been living all this time. Otherwise we are just going to get some fine thinking. There must be an outward movement of her interest, a beginning suspicion, "Well, this really wasn't all necessary and inevitable," before I can expect her to do much real observing of the play of interpersonal movement that probably has characterized her, as it does all of us, all her life. The very lack of outward signs of suffering indicates how early she accepted as fit and inevitable that she should be the slavey in her maternal grandparents' home and that she should in some fashion be kept from associations with other people, presumably because she wasn't good enough or trustworthy enough or just didn't have sense enough. I would lead her to talk a little bit about how she explained this tacit ban on her developing ordinary relationships, and I would expect that she would then hint of her acceptance of her unworthiness for a free life. At this point I would ask, "Well, now, how do you explain college and the rather original choice of subject that you carried through so well?" Then, after I had listened to a good deal of that, I would come down like a ton of bricks on economics. "Well, how about economics? Why has that interest vanished from your life without a trace? You take a Ph.D. in economics, marry an economist, and as far as I can discover, from then on research in economics has been left exclusively to him. Did that suit him? Was that what he insisted on? Did you just accommodate his feeling that it was awkward to have a wife who knew something about his business, or what?"

Thus, by that remote route, I hope that I would begin to get to her resentments toward her husband. They will be so far back in experience, you see, that immediate explosive danger will be diminished by the time she gets anywhere near the present. It seems to me that *the* big

205

problem for the therapist in dealing with a person like this is to close in on areas that inevitably must open her mind to a reassessment of what has been taken more or less for granted as a continuing act of God.

The thing I would be determined that this woman should tell me sometime or other is that she has discussed with her husband just what he had in mind in advising her in long, ecstatic letters of his great love for another woman some years back, and I would try to get her to look at that simply as a piece of research or investigation. "Now here is a very interesting research problem," I would say. "One's husband goes off and becomes terribly enamored of some goddess and writes his wife all about it. Now what was he doing? What did he think he was doing?" She doesn't know, of course; she hasn't had any experience in being anybody's husband. Then I ask her, "But why not find out?" Here again, I hope that I would be pushing on something far enough away and essentially intriguing enough so that she will rather calmly ask him a few questions. I think they will be very profoundly embarrassing questions. My notion of why a husband does things like that is not to the husband's credit at all. And maybe she will have the privilege of seeing him quite disconcerted in explaining this, and maybe that will introduce the idea to her, "Well, this bird who has always said he was horribly insecure and so on, *is* horribly insecure. Why is he picking on me then? Why should I be his whipping-boy?" And I am pretty sure that he will respond very hastily to good management on her part. I may be wholly wrong, but he sounds to me like a person who has been getting away with murder because he was fortunate enough to find one of these incredible women to whom it has never occurred that there is any fun in life or any give-and-take; and I think one starts her education in what I call the *middle distance,* before college and through early marriage, winding up with the great love that came into the husband's life and had to be embalmed in letters to his wife. I do not take an interest in current events with her husband, first, because I wouldn't know what on earth they meant, for she is a poor observer and has carefully looked the other way a great part of her life, and, second, because I wouldn't know what foolishness she might think I wanted her to engage in. You see,

206

I particularly don't want her to get the impression that I think she ought to rough-house him and throw some of the bric-a-brac at him, because the poor man might take flight. He might become completely undone. And I am pretty certain that he is insecure enough so that she will find, to her great astonishment and permanent gratitude, that she can manage with him *if* she proceeds slowly enough along the line I have suggested.

I am not after anything here that is going to be very difficult to recall. It would be well within the realm of reasonable recall for all of us. What I am trying to do with the middle distance is literally to lift her eyes above this tiny little irregular area in which she lives. Part of that will be done by getting her to review this utterly slavey existence that was so convenient for the relations with whom she lived in her girlhood. Why did she never suspect that anything else was possible? Where has she been all her life? What was the doom, the inherent handicap that made her so practically resigned at all stages of her life to what I think is best summed up as an almost complete lack of any fun? There wouldn't be anything at all odd about this woman if she had been born a century earlier in middle New England. She might in that setting have had a placid life. But a hundred little times she seems never to have noticed that life for her in the world of today was a poor imitation of what other people in similar circumstances had been having all this time.

Now I approach the situation in this way because I don't see anything malignant anywhere in it. The husband sounds more like an insecure tyrant than anything else. Maybe he is also schizoid. He also has apparently no grasp on the principle of fun in life than to have an almost classically autistic love affair every now and then; I wouldn't be a bit surprised if some of the women he has been so enamored of have known nothing about it. Also, I do not feel completely discouraged about his perhaps ultimately finding that psychotherapy for himself, though undesirable, is inescapable. I think that he, too, can lift his sights a little bit without any serious upheaval of personality and without this marital group breaking up. I would hope that together they might even emerge from this sort of numb dullness that almost asphyxiates them at times, and get a little bit of pleasure out of life.

The Angry Adolescent

Carl R. Rogers, Ph.D.

From: COUNSELING AND PSYCHOTHERAPY
Houghton Mifflin Co. 1942

CARL ROGERS

Carl Rogers (1902–) is one of the most influential forces in American psychology. He is chiefly identified with a method of therapy which he originated and developed, influenced by the work of Otto Rank, one of the pioneer psychoanalysts who broke with Freud.

The therapy with which Rogers is identified is called non-directive or client-centered. He believes that the therapist must relate to the client (Rogers rarely refers to those coming for therapy as patients) not as a scientist to an objective study, nor as a physician expecting to cure, but as one person deeply involved in the feelings of another. He further believes that the best reference point on which to understand the behavior of any individual is from the internal point of the individual himself.

Non-directive therapy has enjoyed wide popularity among academic psychologists because it is the one therapy which grew completely out of psychology and not out of medicine. It is probably the form of therapy most frequently taught in university graduate courses in counseling techniques. Some believe that it is a comparatively easy technique to learn and that the treatment may be relatively brief. In its avoidance of suggestion or direction and in its emphasis on emotional ventilation and insight, non-directive therapy resembles psychoanalysis.

One of Rogers' greatest contributions in the area of psychotherapy has been his initiation of, and subsequent collaboration in a whole series of researches into the nature of the psychotherapeutic process and its results. Being a trained psychologist and working with trained psychologists, Rogers had the assistance of more individuals trained in research than most of the other psychoanalysts.

In this case, taken from Rogers' book but probably describing the work of a counselor other than Rogers, some of the methods of the non-directive counselor are indicated. The importance of this case is not so much in the technique, which is a little more active than Rogers' cases usually indicate, but in Rogers' emphasis on the development of insight. This case shows how the client develops her own insight into some of the causes of her difficulties.

210

The Angry Adolescent

The development of insight often involves not only the recognition of the rôle which the individual is playing, but also the recognition of repressed impulses within the self. So long as the individual denies certain attitudes which he finds within himself, so long will he keep up compensatory attitudes of a defensive character. When he can face clearly, and can accept as a part of himself, these less praiseworthy feelings, the need for defensive reactions tends to disappear.

An excellent example of the development of this type of insight may be taken from the case of Cora, an adolescent girl of seventeen who was brought to the guidance clinic and to the children's court by her stepfather because of ungovernable behavior at home. The mother was an invalid, having spent periods in the hospital and a sanitarium. The stepfather had assumed much responsibility for Cora, and had also shown a peculiar attitude toward her, being jealous of her boy friends and behaving in ways which indicated a direct sex interest in the girl. As the friction in the home was extreme, Cora was placed in a foster home by the court, and after a short time the girl asked if she might again talk with the psychologist with whom she had had several contacts at the time she went to court. When she came in, she expressed a desire to talk about her family, and much of her conversation revolved about her stepfather. She told indignantly of the way in which he checked on her behavior, even while she was in the foster home, and how disturbed he seemed to be when she had any contact with her boy friend. The interview continues:

Finally counselor said, "Why do you think these things happen?" Cora said, "I think he does it for meanness. I can't understand why my mother doesn't stop him. Why does she always believe him?" Counse-

211

lor said, "I have talked with your mother since you were here. Your mother has talked about this. She understands. Perhaps some day she'll explain it to you. Would you like to have me tell you what your mother and I talked about?" Cora expressed no interest in this, but went right on with the problem of her stepfather's behavior. "I think he just wants me home. I think he wants me to help with the work. I think he's jealous. Several people have said it. The adviser at school said so, you remember I told you. I don't see why he should be jealous; what could he be jealous of? He hates to see me go out with a boy. I don't know how to explain it. I think he's not all there. Sometimes he is, and sometimes he isn't. He doesn't like it if I go with Italians. He doesn't like any boys to take me out. He's jealous. I don't understand it. If he were a boy my age it would mean he wanted me just to go with him. But he's married to my mother. I don't understand it. A boy would come out and say it. He doesn't. He just acts that way. He acts as if he wanted to go with me. Why, that couldn't be true. He's married to my mother. That's hard to think of." She was very disturbed and silent for a long time; became very fussed and fidgeted.

Counselor: "Talk about it some more."

Cora: "I don't know what to say. It seems awfully unfair to my mother if that's it. After all, he married my mother. It wouldn't be fair to my mother. I haven't any feeling for him. I don't see why he should feel that way. I go crazy if he even touches me. He seems so devoted to my mother. I think he is. I realize it's been hard for him, my mother being in the hospital. If he must be like that, why pick on me? He might better go out with someone we didn't know, some woman we didn't know."

Counselor: "Why should he especially like you?"

Cora: "I don't think it's because I'm especially like my mother. People say I am. He says I am. I don't think I am. Maybe I am. There's nothing else to say. It makes me sort of horrified—my own mother. The only reason would be that I remind him of my mother."

She talked about how wonderful her mother was. "He's married to my mother. He shouldn't feel that

212

way. Why doesn't he say something? Why take it out on me? My mother's right there. Why doesn't he give her all his affection? Maybe it's because I'm younger, in better health, or something. I don't think it could be sex, because—unless"—(there was a long pause)—"I know he couldn't have any sex life with my mother. She's sick. I don't even like to talk about such things. What else is there to say?"

There was further conversation along this same line, devoted largely to discussion of the stepfather and his behavior. Two days later Cora came in for her next interview.

Cora looked very sober when she came in. "I'm still in a fog. I've thought and thought. It seems impossible. It's hard to believe. I can see the sense in it. It all adds up, and still I can't believe it. How could that be, when I see that it makes sense?"

Counselor explained to her something of how one could understand how a thing could be and still not emotionally accept it. Cora then said, "It's hard to believe that it's real. Nothing like that ever entered my head. I don't think about things like that anyway."

Counselor: "What is it that is hard to believe?"

Cora: "It's hard to believe, and yet I believe it. It's hard to believe that people would have feelings like that. He doesn't seem clean. When I think about it, I shudder. That was not included in my education. It ought to be for every girl, that there are such things. The idea that my stepfather would have such feelings. I'm not like my mother. I don't see why he should feel that way. I don't know how to say it."

During the remainder of the interview she talked about family frictions, and about the fact that she did not think she would ever wish to go home.

Cora missed the next two appointments which were given to her. It seems entirely reasonable to suppose that the painfulness of this increasing insight was the major factor in her failing to keep these appointments. Consequently, it was two weeks later that she came in for her next appointment.

Cora explained that she had made a mistake about the time of her appointment. "I didn't try to forget it. It was an accident. I've been thinking about what we talked about last time. It all makes sense, but I can't believe it."

Counselor said, "When you were here last time, you were trying to answer the question of what had been your part in creating this situation." (No such statement is included in the counselor's account of the previous interview. If such a question was raised by the counselor, it no doubt accounts for Cora's failure to keep the appointments.)

Cora: "I don't know what it is. I can't think it out."

Counselor: "When your mother was in the hospital, your stepfather did things for you and gave you things and took you places. You were pleased, weren't you? How did you show it?"

Cora: "Oh, I'd jump up and down and be very gleeful. I might have hugged and kissed him. Sometimes I show my pleasure in that way. Sometimes I kissed him and made a great fuss."

Counselor: "Did you ever do something for someone else and have them show pleasure? How did you feel?" Cora thought for a few moments and then gave several examples of having done things for the foster mother. "I felt pretty good that she was pleased." She thought a long time. "I liked her maybe a little harder for a few minutes after that."

Counselor: "Go back again to when you and your stepfather were together and your mother was in the hospital."

Cora talked about the things her stepfather had done for her, particularly taking her places. "He did those things then to please my mother, not for me. I was pleased and showed it. He was pleased because my mother was pleased. When she was pleased, he was more willing to do more for me. Then I got a feeling toward him, hero worship. No, I guess that isn't right. Something different. Sometimes I thought he was very nice, and sometimes I didn't like him. I was also jealous that he had married my mother. I would be grateful to him, but then I would think it was my right that he should do things for me. No, it wasn't hero worship. I

214

can't quite say what it was. He did things for me that pleased me. I guess he was a sort of Santa Claus. You get to expect and expect when people do things for you. Then the person gets kind of sick of it. Then you learn how to get things. I guess that's what I did. I learned how to get things from him."

Counselor: "What did you do?"

Cora showed embarrassment, paused a long time. "Oh, I don't know. I have a lot of tricks. It wasn't hard to get him to go out. He didn't like to sit at home. I'd do a lot of things. When I wanted girls to go with me I'd pick the girls he liked to get him to take them along." She paused a long time and counselor waited, then said, "Anything else?"

Cora: "I suppose my voice was soft and persuasive and my face had a happy expression, the way I knew it would get him to do things." She talked about this for a little while, showing more and more embarrassment.

Counselor: "When you want a boy to take you some place, how do you get it?"

Cora: "I probably look sweet and defenseless." Then very quickly: "I'm not conscious of all this, but I guess I do. I know how to look that way, but it never works on my mother. I guess I learned how to do it particularly in thinking up ways to get things from my stepfather. I didn't consciously bring about this situation." She went back to discuss the idea that her stepfather liked her very much and identified her with her mother, again saying, "It makes sense, but I don't believe it."

Counselor: "Do you like this situation?"

There was a long pause. Cora flushed, fidgeted, and then hesitated. "No, but I do like my stepfather to pay attention to me." She was silent for a long time.

Though the counselor's approach in this situation seems too forceful and directive, the insights gained in this case are of considerable interest. First Cora faces more clearly the fact of her stepfather's sexual interest in her, and the consequent reasons for his jealous behavior. Gradually, however, she comes to recognize that she has herself been encouraging his special interest in her, and that she has adopted various wiles to cause him

215

to continue this rôle of an older "boy friend." It is of interest that as long as her insight is limited only to the stepfather's behavior, she speaks of him with disgust—"He doesn't seem clean." When she is able openly to recognize her own feelings in the situation, she no longer talks in this way, but faces her very ambivalent attitude toward him. In this last interview, a few moments following the excerpt quoted, the counselor asks, "How have you felt toward him?" and Cora replies, "I guess as a Santa Claus, and yet I hate him, but I do like him, too."

In a case of this sort, where counseling treatment has revealed the conflicts which are present, the symptomatic behavior of rebellion, sex delinquency, truancy, and the like becomes more understandable. Also the importance of genuine insight is emphasized. Until Cora was able to achieve a considerable degree of insight, all attempts at treatment were futile. With this insight, she was capable of assuming a more adult rôle, and aggressive behavior was less necessary as a substitute for her conflicts.

It is evident that the insight which was gained was first of all a clearer understanding of her relationship with her stepfather, but the more dynamic insight was her recognition of the tabooed feelings within herself, and the fact that she and the stepfather had each played a part in creating the situation.

PART III

SPECIALIZED PSYCHOANALYTIC TECHNIQUES

The increasing need for the assistance that psychoanalysis can render has led to the development of specialized techniques for the treatment of a broad variety of problems and an ever-widening diversity of individuals.

Some of these techniques are so different from psychoanalysis in its original form that many hesitate to apply the term psychoanalysis to them, preferring to call these specialized techniques "psychoanalytically oriented psychotherapy."

Two of these specialized techniques are described in the cases that follow: brief therapy for a psychosomatic case, and group psychotherapy. Other examples of these specialized techniques would be: psychoanalytically oriented speech therapy, art therapy, and the special modifications used in the treatment of psychotic and borderline psychotic patients. The two techniques presented here are but suggestive of the many ways in which psychoanalysis is being broadened and developed to meet new situations.

217

Brief Therapy

of a

Psychosomatic

Case

Roy R. Grinker, M.D.
and
Fred P. Robbins, M.D.

From: PSYCHOSOMATIC CASE BOOK; The Blakiston Company, Inc., New York: 1954

THE PSYCHOSOMATIC APPROACH

A very important area of the application of psychoanalysis to problems other than those obviously neurotic has been the emphasis on the psychosomatic approach. This approach has made it possible to deal with and treat successfully many cases of apparent organic illness, such as the severe abdominal pains and diarrhea in the present case which resisted other methods of treatment.

Essentially the psychosomatic approach is one which recognizes the relationship between psyche, the mind, and soma, the body. In the particular case described, brief therapy was used. In order to aid the therapy, sodium pentathol, a drug which causes a state of hypnosis, was employed to get to the specific problems as quickly as possible.

While attempts were made by many practitioners after World War II to use sodium pentathol and sodium amytol, a drug with similar properties, for therapeutic treatment, the results have not been as satisfactory as they were found to be under wartime conditions. Most practitioners believe that this brief method is useful only with otherwise healthy patients where the ailment suddenly develops in response to recent acute stress of relatively short duration.

However, one value of the sodium pentathol treatment has been to demonstrate the existence of unconscious motives in the production of illness. It is obvious that the drug administered to the patient in this case brought forth material which had previously not been available to his conscious thought. The expression of this formerly unconscious material caused the disappearance of the symptoms of pain and diarrhea.

Brief Therapy
of a
Psychosomatic Case

An ex-service man, aged 22 years, entered the hospital because of attacks of severe abdominal pain and diarrhea. These attacks had begun while he was overseas in the Army, and resulted in his evacuation through the hospital system to the United States. He was not discharged medically, however, but on "points." The last attack occurred when he was at home awaiting acceptance by a business school, after a discussion with his father over funds for the purchase of an automobile for his own use when away at school. After thorough but negative medical investigation, the internist in attendance requested psychiatric consultation.

The patient was a well-built, tall, handsome young man, extremely pleasant in his manner and interested in getting well. His family had moved to the United States from Canada when the patient was twelve years old and here the father had made a phenomenal financial success. The father was an attractive, dynamic, proverbial type of successful executive who dealt in big business with rapid-fire decisions. The identical pattern of behavior characterized the father in his life at home. The mother was a thin, unattractive, somewhat complaining, shadowy figure, who had had several abdominal operations and frequent attacks of diarrhea. These decreased when her husband took her more frequently on his business trips. A younger brother of seventeen was the only other member of the family. In telling of his family life, the patient considered that there was nothing lacking, that everyone was good and nice. Although not effeminate, he gave the impression of considerable passive compliance and complacency in his attitudes. His war

221

experiences had been uneventful and not dangerous. He had been stationed in England for many months with a quartermaster company, functioning as a driver. He had gone to France long after D-day and had never been in combat. Only once had he been near danger and that was while driving through territory into which German paratroopers had penetrated. He had been a "little scared" but had never seen a German. His first attack of abdominal pain came on ten days later while he was driving a car for his captain.

Because the patient could not remember any conscious emotional attitudes during any of his attacks of pain, it was decided to attempt a reconstruction of the setting prior to the first spell and to uncover the feelings accompanying that particular episode. Accordingly, pentothal was administered intravenously and the patient was told that he was driving his truck on the specific day on which he had been a "little scared."

The patient began talking fearfully of having heard that German parachutists were in the neighborhood into which he was ordered to drive. Suddenly his truck broke down near a hill from behind which shooting could be heard. By regulation he was forced to stay near his truck until help arrived, so after hiking to the nearest ordnance patrol be returned to the vicinity of his truck and sweated out relief in a foxhole. For 45 minutes he remained there alone, in abject fear, although he heard only distant shots. Under pentothal he disclosed his thoughts, never before verbalized, which were those of a little child pleading for God to save him. He was too young to die and besides he had been a good boy, never harmed anyone. What would mother do if he were hurt or killed? As he cried and pleaded to the Almighty for help, he perspired and writhed on the bed and jumped at the slightest noises. In this first exteriorization of the old forgotten stream of thought, there were missing all but minor manifestations of courage and anger. Finally a relief truck arrived and the patient became more aggressive as he directed his fellow soldiers to turn their truck around. As they drove closer to camp he actually became belligerent, and when he saw the guards and machine guns in position he verbally dared those bastardly Nazis to come this way, saying, "We'll kill them like rats."

After the pentothal interview the patient remembered that he had been scared badly but had forgotten all about it. His fear was then dealt with as an understandably normal reaction, and then in a state of emotional exhaustion he fell asleep. Subsequent interviews concentrated on "the little boy within the grown man" and the universality of the fear reaction. A few days later another pentothal interview was undertaken in the setting of the first intestinal attack ten days after the parachute incident. The patient had driven all day long for his commanding officer, an alcoholic captain, who apparently mistreated his men and allowed himself the privilege of women and liquor although he punished his men for identical activities. The patient was his personal driver and often had to support the captain standing or walking, light his cigarettes, and feed him when he was in a state of tremulousness. The captain's alcoholic gastritis and lack of appetite cost the patient many meals for himself.

On this particular day the patient had driven from early morning, over badly damaged roads, until late at night when they stopped at a tiny French village. The captain had ordered the patient to bunk in the truck under the sky while he went into the M.P. station and slept under shelter. The patient kept reassuring himself that there were no Nazi paratroopers nearby, that they all had been cleaned out, that it was perfectly safe, "really perfectly safe," but in spite of this self-conducted psychotherapy he could not sleep for many hours. A few minutes after falling asleep he was awakened abruptly by severe abdominal pains and diarrhea. When the pain became unendurable, he went into the M.P. shelter and sought out his drunken captain who ordered a soldier to take him to the medics. From this local station he was sent through the hospital system, in which he had repeated negative tests for organic disease or infection, and was eventually evacuated home. In the first hospital some guilt regarding his psychosomatic illness caused him to be oversolicitous about the externally wounded soldiers. During this pentothal interview the patient groaned and writhed with his pains. He held his hands over the abdomen; tachycardia, excessive perspiration, and his sickly green color left no doubt as to his suffer-

223

ing. He faithfully reproduced his initial attack in its entirety.

When he awakened we discussed the relationship of this attack to his fear at a second exposure to possible parachutists and his reaction to the captain who had placed him in a dangerous position. He could not see why he should have felt resentful or angry toward the captain, and since there was a strong resistance against anything but the old "It was his right to order me as he wished," another pentothal injection was given in a few days. The patient was placed again in the village square in the dark and urged to express how he really felt toward his captain. After considerable resistance, anger then spilled forth freely and completely. It was documented by countless incidents of discrimination, unfairness, lack of promotion, overwork, etc. The captain who was passively accepted consciously became a "bastard and a no good son-of-a-bitch" who took every advantage of his authoritative position.

After considerable abreaction the patient was interrupted and asked, "And how about your father?" The answer was a surprisingly frank and abrupt, "He's the same kind of a son-of-a-bitch." In the present tense, he then verbally lived through an event of some years past before he entered the Army. The lengthy but emotionally highly charged abreaction will only be summarized. Once when the father was absent from home, the patient's fraternity had held a convention in Chicago and, because transportation was scarce, he borrowed his father's car against his orders. While he was away from home his pet dog had also disobeyed house rules and scampered upstairs into his father's room where it had vomited on a costly rug. On his return the father was very angry and called the patient before him to receive orders for the following punishment: he had to be in the house each night at 6:00 P.M. after high school and could not leave thereafter for any purpose for three months. The patient admitted his guilt, gave his reasonable excuses, and mildly expostulated against the severity of the punishment, saying, "Don't you think it is too severe—yes, I'll take it like a man and not complain," although under the pentothal he sobbed pitifully. Ten weeks later the father was drunk one night and broke the punishment himself by asking the patient to drive him to his club. He invited his son to have a drink with him at the bar and in a maudlin sentimental fashion admitted that the punishment had been overly severe, admitted that the patient had taken it like a man, and asked for forgiveness. They shook hands and the affair was over. But during the pentothal interview the patient gradually worked up into a really angry attitude toward the father which was expressed for the first time. These emotions were remembered and discussed after the pentothal had worn off.

Subsequent psychotherapy was directed toward differentiating between infantile conscious appeasement with unconscious intestinal expression of rage, and adult and manly, normally expressed, justifiable anger. Obviously this was but one episode from a life-long pattern. The father at first denied, in answer to questioning, any arbitrariness in his attitude, but his wife refused to let him avoid the issue and contradicted him at every turn. She and the boy had been compelled by alliance to bolster their defenses against the mutual overstrict enemy and watch always for his weak spots. The father was a boss in his home as well as in his business and issued executive orders in his family or answered requests by a blunt "no" without giving reasons or qualifications. In this manner he had wished to "make a man out of my boy," but actually he permitted no manly semblance of equality, forcing only an infantile obedience and appeasement. Normal emotional reactions could only be repressed. Confirmation of this principle was soon forthcoming as the boy made his first attempt to express his new-found independence, but the father was sufficiently disturbed at least to act the part expected by the psychiatrist.

The result of therapy so far was good in that there was no relapse and the father had developed more respect for his avowed successor. The final outcome will depend on the life-situations of the immediate future and will determine whether this brief therapy has been enough or whether further psychotherapy will be necessary.

This case has been presented in some detail to demonstrate the principles of procedure in brief psychotherapy of acute psychosomatic states. It demonstrates the processes of uncovering the repressed emotional content

225

directly produced by the precipitating cause of the neurosis and its relation to earlier patterns. This patient showed quite clearly a combination of fear, rage, and dependent crying expressed in a psychosomatic symptom in a personality without the expected reaction formation. The working through and the reorientation both of the patient's concepts of maturity and of his human environment was demonstrated. But this occurred in a young, plastic person with little defensive rigidity. His environment had not yet hurt him too badly. We are less fortunate in brief psychotherapy when dealing with middle-aged people who have been habituated to chronic neurotic patterns and have become fixed on the organic nature of their somatic symptoms.

A Group
of
Problem Girls

S. R. Slavson

*Analytic Group Psychotherapy with Ado-
lescent Girls.*

From: ANALYTIC GROUP PSYCHOTHERAPY
Columbia University Press. New York: 1950

GROUP THERAPY

One of the newest developments in the application of psychoanalysis to therapy has been the very rapid growth of group therapy and group psychoanalysis since World War II. Originally psychologists, psychiatrists and social workers turned to group therapy because of the expense in time and money of individual analysis, and in an effort to overcome the lack of trained therapists. The belief was that even a group therapeutic contact was better than none. Today some therapists (including this writer) consider group analysis either alone or in combination with individual treatment the treatment of choice, that is, as often being superior to individual analysis by itself.

Group therapy, it is believed, gives the individual patients the opportunity to operate in a field more closely related to life itself and tends to prevent the development of over-dependence by the patient on the therapist, as it encourages the development of relationships with larger groups of people.

The group described here is from a book by S. R. Slavson whose organizational genius has done much to make group therapy a world wide movement. As Director of the Group Therapy Department of the Jewish Board of Guardians in New York City, Slavson first employed the method in dealing with "problem children." Later he encouraged and publicized the development of group therapy both in the United States and in the rest of the world.

In this particular case the actual therapist was one of the pioneers in group therapy, Betty Gabriel, who dealt with a group of adolescent girls. Increasingly, as the problem of juvenile delinquency becomes prominent, the group therapy approach is being utilized to deal with such problems. However, the use of group therapy is by no means confined to adolescents in social agencies but is being used increasingly in the treatment of adults in institutions and in private practice.

A Group
of
Problem Girls

Sandra was a very attractive girl. Her blonde hair was bleached and touched up to appear "glamorous." She used cosmetics excessively and actually appeared older than her age. She affected a carefree air but grew serious when discussing music and art, in which she had superior talent. She was excessively interested in herself and spoke about her abilities a great deal of the time. She had many phantasies, especially after retiring at night, and frequently spoke of harmonious family life in her home as a reality, which was far from being the case.

Sandra came for treatment through the police department, who apprehended her after a run-away escapade with another girl, Helen. In this Sandra was aided and abetted by her mother, who was in serious conflict with her husband and whom she disliked intensely. Sandra stayed away from home overnight on a number of occasions and picked up sailors on the street. There was constant wrangling in the family about money, the father being a miserly person, giving the family insufficient funds to meet expenses, and grudgingly at that. Sandra truanted from school a great deal until she was transferred to an art school, in which she was interested.

The father was a punitive, rejecting, strict person. He indulged the second of his three daughters, Sandra being the youngest. There was very strong sibling rivalry between these two girls, for which Sandra was blamed by the parents, who considered her a "trouble-maker." The mother, who infantilized the girl and had never given her any responsibilities in the home, complained of

Note: The ages of the girls in this group at the time of referral were 15.6 to 17 years.

229

Sandra's stubbornness and described the girl as restless and as having a very short span of concentration. The father, on the other hand, was distrustful of her and called her abusive names, such as "tramp." Sandra described herself as lazy and "dizzy" and admitted that she got herself into trouble. The father was so restrictive that even on hot summer nights he insisted that Sandra go to bed at nine o'clock in the evening.

The girl was upset by the friction and strife between her parents. The mother was considered inferior to the father, both by him and the daughters. It seemed that the father was unable to meet the mother's sexual demands, and she had sexual relations with other men. (At one of the group sessions Sandra said she wished she could have been somebody's favorite child; she always wanted a father whom she could love; she wanted to be affectionate with her father. She remembered that even when she was a little girl, she could not bring herself to put her hand in his and call him "Daddy." She wished she could call him "Daddy." What does she call him? She giggled self-consciously and said, "Pa.")

Diagnosis: behavior disorder, pre-Oedipal group, conduct type.

Rose, a refugee from Nazi Germany, had undergone a series of traumatic experiences as a very young child, on the flight with her family from Europe. She was raped on at least two occasions during this flight. When she came for treatment, Rose cried frequently for no apparent reason, and was suffering from frightening dreams, nightmares, and "general nervousness." She frequently became irritated and depressed, the reason for which she could not fathom. She was suspicious of people, unfriendly, seclusive, and distrustful of men particularly. Rose bit her nails when excited and had bodily tremors, which dated back to eight years of age, when she also began to scream at her mother and brother.

Rose's father suffered from depression, largely because of the sharp decline in his social and economic status. From his status as a wealthy businessman in Germany, he had been reduced to that of a menial worker here. Rose was very sensitive about and reacted intensely to her father's moods. The father treated her as an infant and was unable to accept her strivings for independence as an adolescent. Rose was an only child for six years, and recalls how her father played with her when she was about four, something he had not done since. Although she had wanted a brother, she resented his coming and vomited at the time of his birth.

Rose was a well developed, attractive girl, who seemed eager for friends but unable to establish relationships. A study of this case revealed that the girl's early Oedipal drives had not been adequately resolved and that her sexual preoccupations were very intense. These she shared with only one girl, her closest friend, who was also under treatment. Menstruation set in at ten years, and had always been accompanied by pains. She knew about menstruation, but did not confide this knowledge to her mother. The girl considered herself a martyr and she saw herself as a mother substitute to her brother from the time she was eight years old. She bathed and fed him, which, it seemed, her parents expected her to do, and took over much of the household duties from the time she was ten.

Diagnosis: psychoneurosis with obsessional elements.

Bertha was a tall, slender girl of sixteen, I.Q. 126. Because of her thin face and prominent nose, she was sometimes referred to by her teachers as "Pinocchio." She had brown hair, often worn in extreme fashion, but seldom neatly combed. She had very attractive large blue eyes. Her clothes were always messy and she was generally neglectful of appearance. Under individual treatment she began to take better care of herself and to use lipstick, wearing a cupid's bow.

Bertha was not self-conscious, related well to people, and spoke with candor and ease, but in a monotone. She seemed to lack affect and talked of all matters impassively, as though she were discussing the weather. She had a strong sense of justice and reacted with anger to anything she considered unjust, whether it was directed against her or not.

Bertha truanted from school and her mother complained that she was "loud-mouthed, stole money from an older sister, and had a quick temper." She kept late hours, lied, had undesirable friends, fought with her seventeen-year-old brother, invoked God when in difficulty, acted in a precocious manner, was always late, even for meals, and was distrustful toward her parents (it was suspected that she knew about her father's extramarital relations).

The parents had been at loggerheads since the beginning of their married life; even when the mother was pregnant with Bertha, the father carried on affairs with other women. The father was attached to and influenced by Bertha to such an extent that whenever the mother wished to get anything from him she asked Bertha to intercede for her. Bertha and the mother, on the other hand, had violent quarrels, and the girl tended to ignore her mother, an unhappy, insecure woman who had borne seven unpremeditated children. She was disappointed in her marriage and insulted and humiliated by her husband, children, and her daughter-in-law.

In Bertha's many altercations with her brother, the mother sided with him, to Bertha's great resentment. She complained that her mother cursed, insulted, and humiliated her even in the presence of her friends. The fights between the daughter and mother were so violent that they threw things at one another, on one occasion breaking a large mirror.

Bertha was brought up on a farm and had come to live in a large city only a year before she was referred for treatment. Before Bertha was born, three children were killed in accidents, and both father and mother felt guilty about it. A maternal aunt was actively attempting to set Bertha against her father.

Diagnosis: behavior disorder, conduct and habit type, neurotic symptoms.

Reva was extremely infantile and felt inferior. Although good looking, she considered herself unattractive, was unable to meet responsibilities such as getting to school on time or keeping appointments, was withdrawn, and felt that no one liked her because she was too quiet. She had no friends, stayed home from school a great deal of the time, and constantly fussed with her face, imagining she had pimples. She was described as nervous, screamed when angry and bit her nails. She used to be afraid of the dark, of strangers and of dogs. Reva was

232

always jealous of her younger brother, who by now was much taller than she and more mature. She frequently fought with him. When Reva began attending school, she cried a great deal and vomited.

Reva saw herself as babyish and having little self-confidence. She did not feel "as good as other people," and said that she was unable to look directly at them. Generally, her attitude toward herself was that she was a failure. Exacerbation of psychoneurotic symptoms had occurred six months before her treatment when a dog that she was taking care of fell from a roof and was killed.

Reva was the oldest of three children, the others being boys. Both father and mother and the next younger brother were all diagnosed as psychoneurotic. The youngest, who was around nine years of age, was also retarded and such a serious behavior problem that he had to be institutionalized. The mother overprotected all the children, while the father, an irritable man, got into temper tantrums and beat them severely.

The central problem as revealed by this girl was her very strong envy of her brother and attachment to her father. It was felt that she was in the midst of the Oedipal conflict and was functioning on the level of a very young child. Reva had not taken on any of the adolescent mannerisms or behavior common to youngsters of her age. She dressed and fixed her hair neatly, but in a childish manner. She was generally insecure and shy, either twisting a handkerchief or pressing it tightly in the palm of her hand when speaking to someone. When she came for treatment she spoke in a confidential tone, complained of headaches and that her eyes got red when she studied or read. In individual treatment Reva was very resistive and proved to be inaccessible. She constantly broke appointments, partly because she was indifferent to the time factor, but largely because she was unable to establish a personal relation.

Diagnosis: psychoneurosis with infantile character development.

Lydia was a tall, slender girl, with a stiff, upright carriage, and an attractive and refined appearance. She wore her hair in a bizarre fashion, with a high pompadour, her lips heavily rouged, harlequin glasses, and stared for long periods without blinking. One of Lydia's characteristics was her lack of affects. Even when she spoke of the death of her favorite grandmother or her hatred for her mother's boy friend there was no change in her expression. She rarely smiled.

Lydia was one of two children; her sister, three and a half years older than she, was married.

In a psychometric test Lydia received a rating of 135. She had an excellent school record, which suddenly deteriorated. The specific complaint was that formerly a quiet and well-behaved girl, she had begun to go around with young people older than herself, kept late hours, and did not disclose her whereabouts. She suddenly changed from a good, studious, rather submissive and obedient girl into an aggressive, quarrelsome individual. She was also enuretic.

The mother and father had been separated since Lydia was about nine years old. The father visited the home after remarriage and made sexual advances to his former wife. Lydia was strongly affected by the separation of her parents. She felt she had been let down by them, especially by her father. The mother, a very strict woman, never seemed satisfied with Lydia's achievements and even when she brought high marks from school, the mother thought that they should still be higher. Lydia was greatly disappointed at this.

She once attempted to run away from home with a girl friend; the latter stole a watch and a ring from Lydia's sister for the purpose, but instead sold the watch and bought clothes for herself.

Diagnosis: latent schizophrenia.

Paula, with a minimal I.Q. of 94, presented a confused picture in her psychosocial development. When she came for treatment, she walked and acted like a boy, spoke in a low-pitched, coarse voice, used profane language as early as the age of twelve. At the same time she dressed prettily and her hair was arranged in numerous curls that hung all around her head. She said she liked to have curls so that boys could pull them.

Paula was a short, stocky, well-developed girl with dark eyes and a small pale face framed by the numerous dark

234

curls. Menstruation began at ten and a half. Paula had an overpowering hostility toward her mother and all women. Women angered her very easily. She adored her father, and was described as "man-mad." She built all sorts of romantic stories about herself in which innocent male friends of the family played unsavory roles. At school, she did poorly, giggled, talked a great deal, and was retarded in some subjects. One of her ambitions from early childhood was to be a policewoman.

As a child Paula tried to push her mother out of bed so that she could get in with her father and even at the time she was in treatment, would call her father in to wash her hair while in the nude. She openly resented her father's attention to the mother. Paula's chief problem was seen as a fairly serious confusion in her sexual identifications. She could not accept the female role and phantasied herself as a boy, largely because her father was the love-giving person in the family, the mother being harrassed, disturbed and authoritarian. The father, on the other hand, had been an irresponsible, youthful person; he was rather fond of Paula, though he had serious conflicts with the two boys older than our patient. There were also two younger girls in the family, one of whom was a baby.

Intensive individual psychotherapy was required for this girl. Transference to a female worker was the chief aim; however, it was found that to enhance her identifications with women, it was necessary for her to have a group experience. She was, therefore, referred at the age of twelve to an activity therapy group in which she remained for four years. This experience was of inestimable value to the girl, both in terms of observable results and her own intense enthusiasm and the feelings of satisfaction that she derived from it. At one point it was found that there were only two women in the world whom she trusted. They were her caseworker and the activity group therapist.

When Paula reached the age of sixteen, she was placed in an interview group. After a year and one half of this, it was decided to terminate treatment altogether and give her an opportunity to test herself against the world, with an option to return if she so desired.

Diagnosis: behavior disorder, Oedipal type, with severely narcissistic character.

At thirteen and a half, Georgia was referred for psychiatric treatment because of general social maladjustment, lack of friends, excessive dependence upon her mother, resistance to going to school, shyness, and bizarre choreoform tics which included facial grimaces, movement of the tongue and lips, head jerk, and involuntary shuffling of the feet. The tics were first observed when she was seven years old and diagnosed as Sydenham's Chorea. The girl received hospital treatment for more than six years. The physicians at the hospital finally suspected psychogenic causes and referred the patient for psychotherapy. After a period of individual treatment, she was referred to group therapy at about fifteen and a half years of age. On referral, Georgia was still subject to tics, spent much time daydreaming, staring into space until her eyes "blurred." As a small child she dreamed of dragons and snakes and had nightmares of dragons crawling on her and lifting her high into the air. When she came for group treatment, her dreams were about boys and dates. She considered herself worthless, had no friends, and was exceedingly hostile toward her mother and older sister.

The parents were seriously maladjusted, the mother being a power-driven, aggressive woman, who managed the household and the children with an iron hand and beat Georgia mercilessly to stop the tics, the cause for which the mother could not understand. Georgia was the butt of her mother's criticisms and fault-finding; she was constantly compared unfavorably with other children and her older sister. In addition Georgia was very tall and the children called her "daddy long-legs."

The father was a narcissistic, infantile, provocative person, given to temper tantrums, and resorted to yelling and screaming. He neglected the family but liked Georgia, though even with her he was usually inconsistent. She was strongly attached to him.

Diagnosis: mixed psychoneurosis with hysterical features, depression, conversion and withdrawal symptoms.[1]

[1] For a detailed anamnesis, full treatment history and outcome

236

Present: Rose, Sandra, Paula, Reva, Georgia, Lydia, Bertha

Paula, Rose, Sandra, Reva and Bertha came on time. Paula did not look well. She had a wan expression on her face and appeared to have lost weight. Sandra told the girls that she had left high school. The girls expressed their disapproval; they thought Sandra should continue with her schooling, but she said she had given the matter a great deal of thought. In fact, she had not fallen asleep until three in the morning before she made her decision as to whether continuing school could or could not help her. She had decided on her future work and school would only hinder rather than help. She wants to be a song writer and, to do this, she needs to have not only time to practice, write the music, orchestrate and arrange it, but she needs to spend time with the lyricist and to contact publishing agencies to sell her songs. She practices the piano a great deal and finds that school interferes. She simply must give up something and it is much easier for her to give up school. (A)

Georgia came in at this point and, not being aware of the content of the conversation, interrupted. She apologized for being absent from the last session. She was very ill, having become ill in the office and her boss was extremely kind to her. She was greatly affected by his sympathy. Since she had a discussion with him on politics, just prior to the elections, he had "treated her royally." In fact, the boss's wife, too, has become a friend of hers. Georgia was wearing a corsage and this was commented on by the girls, to which Georgia responded with much animation. She said that she had had a date with Leon the night before and gave some details about the entertainment. With this she showed the therapist her report card. She was disconcerted not to have received one of the highest marks in shorthand. (B)

The entertainment that Leon had planned for her was not a great success. He had given her three choices of

on this case, see *The Practice of Group Therapy*, ed. S. R. Slavson (New York, International Universities Press, 1947), 197–218. In that report Gloria is named Lilly Sloane, both names being fictitious.

places to go. She had to work all day from nine to five-thirty and was so tired when she got home that all she could do was go to a movie. She displayed her corsage and let all the girls smell the roses. (C)

The therapist said at this point that it was difficult for her to take down all the conversation and wondered about the possibility of having a stenographer at the meetings to take notes. Georgia at once volunteered, saying that it would be very helpful in learning stenography. The girls thought it a splendid idea. The therapist gave Georgia a notebook and two sharp pencils.[2]

By this time Lydia had also arrived. All the girls complimented Reva, who seemed to grow more attractive with each session. She now wore her hair very becomingly and dressed attractively. At this session she wore a very pretty dress and the girls spoke of it. Reva acknowledged their compliments modestly and added that even her mother said that she has a "pretty form" in it. Lydia began to talk about food fads, when Sandra interrupted to tell a dream she had had since the last session. (D)

Sandra dreamed that she was at the piano giving her best efforts to practicing when a small ape, or it may have been a small polar bear, came and stood near her and interfered with her practicing. She was a little afraid of the animal, but actually didn't mind it too much. Finally when it persisted in trying to interrupt her, she ran to her mother's room, but the ape followed her and she begged her mother to take it away. The ape, however, stuck to her. Sandra then ran out of the house, but the ape clung to her. She struck it, and the ape sank its teeth into Sandra's arm. Sandra kept trying to free herself and the struggle continued for some time. Laughingly, she said: "It's just like in dreams," for suddenly there was Helen instead of the ape. Helen said: "Don't go in again and practice. If you do, I'll turn into an ape again." Sandra paid no attention and turned to go back home. As she reached the threshold, Helen changed into an ape again. (At this point Sandra stood up, stooped over, and let her long arms dangle forward and said that

[2] This plan was abandoned after this session by the girls themselves.

238

was just the way the ape's arms were hanging down.) She then awakened.

Sandra herself interpreted the dream. "Just as I have said before, I think Helen holds me down," and the ape is supposed to be a human animal but of low mentality. (Helen had induced Sandra in the past to go on blind dates, pick up sailors, run away from home and participate in other delinquencies. Sandra had often told the girls that Helen was not bright.) Bertha said that Helen clings to Sandra, though Sandra wants to shake herself free of her. Sandra said that she can still recall how scared she was. Lydia said, "Sandra, I believe you're cutting your nose off to spite your face by going with Helen. Helen seems to do you more harm than good." The therapist then asked Sandra whether, instead of the ape being Helen, it might not have been her father. (E)

Sandra giggled briefly and said that when she was little, her father used to frighten her by making faces and threatening her. She said, "I hate him, and I pity him." Bertha said Sandra was involved with her father too much and that he clings to her, too. Her own father, Bertha said, often gets mad at her and then he looks like a beast ready to pounce on his prey. Paula laughed out loud and said, it's queer that Bertha should have said this. Her father sort of frightens her, too. He has a habit of yelling. She thinks that he yells because he is in pain. (F)

Bertha had taken care of her sister's baby the preceding Friday night and arranged to sleep away from home. She told her father about it, also that she would be sleeping with her sister's neighbors. The mother visited her sister and Bertha told the mother that she planned to sleep there again the following night. No one from home telephoned to inquire about her, and her sister commented that it looked as though her parents did not care much about her. When Bertha got home Sunday night, her father was very angry and asked her: "Who the hell said you could sleep over?" He insinuated that she slept "with a fellow." Bertha was almost in tears. Reva asked Bertha why her father didn't trust her. She doesn't know why. She was "giddy in the past," but she had been "acting much better lately." She was so angry at her father that she told him that he was far from being an ideal parent to her; she talked to him at great length. But before she finished, he began to hit her and for once her mother took her part and threatened to leave home if he beat Bertha. Bertha said that her father is jealous of her mother and he used to accuse her of having affairs with other men. It finally got to a state where each accused the other of extramarital relations. Last night, when her father was so angry and beat her, Bertha cast it up to him and reminded him of the kind of environment they were creating for her. She asked him whether he felt that it was the proper thing to do for a growing child. Her father made no reply to this. (G)

Rose said that her father has his peculiarities, too. He "stirs up his anger and then there is murder." Lydia believes there is insanity in her father's family. Her paternal grandmother committed suicide. Two of her paternal aunts became mentally unbalanced. Laughingly she added, "My father is wacky." She described how, when they lived in the suburbs in a beautiful, attractively furnished house, the family were once seated around the dining room table, chatting. Her father suddenly threw a candelabra at his mother. He threw his lighted cigar at her and then broke the dishes and windows. In fact, he wrecked the house. Lydia described in detail the lovely carved oak furniture, the gold-lace curtains, the candelabras. The cause of his anger was an argument between her mother and the grandmother. Lydia said that her sister had the same kind of temper. Sandra said that while in her family things do not reach such extremes, her father, when he gets angry, throws the silverware at her. Georgia recalled distinctly that when she was a little girl, her father used to be like that, too. He would wreck things, kick at the door, and was generally pretty destructive. (H)

Bertha said that listening to all of this and thinking about it, has made her realize that she never loved her father, but like Sandra, she pities him. The reason for this conclusion is that she senses weakness in him. Today her father humbly apologized to her and sort of offered to buy her off by telling her that she could buy whatever clothes she wishes.

Sandra said that at this point she couldn't sympathize

with her father very much, she felt angry at him. Why angry? Because when she returned home after her runaway, he suspected her of having had sexual intercourse. Rose asked Sandra what else could she have expected. Sandra very angrily asked, "What do you mean?" Rose said that her father apparently was aware of her habit of picking up sailors, but she could understand why Sandra ran away. Sandra said: "Well, why not? I did it to make up for the love I don't get at home." Lydia asked if Sandra felt like an outcast in the family, and added, "Sandra, I guess it is hard to break a vicious circle." Sandra said that her father should have realized that people run away from home because they are unhappy, not because they want to be bums. (I)

At this point Sandra said timidly that she had been rewriting her biography, and the girls asked her to read it to them. All sat in rapt silence as Sandra read it. Rose and Lydia seemed most impressed by Sandra's talent. The others, as well, gave Sandra a great deal of praise. Reva (not to be outdone, it seemed) raised her voice and said that she, too, was writing. Hers is not a biography but a short story. The girls asked her to read it, which she did. The same attention given Sandra was given also Reva. When Reva read her story, the girls were so affected by it, that Georgia said it brought tears to her eyes and she had noticed that several other girls looked tearful too. Reva read with much feeling and at the end, Paula offered to type as much of Sandra's biography as was ready, and said she would continue typing it until it was completed. Sandra handed the sheets over to Paula. At this point, Bertha offered to type Reva's story.

The girls commented that though Reva's story was very nice and very interesting, she had made a few grammatical errors. Bertha asked whether Reva would mind if she corrected them while she typed. Reva said she would be very glad; she was aware of having made some errors. Lest Sandra feel underpraised, the girls again gave her a great deal of credit for her biography. They said they recognized that in her description of the delinquent girl, she was talking about herself. (Sandra displayed no affect when this was pointed out to her.) (J)

Rose returned to the discussion of fathers. She said she was still thinking about her relationship with her father.

241

She repeated an incident she had narrated many months ago in individual treatment. When she was a little girl and misbehaved her father used to threaten to make her poor, to throw her out of the house so that she would become a beggar. With a note of sarcasm in her voice, Sandra said that her father used to threaten to cut off one of her braids, so that she would look grotesque.

The therapist said that it seemed that all the girls fear their fathers and asked what it is they are so afraid of. Paula interrupted to say it is not only the fathers. Her boy friend Jim told her that her mother is "sinister." Paula did not know the meaning of the word. The girls looked it up in a dictionary on the therapist's desk. Paula said with a sad expression on her countenance, "I've been jipped." She added, "You see, it isn't only the fathers; it's the mothers, too."

When Paula's father saw her on Jim's lap, he told her to get "the hell off his lap." Paula argued with her father and questioned why he should feel like that about it; they weren't doing anything. Her father ought to be glad that she sits on Jim's lap in his presence rather than when his back is turned, but her father called her vile names just the same.

Bertha said she could never pet or fondle a boy friend or sit on his lap in the presence of her father. In fact, she can't even let a fellow hold her hand. Lydia said that in the presence of all, the family and friends, she sat on Max's lap and went *into* Joe. Paula didn't let her finish and said, "Lydia, I think you want what Joe has." Lydia said she doesn't want anything that Joe has. Paula asked her how long had she been going with Joe. Lydia said from February to June. Paula then said, "Lydia, I think you want Joe's penis." Lydia raised her head challengingly and said, "Not if it were offered to me on a silver platter." She tried to explain what she had meant to say, but Paula sort of laughed her down and said: "Anyway, Lydia, you made a nice slip ('into')." Lydia denied that it had any special meaning and said that she kicked Joe out of the house only last night. Lydia went on to say that she had moods when at school. She was not interested in boys; boys did not affect her as much as they seemed to affect the other girls. Sandra and Rose

242

both said they had moods and "can imagine things and cry over them."

Reva had tried several times to say something and finally got her chance just before the end of the session. She has met several times the sailors (of whom she had spoken to the group before), and spent some time talking with them. (This was during World War II.) They were very nice, respectable boys and Reva enjoys talking to them, but her father acted strangely about it. He yelled at her so that he scared her, he was so angry. He told her that she must never see them again. Reva tried to explain that she had made no dates; she never knows when she will meet them. She can't help it if they happen to be on the street when she is, but her father was adamant and said she must not see them again. She will, of course, do as she is told, but if the boys meet her, she will talk with them. However, she soon will not have to worry about it because their furlough is up and they will be leaving. As to whether she will write to them, she thinks she may. She sees no harm in it whatsoever. "I'm not marrying them," she said. (K)

Because the hour was late, the therapist terminated the session rather abruptly.

INTERPRETATION

(A) Sandra is still in conflict and feels guilty about quitting school; she brings her problem to the group as she would to a good mother. I have already reported that a therapy group can be a substitute for a mother in some patients' unconscious. Actually Sandra is hoping for but does not receive approval. The discussion illustrates clearly sibling transference. Leaving school is a regressive act, the meaning of which becomes clearer when later she interprets her running away as seeking love. Sandra's ego is weak and she tends to run away from difficulties.

(B) Georgia comes in all excited and acts hastily. The excitement stems from guilt because she had gone out with a boy the night before; she was disloyal to the girls in her (homosexual) relation to them and to the therapist (mother), Leon symbolically represents her father and she has to placate the therapist (mother).

243

She begins by explaining (apologizing for) her being absent so that the therapist will not be angry with her. She directly tells how her boss and his wife were good to her, suggesting that the therapist, too, should be good to her and not punish her. She proceeds to further placate the therapist by displaying her school report card (an act of submission), expresses her dissatisfaction with herself for not being better than she is, thereby fending off any possible criticism (punishment), and holding out a sort of promise that she will be a good girl.

The therapist did not perceive Georgia's intention, namely, her need to be forgiven and does not respond. The therapist should have in some way reassured the girl by saying something like, "I hope you had a nice time." The therapist could also have interpreted the transference by asking, "Do you find it necessary to apologize for going out with Leon?" But this may be rather risky at this point. Georgia's "animation" when the girls call attention to her corsage is really a manifestation of anxiety which she seeks to allay by offering them all a smell of the flowers.

(C) Not having received the forgiveness of the therapist, Georgia seeks here to placate her and the girls by saying that she really did not have a good time (therefore deserves no punishment). Her sin gave her no pleasure.

(D) Georgia's spending an evening with her boy friend activates sexual phantasies in the girls. The object becomes Reva, the most feminine, demure, and "sexy" (the girls' own characterization of her). Interest in her appearance, dress, hair, unmistakenly stems from homosexual trends. Sex seems to disturb Lydia, which is transmuted into oral preoccupation and food. As a result of the attention she had been receiving from the girls in the group, Reva, who had been an untidy, infantile, unpunctual, and irresponsible girl, sloppily dressed, has greatly improved in all these areas and now derives ego satisfaction. She is now even able to accept praise without being disturbed. Reva's mother comes to mind (since her nuclear problem is Oedipal involvement with her father and her intense desire to displace her mother). She says in effect, "I am worthy of my father, even my mother admits it." The sexual content of the conversation activates Sandra to associate it with a dream, which can be expected to have sexual connotation.

When the therapist introduced so peremptorily the question of a stenographer, she changed the course of the girls' free association. When administrative matters must be brought in, it should be done at the end of the session, not in the beginning or during the group interview.

(E) In this dream, and because of the sequence in which it is told, Sandra brings forth her homosexual involvement with Helen. The fact that the two girls go out, pick up sailors, and run away from home together, is evidence of the homosexual attachment between them. The symbolism of the monkey or bear, is quite evident (pubic hair), and the dream expresses her struggle against Helen's seductiveness which prevents her from being "good." When Sandra speaks of wanting to go back to play the piano, she means she wishes to be "good," but Helen arouses forbidden impulses and these are evil as the monkey (sex) is evil, and she is afraid. The therapist had rightly recognized that Helen was a displacement for Sandra's father and has given an interpretation which is entirely correct, if we are to judge by the sequence of the interview. Note also that in the dream Sandra runs to her mother for protection (against her sexual impulses), but her mother is not there.

(F) Sandra's giggles confirms the correctness of the therapist's surmise which is still further confirmed by her childhood memories of her father. In her unconscious, the monkey, the "bad" impulses, the father's "monkey faces" that so impressed themselves on Sandra are all related. Her father arouses in her evil impulses that are symbolized in the monkey "or bear." Bertha interprets Sandra's problem correctly. Sandra and her father cling to each other too much. Bertha too visualizes her father as a beast (one who can attack sexually) and Paula expresses her death wish towards her father when she says that when he yells she thinks he does so because he is in pain (for pain is a preliminary to death).

The noteworthy element of this passage is the way members of the group interpret each other's unconscious. We see how correct are their insights and how they help one another in releasing and understanding impulses and phantasies. Catharsis, identification, universalization are all present in this. The flow of the interview demonstrates further the importance of grouping patients on the basis of a common syndrome, in this case incestuous strivings toward their fathers. This similarity favors mutual understanding, support, catharsis, and insight.

(G) Bertha vaguely perceives the sexual involvement between her and her father. The fact that he suspects her as well as her mother of illicit relations places her in the same category with her mother and his other women. The father's beating Bertha, as it appears in the context, can be interpreted as a form of sexual aggression. The objectivity with which she now deals with her father reflects considerable emotional growth in the girl. It also demonstrates the principle of cathexis displacement.

(H) Lydia, whose schizophrenic process has been held in check through individual and group therapy for almost ten years, gets very close to her problem. She is preoccupied with insanity, and is also able to perceive the relation between incest and insanity. At a previous session, the twenty-ninth, Lydia recalled that as a very small child, somehow her face was covered over by a blanket and she began to choke in her sleep. She clearly recalls the terrible fear she had experienced. She related also other terrifying experiences. She said once that she was born with a tumor on her head, "which was removed by X-rays." She then laughed and added, "maybe some of it is still there." The therapist asked her what she meant. Smilingly, Lydia said, "Maybe I still act kind of crazy." The therapist asked, "Do you think you do?" Lydia laughed without answering. Much later in treatment it was Lydia who revealed that once she cut a cat across the abdomen and that for some years she had regularly stolen from stores. Reva made no comment during the entire conversation about fathers. Her involvement with her father is too great at this point for her to be able to talk about him so directly.

(I) Bertha's statement about her father indicates considerable improvement. She now sees her father realistically, having been helped to do so through psychotherapy. She no longer idealizes him and her ambivalence is decreasing. She is clearer about him (cathexis displacement). She sees him as a weak person (which he

246

actually is). Sandra too is beginning to be more objective about her father. She no longer feels guilty about her hatred of him, which is justifiable in terms of the real situation. Stimulated by the views of the others, Sandra reveals excellent insight into her motive for picking up sailors and for running away from home. Lydia who is a very perceptive person, characteristic of schizophrenics, makes the significant remark about breaking the vicious circle. In later sessions the girls discuss this thought and their role in it.

(J) When Sandra speaks at this point of her biography, she is actually continuing the story of her relation to her father. Her biography dealt largely with the intense suffering that leads to delinquent behavior and the struggle a girl goes through in her attempts to avoid it. Since all of the girls, and especially Sandra, were on the threshold of establishing the association between delinquent acts and relationships with fathers—all of this session was really devoted to it—the therapist should have attempted to bring this relation out into the open. Such interpretation might have been appropriate and desirable at this point. Sandra gave the lead in her previous statement that her behavior stems from her cravings for love.

The close attention of the girls as Sandra reads about the psychological basis for delinquency and the struggle with her environment and her own impulses indicates the girls' identification with her. This is valuable to Sandra and to the other girls. Sandra's ego is built up by the recognition and the impulses and feelings of all are clarified by the story. This is therapy through identification. Sandra's narrative was so written as to describe and interpret each girl's feelings much as a therapist would do.

Reva (who came to the group as a demure, shy and withdrawn "yes girl," as she had been characterized by the others) has now become assertive and is able to enter into open rivalry with Sandra, for Sandra places her in the subsidiary position she is forced to take toward her mother in relation to her father. This demonstrates again the variety of transferences that emerge in a group when a fellow patient may become the recipient of one's feelings toward parents. The identification with

247

the story as revealed by the girls' tears takes the form in Paula of actual participation in typing it.

(K) In this interchange the girls' real castration anxieties appear. To Reva, being turned out of the house and becoming a beggar is to take away the security which she received from the father, while Sandra's fear of losing one of her braids has quite evident meaning. This is confirmed later when Lydia and Paula speak plainly about wanting "what Joe has." Castration anxieties are clearly shown by the girls, as demonstrated by the following incidents. During the sixth interview, Lydia said that she is especially concerned about her subway travel, because there are many men on the subways who get close to her. At this, she drew out of her purse a hat pin which she said she always carries for protection. The others laughed, and each of the girls took the pin and handled it. With the exception of Sandra, all the girls said they carry long pins with them. The adolescent girls' preoccupation with castration is demonstrated in another group. Betty asked Ella whether she was wearing a real man's shirt. (Ella also wore men's ties.) Ella rather proudly stuck out her chest and said: "Yes, and it buttons down the front." Anne said, "She even has a fly on her skirt." At that, Ella seemed quite disturbed and vehemently denied it. There had been pencils and paper on the table and the girls took them up and remained silent for a period. . . .

An even more direct expression of adolescent girls' preoccupation with castration is revealed in the following story, written by Yolanda. The story takes place in the year 2040.

"After the war which the Allies won, there was a battle of the sexes. The women won and now their positions are reversed. The men have the babies, do the housework and do everything connected with the home, while the women work and earn a living. Now the scene opens in an office. A woman presses a buzzer, in comes a man to take dictation. Mr. Jones sits on the boss's lap to take the dictation. Says Mrs. Smith to Mr. Jones, 'What are you doing tonight, honey?' She's just about to kiss him when in walks her husband with a gun: (Haaa, haaa, these women, you can't trust them!) He bangs Mr. Jones on the head. Jones falls. He is worried: 'I've killed him;

248

now who'll take care of the children?' The wife says: 'I'll protect you.' They go to the policewoman, who puts them through a third degree." Here Yolanda demonstrated how the policewoman sticks pins into Mr. Jones.

At another session, Betty said with much feeling: "They [women] are paid less for the jobs they do as good as a man and even better." She went on to say that when she reaches the top of the ladder she will fix men. They are impolite, stupid. "Even my father [stepfather] is stupid for living with my mother," and she gave a number of illustrations of the neglected home and her mother's inadequacy and neglectfulness. Betty feels sorry for her stepfather for marrying her mother. He is a nice man, good and kind, but has a "rotten life" with her mother.

Returning to the dialogue in the record, we find revealed the close association between fathers and boy friends and the ready substitution the girls make one for the other. The incest drives toward the father are now displaced. Bertha conveys this when she confesses to being too guilty to pet or fondle her boy friend in the presence of her father. She is vaguely aware of her father's interest in her and her interest in him, and to come in physical contact with another man in his presence is an affront to and a sexual rejection of him. She is afraid of hurting him and suffer his wrath that would follow. Lydia, on the other hand, is characteristically narcissistic and has a less sharpened awareness of the effect on others. She does not inhibit her actions. She unintentionally reveals her penis striving which Paula at once recognizes. When faced with it, she vehemently denies it. Lydia also reveals her autistic character when she avers that boys do not affect her as they do the other girls. Reva's description of her father's reaction to her seeing the sailor boys in the neighborhood reveals his attitudes toward his daughter. Interestingly enough, she ends up by saying, "I am not marrying them," which is to say that "my father need not be afraid that I will marry them; I will marry him." In the light of this girl's basic problem, namely to replace her mother, this statement is significant.

Paula's sexual confusion and intense striving to have a penis makes her readily aware of a similar striving in Lydia, and she at once recognizes and interprets Lydia's

249

unconscious. She also understands the significance of the word-error "went *into* Joe." Both statements strike a responsive note in Paula. By sitting on Jim's lap, Paula acts out her basic infantile unawareness of the significance of sex and her general infantile character. But there is in it also an element of seductiveness toward her father. The girl is strongly fixated on her father, who was the more kindly of the parents, and by sitting on Jim's lap in his presence she seeks to make him jealous, in which she succeeds.

The therapist attempted to stimulate the girls to further exploration of their incestuous strivings by asking why they are afraid of their fathers. Paula blocks this line of discussion, since her attachment to the father makes it necessary for her to see him in a better light, and she throws the onus on mothers as well.

DISCUSSION

This record is fairly typical of a group interview of adolescent girls when the conflict between Oedipal drives and the normal sexual interests are at their greatest. We see the girls' dependence upon, and death wishes toward, their parents. This is quite clear in Paula, though less evident in the others. We must note the easy catharsis, free association, and associative thinkings, and the low levels of resistance. The girls are singularly free of "shame," and their revelations of "bad" impulses meet with no disapproval. Identification is very clearly demonstrated here in all the problems discussed; emotions are acted out, as well as talked through.

The girls act as therapists to each other, giving clear and sometimes profound interpretations of unconscious motivations. This type of interview leaves very little for the therapist to do, since the therapeutic flow occurs without her participation. The therapist is passive, but at appropriate times she brings out a point to help the patients toward insight and further catharsis.

Expression of the girls' hostility toward the parents was made possible in this session by cathexis displacement facilitated by the acceptance, security, and affection and closeness that the girls feel toward each other and toward the therapist.

250

Spotnitz,[3] who has analyzed the basic trends of the interviews of this group of adolescent girls, has found that they were motivated, in part at least, by two forces. "Those forces which tended to bring the group together, and those forces which tended to disrupt the group and break it up," and that these forces were the same. They were emotional drives associated with "the reproductive constellation" which was counteracted and disturbed by the girls' feelings of inadequacy as potential mothers. Spotnitz characterizes the latter as "the inadequacy constellation." He has found that "after about two years of [group] therapy, in the main, there had been a definite movement from a curiosity about children and how they are made, to a greater interest in producing them and in properly taking care of them." This change occurred because the girls found "that many of their fancied inadequacies were not inadequacies but based primarily on social disapproval, and as they learned to tolerate the group disapproval and came to understand themselves, many inadequacies turned out to be assets and others tended to disappear."

I believe this analysis applies very well to this group of girls.

[3] Hyman Spotnitz, "Observations of Emotional Currents in Interview Group Therapy with Adolescent Girls," *Journal of Nervous and Mental Diseases,* November, 1947. From a paper presented at the Fourth Annual Conference of the American Group Therapy Association.

Conclusion

This book was prepared in an effort to show the growth of psychoanalysis by the presentation of case histories from the practice of those who have had most to do with its development; but the study of these cases reveals in addition the rich variety of ways in which psychoanalysts think about their patients, and by the same token, demonstrates that there is no rigid new orthodoxy in psychoanalysis. All psychoanalysts do not have one answer, and unhappily for those who lust for certainty in an uncertain world, there is no single analyst who believes that he has the one answer that will apply to all his patients. Instead, the modern, well-informed analyst gives himself greater flexibility in his arduous therapeutic task by utilizing theories and techniques borrowed from many schools.

The development of psychoanalysis may profitably be studied in many ways. It could be viewed in terms of its change from the essentially biologically oriented theory of Freud to the increasingly social orientation of Sullivan and Karen Horney. Or it could be examined by observing the shift in emphasis from the minute examination of early childhood trauma and the subsequent specific investigation of latter-day neurotic symptoms in connection with such trauma, to the more frequently practiced present-day emphasis on the entire individual. But one of the difficulties with such convenient schemes of organization is the remarkable quality of Freud's mind. The broadness of his thinking led him to forecast almost every major development in modern psychoanalysis. While it is true that in practice his own emphasis was primarily on the biologically based instincts, he was aware of and pointed to the necessity for investigating the whole individual, including his social condition.

If one reads only the case material, the overwhelming impression is that the analyst has shifted his role from that of the cool, objective observer in an antiseptic atmosphere of clinical neutrality to the involved participant in the vicissitudes of the analysis. Freud and his early followers, Abraham and Ferenczi, write like psychic surgeons describing their unemotional explorations of the illnesses in the minds of their patients. In theory, their emphasis is on maintaining analytic anonymity so that the patient sees the analyst as a blank screen on whom he can project his emotional distortions. But at least some of this objectivity on which Freud prided himself is more apparent than real. Even so critical a writer as Joseph Wortis (*Fragments of an Analysis with Freud*) describes him as "mild, earnest, and friendly." On the other hand, Lindner, still basically a Freudian, openly involves himself directly and emotionally with his patient, as does Sullivan, a dissenter. The crucial difference in approach is that Freud's involvement with his patients seemed to be due to his own personality rather than being a deliberate action based on theoretical conviction.

The quality that distinguishes psychoanalysis from all other forms of treatment is that it is essentially and consciously a personal form of treatment. Its failure or success rests upon the nature of the relationship between the analyst and his patient and their combined ability to communicate with each other. While it is true that this relationship is probably always present as a potent factor between healer and afflicted, only psychoanalysis recognizes this as the curative factor. On this one principle I believe it is fair to say that analysts of practically all schools might agree.

At the present time a number of analysts of differing psychoanalytic backgrounds are striving for the maximum involvement with their patients as conscious therapeutic strategy. Some of them have found support for their beliefs in the philosophical theories of modern existentialism and ancient Zen Buddhism. Others, while doubting the scientific validity of either existentialism or Buddhism, still work to eradicate the gulf that traditionally existed between analyst and patient.

Looked at in this way, it seems to me possible to see one unifying concept in all of the psychoanalytic theories. Basically all analysts agree that the greatest single cause of mental distress is the absence of growth-fostering love and acceptance in the development of the individual; therefore they see the analyst's task as being one which needs to supply such growth-encouraging love in the form of deep understanding. This love must not be exploitative, possessive, or incapacitatingly overprotective but must take the form of acceptance and understanding.

When we approach the development of psychoanalysis with this concept, it is possible to see that Freud provided growth-fostering love by understanding and accepting the formerly rejected emotions and fantasies of sexual love and hate; successively, Adler accepted competitiveness and the wish for dominance, Sullivan and Horney the variety of ways in which individuals interact with each other in society, Jung the different aspects of the individual's way of being. Finally Rogers attempted to go even further by not interposing any theory of personality between himself and his clients, but by permitting them the fullest latitude of expression while trying to feel with them. All of these creative thinkers in the field of psychoanalysis base their approach on displacing censorious judgment and criticism with the effort to accept and understand.

A major development in psychoanalytic practice since World War II has been the rapid growth of group therapy, or group psychoanalysis, as some prefer to call it, in order to indicate that they believe it can reach the same deep levels of understanding as individual analysis. In the group setting the analyst is committed to the fullest possible participation with his patients. No longer can he take refuge in the faceless obscurity of his position behind the couch but must reveal himself as a living, feeling being who is deeply involved in the human drama that takes place before his eyes. His patients can observe him in interaction with others than themselves as he can observe them in interaction with others than himself.

In the group the analyst is stripped of much of his magical powers, he has no choice but to share his limitations, as well as his strengths, with the group members. The group presents the best medium we have to date for observing the patient in a situation as close to real life as it is possible to arrange within the limitations of office and institutional practice. It is within the group

255

situation that the analyst has the opportunity of studying the interaction between the individual and the group, and how this interaction contributes to health as well as to pathology. Perhaps from this study we may contribute to an understanding not only of how to help individuals to function in society but to the creation of a society which will produce fewer disturbed individuals.

A significant conclusion one can come to as a result of studying the case histories contributed by the founders of psychoanalysis is how much, many of the present innovators owe these pioneers. It is difficult to find any brave new approach that does not derive its basic premises from these forerunners. What seems to have happened is that the newcomers have chosen to concentrate on one area of Freud's epochal discoveries. Carl Rogers, for example, who has had great influence in the development of the present-day encounter group movement, states in his book *Humanistic Conceptions of Man* that he was very much influenced in his work by Freud, Adler and Rank. Fritz Perls, the founder of the "Gestalt" Therapy movement had his basic training in psychoanalysis which he skillfully wedded to Moreno's psychodrama. Wilhelm Reich, and Alexander Lowen, the bio-energetics "gurus," emphasize the sexual area that Freud first laid bare. Eric Berne, the founder of Transactional Analysis, was originally a psychoanalyst who translated the often archaic language with which Freud's English translators saddled his simple clear German back into simple clear English. When I had the opportunity to watch Berne work, he sounded to me like a skilled psychoanalyst who chose to conduct his analyses in a group context. John Rosen, the direct analyst, was able to supply psychoanalytic concepts to the treatment of psychosis.

In my own work (*Decision Therapy*, Pete Wyden, Inc., 1973) I have chosen to emphasize the decision factors in therapy. After studying both the cases of the masters here included and the patients I have worked with for over 20 years, I came to the conclusion that the crucial turning point in any successful therapy came when the patient was able to make a decision to change and then put the decision into effect. While my approach is a direct one, I cannot claim that I could have developed this theory without my knowledge of psychoanalysis.

256